I0802182

THE LOST YEARS OF

William S. Burroughs

THE LOST YEARS OF

William S.

NUMBER TWENTY-ONE:

TARLETON STATE UNIVERSITY

SOUTHWESTERN STUDIES IN

THE HUMANITIES

William T. Pilkington, General Editor

ROB JOHNSON

Burroughs

BEATS IN SOUTH TEXAS

TEXAS A&M UNIVERSITY PRESS

COLLEGE STATION

Manufactured in the United States of America

Second printing, 2008
The paper used in this book meets the minimum requirements of the American National Standard for Permanence of Paper for Printed Library Materials, z39.48-1984.
Binding materials have been chosen for durability.
♾

Portions of this work first appeared in "William S. Burroughs: South Texas Farmer, Junky, and Queer" in *Southwestern American Literature,* Volume XXVI No. 2 (Spring 2001): 7–36. Reprinted by permission.

Library of Congress Cataloging-in-Publication Data

Johnson, Rob, 1961–
The lost years of William S. Burroughs : beats in South Texas / Rob Johnson. — 1st ed.
p. cm. — (Tarleton State University southwestern studies in the humanities ; no. 21)
Includes bibliographical references and index.
ISBN-13: 978-1-58544-517-2 (cloth : alk. paper)
ISBN-10: 1-58544-517-7 (cloth : alk. paper)
ISBN-13: 978-1-58544-547-9 (pbk. : alk. paper)
ISBN-10: 1-58544-547-9 (pbk. : alk. paper)
1. Burroughs, William S., 1914–1997—Homes and haunts—Texas, South. 2. Beat generation—Texas, South. 3. Novelists, American—20th century—Biography. 4. Burroughs, William S., 1914–1997—Friends and associates. I. Title. II. Series. PS3552.U75Z715 2006 813'.54—dc22 [B]
2006001538

CONTENTS

LIST OF ILLUSTRATIONS

THE LOST YEARS OF

William S. Burroughs

PROLOGUE

It's April of 1949 in the South Texas Valley, but it's not spring: It's already summer and will stay that way for the next six months. In the town of Pharr, two miles from the larger, rival city of McAllen, Constable Tom Mayfield drives a beat-up black Oldsmobile 88 down Highway 83. Tom has found an old cherry-top siren in a junkyard and rigged it on top of the 88 with some baling wire, but it's not hooked up to anything. At the corner of Highway 83 and Cage Road, he stops for coffee at the Hub Café. A red-haired, cross-eyed carhop waitress named Nevada ("Ne VAY duh" she corrects you if you try to call her by the state's name) hands him his dime coffee. Tom thanks her in the rasping voice that has earned him the nickname "El Ronco" [the hoarse one] with the Texas Mexican population. Among the Anglos, he is "Whisperin' Tom." Tom drinks his coffee, then drives west in the direction of McAllen.

The road follows the railroad tracks that, back in the early 1900s, first connected the upper Valley to Brownsville, Corpus Christi, and beyond. Laborers are loading train cars at the San Pat Vegetable Shed, where local produce is packed and shipped out of the Valley. Inside the shed office, Walter Benson has a phone on each ear and is simultaneously taking produce orders from two buyers. His memory is so good he doesn't even need to write down the complicated instructions entering both sides of his head. John Snider, a cash buyer for the shed, marvels not only at Walter's memory but also at the fact that Walter can think at all after a long night of drinking in Reynosa's famous *Zona Rosa* [pink zone], the tourist area just over the border from McAllen.

There, in Reynosa, at the intersection of Miguel Alemán and Paseo de los Pirreyes, the heart of the Zona Rosa, the cab drivers who have served all night as purveyors of entertainment for gringos such as Walter Benson are giving the business to Manuel, another cab driver. He has once again returned a drunken fare named Billy back across the border to Pharr. Billy's nickname is Willy "El Puto" — Willy the Queer. Carlos makes a big show of sniffing Manuel's crotch and asks him, "What have you been doing with Willy?" They are hanging out in front of Joe's Place, one of the border's premier restaurants and nightclubs. On the back patio of Joe's, Roberto Perez, the *domador,* or lion tamer, is feeding raw meat to six African lions Joe keeps in a pit inside his restaurant. Sometimes Joe leads them through the dining room on a gold chain, amusing the gringos.

From Reynosa, you cross the border and drive a motel-lined highway ("the nickel-plated highway to Hell") eight miles north to McAllen, the border town on the U.S. side. McAllen is a small but prosperous town run by citrus farmers, land developers, and bankers. Clint Murchison Sr., already "cured" many times over as a millionaire in oil and gas, steps outside the McAllen State Bank, which he owns, and joins a group of men shooting the breeze. They discuss a story in the *McAllen Evening Monitor* about Sen. Joseph McCarthy's latest attack on communists. Clint has recently sent Texas' unofficial "third senator" a hefty campaign contribution. He's worked too hard for his money to have a bunch of goddamn commies take it away.

At the *Monitor* offices, Bryce Armstrong is writing a story about a new report from Austin criticizing South Texas farmers for their use of illegal laborers. The authors of the report call the practice of hiring the "wetbacks" a "quagmire" that will drag down the entire region. Later that day, after the high school lets out, Jim McKone will play cub reporter and run some errands for Armstrong.

Just northeast of McAllen in Edinburg, the county seat, Carrol Norquest is trying to get a crop of onions picked. He has hired a crew of illegals who swam the river the night before and were then transported to Norquest's farm in a flatbed truck. Normally this is business as usual in the Valley, but lately the number of roundups by *la chota* — the Border Patrol — has been increasing. That morning, when Norquest's "wets" see la chota coming, they scatter into the brush. This time Norquest is lucky: The Border Patrol agent is nearing retirement and has known for years that part of his job is not to do his job. He also knows that if Norquest can't get his crop picked, it could spell disaster for him. The agent tips his hat to Norquest and drives on.

Kells Elvins owns farmland in Edinburg, too, but unlike Norquest, Elvins has little to do with the actual farming. He's a transplanted Midwesterner of independent means: a "gentleman farmer," as the old-timers in the Valley would say. Elvins lives in Pharr in a house surrounded by citrus groves. He's dating a local girl named Marianne Standing, the daughter of a librarian in McAllen. Mrs. Standing has warned her daughter against dating the older, dashing Elvins, whom she considers a rake. But Elvins has a date with her tonight.

Marianne first met Kells through his friend Eugene "Tiger" Terry. Terry, in his early twenties, is also tending his father's farm, a job he was assigned after he flunked out his first semester at the University of Texas and had no other prospects. The Valley is a good place for guys like Kells and Terry. They spend a lot of time together over in Reynosa. Terry's favorite spot is Joe's Place. José Ortega, its owner, says the rough-and-tumble Terry is like a son to him, and he indulges the boy when Terry wants to "pet the cats" — Joe's pet lions.

The weekend before, Kells, Gene Terry, and Kells's odd and erudite childhood friend Billy (aka Willy El Puto) drove to Corpus Christi and hit the waterfront bars. One of Billy's favorite pastimes is to organize skits among his drinking buddies, and that's how Gene Terry got his nickname — "Tiger" Terry, the punch-drunk boxer, who was a character in one of their improvised routines.

Billy is William S. Burroughs, of St. Louis, Missouri, and he and Kells are in business together — of sorts — as farmers. Billy lives just behind Kells's orange groves in a ranch-style house on Route 1 in Pharr. He needs to go to the San Juan drugstore to buy his common-law wife, Joan, a case of asthma inhalers. Joan will break open the inhalers, pull out the Benzedrine-soaked strips inside, wad them up, and swallow them with a cup of coffee. She is addicted to Benzedrine, and Billy is, off and on, a heroin addict. He's off now and feeling a little junk-sick. Before the day gets too hot, he steps outside, strips down to his underwear, and heads into the orange grove on Kells's property.

There is what appears to be a refrigerator set up in the grove, and Billy climbs inside it. The dying cell gravitates to the Valley, Billy believes, and he has built an orgone accumulator in order to soak up what little life essence there is in the deadly atmosphere of the place. Wilhelm Reich's healing orgones immediately begin their work, sending a tangible charge of energy first felt on the back of Billy's neck. If he can help it, he isn't going to die in a place he describes that day in a letter to Jack Kerouac as "this Valley of heat and boredom." He isn't going to die there, not as Gene Terry would, killed a year later by one of Joe's lions, nor as his friend Walter Benson would die several years down the road, shot three times by his father-in-law in his own home in Pharr. And he won't be buried there, as will his best friend, Kells, twelve years later.

On the sidewalks of Pharr, Tom Mayfield shows a wide-eyed kid the nineteen notches on his pearl-handled revolver.

“THE BEATEST STATE IN THE UNION”

William S. Burroughs in Texas

William S. Burroughs was a junky, queer, and writer, famous for writing (not coincidentally) *Junky* and *Queer,* as well as *Naked Lunch* and many other contemporary classics. His reputation as a writer lands him on just about everyone’s list of important American writers of the twentieth century, and internationally he stands alongside avant-garde and experimental writers such as Céline, Beckett, and Joyce. A famous buddy of Jack Kerouac and Allen Ginsberg, Burroughs is one of the godfathers of the Beat movement, although he never really called himself a Beat.

Burroughs’s biographers have detailed his boyhood and adolescence in St. Louis in the 1920s; his years as a student at Harvard and abroad in Europe in the 1930s; his days as a junky in New York in the 1940s; the accidental shooting of his common-law wife in Mexico City in 1951; his writing of *Naked Lunch* in Morocco in the midfifties; his development of a theory that language is a virus in his science-fiction novels of the sixties and seventies; the unexpected writing of his late-life masterpieces, a trilogy of books beginning with *Cities of the Red Night* (1981); and his emergence in the 1980s and 1990s as one of the world’s most visible counterculture figures. In 1981 he was introduced on “Saturday Night Live” as the greatest living writer in the United States — a fact that might have shocked some viewers, who probably thought the author of *Junky* was long dead. Appearances in films such as *Drugstore Cowboy* (he plays a junky priest) and duets with rock stars such as Kurt Cobain have ensured his continued celebrity status with a young, hip audience. His gaunt, erudite person was so well known that Nike paid him to hawk sneakers in a controversial 1994 commercial. Burroughs died in 1997 in Lawrence, Kansas, where he lived close by his longtime companion and now literary executor, James Grauerholz. He was eighty-three years old.[1]

All of this is familiar to Burroughs’s fans and fanatics, of which there are hundreds of thousands all over the world. They can tell you with the accuracy of literary historians the most minute details of his life and work and his associations with the Beat Generation cast of characters. However, if there is a lost chapter in Burroughs's life, one that has not been told and retold, one not generally known to Burroughs enthusiasts, it is the one I tell in this book: The story of Billy Burroughs on the Mexican border in South Texas. I have turned that chapter of his life into an entire book because I have discovered that, if you look closely at any period of the life of this fascinating man and brilliant writer, you find much more than you expected.

Unless you are a hardcore Burroughs-phile, you may well be surprised to learn that from 1946 to 1950 Burroughs prepared himself for the writing of his first books by, among other pursuits, being a farmer in Texas. In New Waverly, Texas, north of Houston, he was the kind of "farmer" you might expect the author of *Junky* to be: He raised marijuana and opium poppies and entertained Beat visitors such as Allen Ginsberg and Neal Cassady. Burroughs's "farmhand," the famous junky Herbert Huncke, writes about this misadventure in *The Evening Sun Turned Crimson,* and the New Waverly farm also figures in Ginsberg's early poetry and biographical stories about Cassady.[2]

Less well known, however, are the stories about Burroughs's other farm, the one in the South Texas Valley. In comparison to the New Waverly "ranch," this was a serious farm, and Burroughs raised legal crops such as cotton, carrots, and peas. None of the Beats ever visited Burroughs there. Kerouac intended to but was sidetracked. In a 1949 letter, Kerouac rather vaguely described the location of Pharr, Texas, where Burroughs lived off and on, as "down near Monterrey [Mexico]," completely overlooking the United States.[3]

Accordingly, the Valley is not the most famous setting for Burroughs's books, which take as their inspiration various exotic and world-class cities where he lived and wrote — New York, Tangiers, Paris, Mexico City, and London. Pharr, Texas, stands out in that list. Even in Texas, most people do not know where it is. ("You've Gone to Pharr — Pharr, Texas, That Is!" a chamber of commerce bumper sticker reads.) Barry Miles, in an otherwise impeccable biography of Burroughs's friend Allen Ginsberg, tells readers that the Valley is in *East* Texas, not South Texas.[4] Burroughs's biographer Ted Morgan was also challenged by Texas geography and says the Valley is in "East Texas near the Mexican border."[5] To make things more confusing, there is no "valley" in South Texas, only a landscape described today in the real estate ads as "laser level."

I originally went looking for signs of Burroughs's stay in the Valley when I was doing background research on Beat writers and spotted, to my surprise, Pharr, Texas return addresses on several letters collected by Oliver Harris in *The Letters of William S. Burroughs, 1945–1959*. You see, Pharr was just down the road from my house in McAllen, Texas. Later I found Burroughs's farm in nearby Edinburg, and it was only four miles from the University of Texas–Pan American, where I teach. However, no one I spoke to at the university had ever heard anything about Burroughs being down here. The Valley was simply not on the Beat Map. Therefore, I'm probably the first person who has read *Naked Lunch,* walked around on Burroughs's fifty acres of "the finest land in the Valley," and known that it was farmed by El Hombre Invisible.[6]

For those who do not live in the Valley, if you want to take a look at Burroughs's land, you first need to drive to the bottom of Texas on Highway 281 South. In Edinburg, take the Monte Cristo exit, drive east past the stockyards, a boys' reformatory school, and a golf course, then go south on César Chávez (formerly Morningside Drive) for a quarter mile. Burroughs owned the north ten acres of that lot and all forty on the lot to the south. It's still farmland.

I took my graduate students there on a day the wind was blowing hot from Mexico, raising dust on the caliche road. They had read *Junky, Queer,* and *Naked Lunch,* all three of which have important Texas sections, and standing there in the dusty intersection between the farm fields, they were as excited as if they were in Poets' Corner. One student handed out empty film canisters to put soil in as a memento of our field trip. A Ford F-150 drove by us slowly, the men inside wearing the signature South Texas ranchero hat (a white cowboy hat). I huddled the students next to a barbed-wire fence and read to them from Burroughs's letters about South Texas and from a section of *Junky* cut out of the original edition because, as Allen Ginsberg says, a "literary description of Texas agricultural society was . . . not . . . germane to the funky harsh non-literary subject matter."[7] (The description was restored in the 1977 edition.)

Of the farming operation run by him and his business partner, Kells Elvins ("Evans" in the book), Burroughs says, "The farmer did all the actual work. Evans and I would drive around every few days to see how the cotton was looking. It took us about an hour to look at all our cotton because the fields were scattered around from Edinburg to the lower lift, almost on the river." Burroughs's land on Morningside was at the northern end of this drive. He describes the extent of their labor as follows: "There was no particular point in looking at the cotton since neither of us knew the first thing about it. We just drove around to pass the time until five P.M., when we started drinking. . . . Exactly at five, someone would bang a tin pan and yell 'Drinking time!' and the others would jump up like fighters coming out at the bell."[8] Standing in Burroughs's former field, looking south toward Pharr and Mexico, my students and I could almost hear the echoes of that tin pan and the call of "Drinking time!"

Since locating Burroughs's land, I have become the local Burroughs-in-South-Texas authority and have, over the past several years, tracked down a dozen or so South Texans and Mexicans (mostly now in their late seventies and early eighties) who knew Burroughs or his business partner, Kells Elvins. None of these people had ever talked to a literary researcher about Burroughs, and most of them were astonished to hear that "Billy" was a famous writer. They were even more surprised to learn that he had actually written about a few of them in the South Texas portions of books such as *Junky* and *Interzone.*

Among the people here who know Burroughs's work (or have heard of it), the reaction is always the same when I tell them Burroughs lived in the Valley: First, they think it's a joke; then they are genuinely thrilled. Norman Mailer said William S. Burroughs was the only writer of his generation "possessed by genius," and this internationally famous author not only lived here but also wrote about this place. There is talk of an annual literary festival in either Pharr or Mexico.

As a setting in Burroughs's work, the Valley is central in *Junky* (first published in 1953), "Tiger in the Valley" (an unpublished 1955 short story), and, to a lesser extent, in *Queer* (1985), but the Valley recurs as a setting in almost all of his books in one form or another. Most of these references to the Valley are so local that their significance has escaped the attention of critics and biographers. However, Burroughs's experiences in South Texas are of key importance in understanding his life in the period just before he began writing his first book, *Junky*. In fact, the original manuscript of *Junky* ends with Burroughs failing as a farmer in South Texas and moving to Mexico. Farming in South Texas convinced him that the United States was rapidly becoming a communist-style police state, and he couldn't wait to move to the "free" country of Mexico, which offered an escape back into the past of the American frontier, when everything was allowed and people minded their own business. There, in Mexico, he began writing the books that would transform him from Billy Burroughs into William S. Burroughs, writer.

Today, looking back at Burroughs's life, it seems as inevitable that he would live in the Valley in the late 1940s during what is sometimes referred to as the "wetback era" as it does that he would live in Morocco in the midfifties (during the end of colonial rule) or in New York in the midseventies (during the rise of the punk rock movement). But what brought him to the Valley? In some ways, the answer is simple: He was running from his past, and Texas (especially its border with Mexico) has always been a good place to run to. Therefore, as you might suspect of someone who moved from New York City to the Texas-Mexico border, he was here because of run-ins with the law back East. In fact, he came here twice to escape the clank of iron.

Before moving to Texas in the late fall of 1946, Burroughs had been living in New York City and hanging out with a crowd of small-time criminals, junkies, and bohemians. Through his friends Jack Kerouac and Allen Ginsberg he met Joan Vollmer (later Joan Burroughs, his common-law wife). Vollmer was brilliant and a Benzedrine addict, and her apartment was a kind of salon for Burroughs, Ginsberg, Lucien Carr, Kerouac, and many other characters in the Beat Generation. She and Burroughs became close companions in part because, as their friends observed, Vollmer was the only woman he had ever met who was his intellectual equal.

Life among this crowd was unstable at best. There was lots of drinking and heavy use of the stimulant Benzedrine, which they obtained by cracking open over-the-counter asthma inhalers and eating the drug-soaked strips inside. Drugs, especially opium, had long fascinated Burroughs even before his brief tenure as a medical student in Vienna in 1936. In the fall of 1945, he began "studying" addictive drugs and, under the tutelage of Times Square hipster Herbert Huncke, became hooked on morphine. To support his habit, he and a pal of Huncke's named Phil White (later identified as the psychotic "Mad Dog Noonday Killer") rolled drunks in the New York subways "working the hole," as they called it in their subterranean lingo. Burroughs's first narcotics arrest, or "fall," took place in April 1946 when he misspelled Dilaudid as "Dillaudid" on a prescription pad that Huncke had stolen. (A suspicious pharmacist turned him in to the police.) Burroughs, a first-time offender, was granted probation but, with no visible means of support, was ordered to move away from Times Square and the Columbia crowd and back to his parents' house in St. Louis, Missouri, where he had grown up. Burroughs was thirty-two years old.

In St. Louis, he soon hooked up with an old friend named Kells Elvins, who considered Burroughs the funniest man alive.[9] While Elvins was a graduate student at Harvard in the late 1930s, he and Burroughs had collaborated on a comic routine (still very funny) titled "Twilight's Last Gleaming." In the summer of 1946, Elvins had just returned from a place about as far away from the junkies and subways of New York as is possible in the United States — deep South Texas. Elvins, a brilliant but restless young man who had been an accountant, a psychologist, and a marine was now a farmer living in the Valley, having inherited some citrus groves in Pharr, Texas, from his father, Politte. Elvins quickly convinced the currently unsettled Burroughs to go in with him on the South Texas farming venture. Herbert Huncke described Kells's irresistible pitch to Burroughs: "His [Kells's] father had sent him down to Texas, and of course he had nothing more to do than just sit back and collect. These people live on elaborate farms or plantations in big, comfortable houses, and they have people working citrus fruits or tomatoes. It's a very good business. This sounded good to Bill." Burroughs's parents also liked the idea, hoping that their wayward son would settle down into an acceptable profession.[10]

Burroughs first visited the Valley in late June of 1946 and stayed with Kells in Pharr, where they began a farming project together that, for Burroughs, would continue until 1950, when he sold the last of his South Texas land. To start off as a farmer, he purchased fifty acres of farmland with money his parents advanced him. According to a letter he sent Allen Ginsberg in October of 1946, he was growing citrus and expected to make ten thousand dollars in the mail-order business: Shipped all over the United States, baskets of grapefruit, oranges, and pecans from the Valley were (and still are) popular holiday gifts. During this initial stay in the Valley, from June to November of 1946, Burroughs probably met many of Kells's friends, such as Pat Paris, Walter Benson, and Ted Marak. They golfed, swam, and made trips to Reynosa throughout the warm South Texas fall season.[11]

In November of 1946, disturbing news took Burroughs back to New York City: His friend Joan Vollmer had been institutionalized with a Benzedrine-induced psychosis and was unable to take care of herself or her daughter, Julie, from a previous marriage. Burroughs rescued her and brought her and Julie back with him to Pharr. Bill and Joan would not be separated again until her death in 1951, and in Pharr they began what amounted to a common-law marriage. Valley residents from that period who recall the 1946 visit remember Joan as "nice," but Julie appeared unkempt and neglected. The three of them lived together in a run-down McAllen motel.

While the oranges and grapefruits were being picked and shipped, Burroughs evidently came up with an even better idea for a cash crop: marijuana. However, the wide-open landscape of the Valley made a marijuana crop difficult to hide. What he needed was a more thickly wooded area. East Texas, where Burroughs had visited Kells in 1939, fit the bill.[12] In November or December of 1946, Burroughs bought ninety-nine acres in New Waverly, near Huntsville, about four hundred miles north of the Valley. Burroughs, Joan, Julie, and later Billy Jr. (who was born in Conroe, Texas, on July 21, 1947) lived in New Waverly for a year on this East Texas "ranch," as Jack Kerouac romantically called it. Joan viewed the ranch less romantically: In a letter to Allen Ginsberg in 1947, she complained about the scorpions infesting the property, calling Texas "the beatest state in the Union." The main work on the property was the raising of marijuana and opium poppies. Both agricultural efforts flopped: Burroughs failed to cure the marijuana properly, and the opium poppies did not take to the East Texas red dirt.[13]

Although his illegitimate "farming" enterprise in East Texas had fallen flat, Burroughs did not give up on his legitimate farm in South Texas, and in May of 1948 he traveled to the Valley, bought forty more acres, and consolidated his holdings with Elvins. At the time, he might have been thinking of moving his family back to the Valley, but an incident occurred on the drive down to Pharr that changed his plans. As Burroughs describes it, "I lost my Texas driving license for driving while drunk and public indecency." More graphically, he and Joan had been caught by legendary South Texas lawman Vail Ennis while having drunken sex beside their parked car. Pleading guilty to drunkenness and lewd behavior, Bill got off with a fine. However, the arrest forced him out of Texas altogether because the judge in Beeville suspended his Texas driver's license. Burroughs decided that "things [were] very uncool in Texas."[14]

After the arrest, Burroughs sold his East Texas ranch (but stayed in business in South Texas) and, in the summer of 1948, moved to New Orleans. Since January 1945, he had been on and off heroin. In New Orleans he could smell the dope, and he quickly developed a fresh habit. However, the city turned out to be a dicey place to score: The dope scene was a small one, and addicts were easily spotted. To avoid being too obvious, Burroughs used his connections all over Louisiana, Texas, and Mexico to keep the monkey off his back. Some beautifully poetic passages in *Naked Lunch* describe his frantic trips from New Orleans to Houston (to buy paregoric, an opium-laced liquid) or to South Texas and Mexico:

> On through the peeled landscape, dead armadillos in the road and vultures over the swamp and cypress stumps. Motels with beaverboard walls, gas heater, thin pink blankets. . . . Came at last to Houston where I know a druggist. . . . [H]e looks up and makes me with one quick look and just nods and says: "Wait over at the counter. . . ." So we pour it [paregoric] in a Pernod bottle and start for New Orleans past iridescent lakes and orange gas flares, and swamps and garbage heaps, alligators crawling around on broken bottles and tin cans, neon arabesques of motels, marooned pimps scream obscenities at passing cars from islands of rubbish. . . . Back through Lake Charles and the dead slot-machine country, south end of Texas, nigger-killing sheriffs look us over and check the car papers. Something falls off you when you cross the road into Mexico.[15]

In spite of his attempts not to "burn down" his New Orleans sources for heroin, Burroughs took a second fall for drug possession on April 6, 1949.[16] He was released pending trial, and for the second time after a fall, he moved to the Valley to get away from the junk scene. He also wanted to be in the Valley to be close to the Mexican border in case his upcoming trial in New Orleans appeared as if it would go badly.

Burroughs and Joan and the kids holed up in the Valley for six months, from April to October of 1949. Maybe it was just withdrawal sickness, but Burroughs found the Valley dull and oppressive. When you pour yourself a glass of milk in the morning, he says, it sours before you even get it to your lips. But it was more than just the heat. Burroughs, who was a believer in Wilhelm Reich's "orgone" theory, felt that the Valley was plagued by a particularly deadly atmosphere: "Whatever it is — orgones, life force — that we all have to score for all the time, there is not much of it in the valley. . . . Death hangs over the Valley like an invisible smog."[17]

In *Junky*, Burroughs's description of the Valley is thus a harsh one. He sees it as a flat, desert landscape with depressed towns scattered like recently pitched carnivals or camp meetings (La Feria [the fair] is the name of a lower-valley town). The name itself for the region — "the Valley" — is deceptive, part of the basic con in a land-development scheme set up for unsuspecting "marks," says Burroughs. "During the Twenties, real estate operators brought trainloads of prospects down to the Valley and let them pick grapefruit right off the trees and eat it. One of these pioneer promoters is said to have constructed a large artificial lake and sold plots all around it. 'The lake will sub-irrigate your groves.' As soon as the last sale closed, he turned off the water and disappeared with his lake, leaving the prospects sitting there in a desert."[18]

Forty years later, in his allegorical *The Western Lands* (1987), Burroughs tells this story from the Valley in order to illustrate the cons awaiting pilgrims journeying to the "City of Knowledge": "Other societies prey on the pilgrims, for the area is infected with every variety of faker and swindler selling spurious Western Land plots and villas and condominiums. There you are in your beautiful villa, straight out of Disneyland, on a clear blue lake that drains away, while you sit, with a last derisive gurgle . . . *'suuuuuugggger.'*"[19]

As a display in the Hidalgo County Historical Museum notes, the locals sometimes referred to real-estate investors from the Midwest as "Valley suckers." The most famous Valley land developer, John Shary ("the father of the Texas citrus industry"), lived on an estate that doubled as a hotel for his visiting prospects. The estate, now located on Shary Road in Sharyland, was set amid thousands of acres of citrus groves and fronted by an artificial lake.

By the late 1940s, Burroughs and Kells were at least the third generation of Midwestern suckers in the Valley. The pitch was still the same: a year-round growing season, a climate perfect for citrus, cheap and abundant labor, and irrigation from the Rio Grande — a winter garden. In 1948, Hidalgo County (where Pharr is located) produced more cotton than any other U.S. county and also grew a large part of the Valley's one hundred million dollar citrus and vegetable crop.[20]

At the time Burroughs and Kells were living there in the mid- to late forties, the Valley had a population of approximately 200,000, a fairly sparse number compared to the huge area of land the Valley covers — 120 miles of the Texas border from Brownsville on the coast all the way up the river to Rio Grande City.[21] To the north of Burroughs's and Kells's farms, for about 200 miles up to San Antonio, was nothing but "brush country" (mesquite trees, cactus, and not much water) and ranches, the most famous of which was the 1.2 million-acre King Ranch, about an hour and a half north of McAllen. To the south, about 6 miles from Pharr, Texas, was the Rio Grande River, the Mexican border town of Reynosa, and northern Mexico beyond. Three hours south in Mexico was the industrial city of Monterrey, and another day of driving southward brought you to Mexico City, then a city of 2.5 million people. In Pharr, Burroughs actually lived a few miles closer to Mexico City than he did to Dallas, Texas, and its oil-rich millionaires.

The eastern boundary of the Valley is the Gulf of Mexico and a long barrier island called South Padre Island. In the 1940s, the island was accessible only by boat and was completely undeveloped. Today it is a huge spring break and summer vacation spot with miles of beachfront hotels and condos. In his day, Burroughs and friends went to Boca Chica beach, just south of Padre Island and twenty miles east of Brownsville, the southernmost city in Texas. He also traveled up the coast to Corpus Christi, where he would party with oilmen in waterfront bars.

Traveling west on Highway 83, you would have passed through towns that Anglo land developers had established at the turn of the century and into the teens, when barren ranchland was transformed by irrigation into some of the richest farmland in the United States. These towns include Donna, Weslaco ("Western Land Company"), and McAllen. In *Junky*, Burroughs describes the layout of the Valley along Highway 83 in these terms: "A three-lane highway runs from Brownsville to Mission, and the towns of the Valley string out along this highway. . . . The whole Valley has the impermanent look of a camp, or carnival."[22]

At the western and northern ends of the Valley, you passed through Zapata County, where, in 1948, county judge Manuel Bravo helped Lyndon Baines Johnson secure a seat in the U.S. Senate by "finding" seventy-one extra votes.[23] One hundred miles up the river, you reached Laredo, Texas, the site of Jack Kerouac and Neal Cassady's famous crossing into Mexico in *On the Road* in the summer of 1950.[24]

The local setup for Burroughs was Kells's farm on the McAllen-Pharr city line and a quarter mile south of Highway 83 on Jackson Road. Burroughs lived in a falling-down house north of Kells's property, on Route One in Pharr. Larger than Pharr, McAllen claimed a sophistication that the smaller town was evidently lacking. Socially, in Pharr you made the rounds between the Hub, an all-night drive-up hamburger joint; the Covered Wagon, a sometimes rowdy dance hall and restaurant; and Joe's Place in Reynosa, an upscale restaurant with fabulous nightclub acts and African lions roaming the premises while restrained on gold chains. Kells was a member of the McAllen Country Club, so Billy could golf and swim there or at the golf club in Edinburg. For Joan's three-Benzedrine-tubes-a-day habit, Billy probably went to the San Juan drugstore, located down the road a couple of miles from Pharr.

Agriculture was the mainstay of the economy in the Magic Valley, so-called because the temperate climate allowed for a year-round growing season. During World War II, an all-out effort to keep the troops supplied in "food and fiber" (vegetables and cotton) led to a profitable boom for Valley farmers — men such as Burroughs's fellow St. Louis native, John Noser, known as the "Carrot King," and others who made a lot of money very quickly on huge sales of some in-demand commodity. However, after the war, when Burroughs started farming, demand decreased, and costs for farmers rose, leading to a price-cost squeeze that, along with some rare, severe freezes, eventually ruined his and Kells's agricultural enterprises.[25]

Before moving to South Texas, Burroughs knew nothing about farming, but he approached it seriously. For example, he appears to have been involved in many of the day-to-day operations of the land he farmed and owned. He oversaw the hiring of Mexican laborers, and he says he took care of them by providing them food, shelter, and medical care. At harvest time, he, Kells, and Ted had a camp of more than two hundred field hands. When he made a profit, Burroughs says in a letter to Allen Ginsberg, he shared it with the workers, a cooperative business practice that would have made the local farmers suspicious of him and even angry. As he had studied many other subjects, he now studied farming, and he experimented with ways to run his operations fairly and profitably. This was not a light subject with him: Burroughs was genuinely interested in developing a social and economic system that would do away with the tyranny of the upper classes while preserving the right of people to benefit from their own talent, initiative, and hard work.

Part of the magic of the Magic Valley, though, was the ready availability of dirt-cheap laborers from Mexico — so-called wetbacks. Burroughs and Kells, like every other farmer in the area, broke the law by hiring them, but the Mexicans labored right under the nose of the Border Patrol. Burroughs felt so hypocritical about this aspect of his noble life as an upstanding American farmer and son of the soil that he declared himself, in a letter to Allen Ginsberg, to have been more honest as a heroin dealer than he currently was as a cotton and carrot farmer. Also in letters, he noted instances of brutal mistreatment of these workers, while at the same time disclaiming responsibility and painting himself as a fair and generous *patrón* [employer]. However, as a "gentleman farmer," Burroughs maintained a clear separation between himself and the Mexican farmworkers he hired. Nowhere in his letters or books, for example, does he write about the clear segregation of Mexicans and Mexican Americans in the Valley. Well into the 1950s, for instance, in certain parts of the Valley, some restaurants still refused to serve Mexicans, and "whites only" swimming pools were common.

In other respects, though, Burroughs's picture of the Valley in his letters and books is accurate and compares favorably — as authoritative, regional literature — to works by indigenous Valley writers from that period, such as Américo Paredes's *George Washington Gómez: A Mexicotexan Novel* (circa 1945, publ. 1990), Hart Stilwell's *Border City* (1945), and John Houghton Allen's *Southwest* (1952). In particular, Burroughs has an affinity with the eccentric John Houghton Allen, a trust-fund artist who ranched land he had inherited from his father (a University of Texas regent) near Laredo in the 1940s. Like Burroughs, Allen found the Valley depressing and dealt with it (as did Burroughs) by drinking heavily: "The best way to see the Southwest is through the bottom of a glass," Allen wrote in *Southwest*.[26]

As is true of all of these Valley writers of the 1940s, Burroughs has preserved key details from that period. For example, characters such as Roy in *Junky* have only recently been identified as well-known people from the Valley. Roy L. Hines was a land agent for the Bentsen family, and he sold Burroughs his fifty acres of farmland in Edinburg in May of 1948. Roy has a key line in this first novel by Burroughs. Burroughs tells the very typical Valley story of a man who tries repeatedly to leave the Valley but is always drawn back here by some invisible force: "But he couldn't keep away from the Valley. He would run like a hooked fish until the drag of his dying cells tired him out, and the Valley reeled him in." Comments Roy, "That man is crazy. . . . He don't know what he wants." Such details in Burroughs's work accurately re-create the Valley of that time and ring true today for those of us who live here, for the place is still famous for mysteriously "reeling in" people who try to leave and keeping them here in spite of their best interests.[27]

Roy Hines was a solid Valley citizen, but the majority of the characters Burroughs knew in the Valley were eccentric and even wild — more like the characters Burroughs knew in Times Square, circa 1945. They were Kells Elvins's friends for the most part, and Kells was famous for collecting characters around him. James Grauerholz's 1974 interview with Burroughs reveals the identity of some of these men: "So I'm over in the Rio Grande Valley . . . and I stayed first in several houses of friends of Kells that were out, that were away — one was Phillip something-or-other, and Walter Benson, who was later shot. He was living with this woman, and her father didn't think he was treating her right — came over there, put six bullets in him and killed him. And some schoolteacher who was there at the time was shot in the knee and later turned up in Mexico — [hit] by one of the bullets. . . . And this went on for almost a year. I was staying first in Walter Benson's house, then Benson came back, then in Philip's house, then I rented a house. Billy was talking at this time, quite fluently — this is when the Tiger Terry incident occurred."[28]

In 1956 Walter Benson was shot in his own front yard by his father-in-law, a justice of the peace. Tiger Terry, also one of Burroughs's South Texas friends mentioned in this letter, was killed by a pet lion at Joe's Place restaurant in November of 1950, when he climbed into the lion's cage and provoked one of the females who had just given birth to cubs. Burroughs later wrote a short story about Terry's death. In fact, those who are familiar with the tragic and bizarre stories of Burroughs's Beat associates back in New York in 1945 will see a pattern. His circle in the Valley was just as Beat, just as excessive, and even dangerous at times. They scared the locals with their wild partying and eccentric lifestyles, much as more staid New Yorkers had been frightened by the dangerous antics of the 1940s' Columbia crowd of 118th Street.[29]

They were an unconventional group of Anglos in South Texas, pushed up against the end of the United States all the way to the border — *la frontera*. Many old-timers remember it as "the Wild West," a frontier with a law all its own. Burroughs, as an outlaw himself, evidently relished this Wild West atmosphere and liked to play Billy the Kid and shoot oranges that Kells and Ted Marak threw into the air. As an outlaw, though, he needed some tough lawmen to complete the cast of characters, and men such as Sheriff Vail Ennis of Beeville, Texas, and Constable Tom Mayfield of Pharr, Texas, stood in for the Bat Masterson types Burroughs had read about as a teenager in Jack Black's *You Can't Win* and in pulp Westerns. Burroughs wanted to believe in the Wild West, and he hardly wanted to deromanticize these classic Western lawmen.

This Wild West atmosphere left room for behavior that would not happen — or be tolerated — in other places in the States. It also gave rise to an atmosphere of free thinking. Kells's front porch was the meeting place for the Valley's characters at the time — Billy Burroughs, Gene Terry, Ted Marak, Obie Dobbs, T. L. Reed, and many others. They sat around at Kells's and conducted what Billy's friend Ted Marak called "the Think Tank" — although, since these sessions were fueled by Kells's homemade gin, "Drink Tank" might have been more appropriate. The members of the Think Tank would drink gin, smoke pot, eat bennies, and come up with all kinds of miracle cures, get-rich-quick schemes, and stupid diversions, such as building a life-essence trap designed by Wilhelm Reich called an orgone accumulator, starting a cockroach farm in order to provide "food on the hoof" for Kells's chickens, or creating an "indestructible" fabric from the Egyptian ramie plant.

Some of these schemes were more legitimate, such as Burroughs's attempts to find oil on his property in Edinburg, an experience that ended up inspiring the Texas oilman routine in *Queer*. Other stories about Texas wildcatters show up in interviews with Burroughs's biographer Ted Morgan, for whom Burroughs re-created the late 1940s' boomtown atmosphere of Corpus Christi. Like Burroughs, Kells, and other "South Texas Beats," men such as David "Dry Hole" Byrd (Dry Hole Dutton in *Queer*) were radical individualists who did whatever they wanted to do.

The place to do what you wanted to do in South Texas was across the border in Mexico at fabulous nightspots such as Joe's Place or informal drinking spots such as the tent-covered Patio. Burroughs was known to drink heavily at Joe's Place, a bar famous for its owner's never-ending quest for original diversions and novelties, such as a rotating bar and risqué after-hours entertainment. Sometimes Burroughs drank there in the company of Kells and Obie Dobbs (Kells's live-in woman), but he also often drank there alone. He would have loved Reynosa's Zona Rosa in the forties since it was a place where there really were no limits. Booze, drugs, women, and boys were all available. At some point Burroughs must have requested the latter, for local Reynosans still remember him as "Willy El Puto" [Willy the Queer]. These trips across the border from McAllen to Reynosa undoubtedly served as a dress rehearsal for his later life in Mexico City since his behavior in Reynosa closely resembles his description of himself in *Queer*, written a few years later in Mexico City.

In this respect — the desire to do whatever he wanted — Burroughs was reflecting a political view that today would definitely be labeled conservative or libertarian. He hated FDR liberalism, and, in fact, next to "communist," "liberal" is the dirtiest insult he can come up with in his letters of the 1940s. He was after all the grandson of the man who had perfected the adding machine and established a family fortune on the basis of his own hard work and ingenuity. In postwar America, though, the grandsons of these laissez-faire capitalists now saw their ideas and schemes endlessly foiled by government regulations, bureaucracy, and police-state tactics. In particular, Burroughs hated the New Deal farm legislation that tied his hands as a farmer by telling him what, when, and how much to plant. He also felt caught by what he called in a letter to Allen Ginsberg "the wetback deal." The farming game was rigged against small farmers by the "big holders" in the same way a dice table always plays in favor of the house, he wrote in *Junky*.[30]

In late 1949, to paraphrase the opening lines of *Naked Lunch*, the heat closed in on Burroughs as a farmer: The wetback deal and government regulation of farming were — to him — intolerable limits, and he yearned to live in a truly free country. He sold his fifty acres of the "finest land in the Valley" to Kells Elvins in May of 1949; by 1951 Elvins himself was pretty much out of business, his citrus groves having been decimated by drought and consecutive years of hard winter freezes in the Valley.[31]

The law was also closing in on Burroughs: His possession case in New Orleans had been pending during the six months he lived in the Valley in 1949 and was set for trial at the end of October. Burroughs took his lawyer's off-the-record advice, and by late fall of 1949 he had an apartment in Mexico City, where he would live for the next several years.

Burroughs loved Mexico for all of the reasons South Texas had taught him to hate the United States: People in Mexico minded their own business, he said, including the police. "What a relief to be rid of the U.S. for good and all, and to be in this fine free country," he wrote to Jack Kerouac. "I am selling my property in Texas. . . . I have been writing a book about junk."[32] Such glowing letters about Mexico, in turn, greatly influenced Kerouac's view of that country in *On the Road*, which he wrote almost immediately after reading the book Burroughs refers to — *Junky*. This letter to Kerouac, by the way, is Burroughs's first mention of writing *Junky*: Freeing himself of the United States and his Texas farming ventures had also apparently freed him to write the book that would become a classic account of America's emerging police state. Junk and cotton were really not that far removed.[33]

I can't say that Burroughs remembered the Valley fondly. In fact, his experiences here convinced him to leave the States altogether. But I have my own ideas about that: William S. Burroughs thought he understood every con in the world and that no one could beat him. In the Valley he was beaten — beaten at trying to play the game honestly.

He thought he knew the game in Mexico, but he slowly realized that it was against him there, too: As an American, he could not own property without a Mexican partner, thus spoiling his plans to open a bar or go into ranching. It was another game, however, that would ultimately force him to leave Mexico for good: In September of 1951, at a party in Mexico City, he attempted to shoot a drink glass off Joan's head in a game of "William Tell." He missed, hitting her in the forehead and killing her. The New York newspapers picked up the story because of the William Tell angle and because Burroughs was related to the inventor of the adding machine. And what was Burroughs's occupation at the time of the shooting? Said the *New York Daily News* of the man who would, eight years later, be known as the internationally famous author of the novel *Naked Lunch,* "Burroughs is a wealthy cotton planter from Pharr, Texas."[34]

THE SOUTH TEXAS BEATS

If you are reading this book, you probably know at least something about the Beat legend of New York City, which arose in Times Square in the mid-1940s. There was Jack Kerouac, twenty-two years old and already the author of more than a million unpublished words; beautiful Lucien Carr with Dave Kammerer stalking him; Bill Cannastra, the self-destructive, alcoholic lawyer who slept with Tennessee Williams and died in 1950 trying to climb out a window of a moving New York subway train; and Allen Ginsberg, an aspiring poet with William Blake–inspired visions and lusting after Neal Cassady. There were also the criminal-world types, such as the junky Herbert Huncke, described by Kerouac as a "true genius" storyteller; Phil White, who worked "the hole" with Burroughs in New York City; small-time thief and hustler Little Jack Melody and his girlfriend Vicki Russell, who taught them all how to get a Benzedrine high on asthma inhalers.

You had that whole cast of characters. Their story has been told by Jack Kerouac, Allen Ginsberg, John Clellon Holmes, William S. Burroughs, Carolyn Cassady, Joan Haverty, Joyce Johnson, and a host of other lesser-known novelists, poets, and memoirists. In addition, their stories have been retold in numerous biographies and interviews. Lately — and it seems to me somewhat belatedly, considering how interesting these people's lives were and how predictive they were of future lives — these Beat characters have become the subject of several films, emphasizing of course their extreme behavior, sexual promiscuity, good looks, and use of drugs and alcohol.[1] The fact that many of these original Beats met early deaths, often in bizarre fashion, only makes the tale that much more intriguing. Allen Ginsberg eulogized them in his poem "Howl," beginning with the line "I saw the best minds of my generation destroyed by madness" (which makes you wonder about the overall quality of those who survived).

Perhaps I'm overstating it, but a similar group of Beats was down in South Texas when Burroughs was living there. In fact, South Texas, hundreds of miles from the nearest major U.S. city and only minutes from a whole other country, Mexico, was the perfect setup for extreme characters living lives far out on the fringes of bourgeois, postwar society.

The South Texas Beats were a rich cast of individualists, eccentrics, and iconoclasts, including the happy-go-lucky hell-raiser Eugene Terry, who got his first taste of junk in the army; Ted Marak, who had been framed by a conman in Vegas and had to hide out in the Valley, where he had family; Walter Benson, who was a Jekyll-and-Hyde alcoholic but tremendously intelligent; T. L. Reed, a former New Orleans pimp who dressed immaculately and wouldn't get in the orgone accumulator because he was afraid he would mess up his manicured nails; and Obie Dobbs, Kells's live-in girlfriend, who made her way through life on her beauty but with a reputation following her. These people stood out even in a place already full of real characters. Ted Marak told me Kells himself was a "walking controversy." Again, the fact that several of these people died young, violently, and bizarrely — Walter Benson, Joan Burroughs, Gene Terry — only adds to the legend. However, unlike the New York Beats, whose lives were immortalized by the writers who hung out with them early on in their careers, these South Texas characters have never been celebrated.

The South Texas Beat scene centered around Kells Elvins, the learned psychologist and "alcoholic playboy of the Western World" (as his only son, Peter, described him to me).[2] Kells brought them all together in the Valley, including Billy Burroughs. Burroughs, in fact, had been following Kells's adventures for years. Long before their South Texas days, Burroughs and Elvins had been boyhood friends, growing up together in a tony St. Louis suburb. Then, from 1932 to 1936, they were both students at Harvard, and they remained close friends thereafter. In the summer of 1939, Burroughs visited Kells in Huntsville, Texas, where Kells was interning as a prison psychologist and working on his master's thesis at the University of Texas. Kells had also been living in South Texas off and on since 1936, and it is possible that Burroughs visited the Valley with him during the Huntsville trip.[3]

Kells first came to the Valley in the mid-1930s, when his father, Politte, "retired" there — in somewhat unusual circumstances. Politte had been a successful lawyer and was, at one point, the head of the Republican Party in Missouri. However, he suffered from paresis, a mental disorder caused by syphilis. "He was as mad as a hatter," Peter Elvins told me in a letter. In 1934 Kells's mother institutionalized Politte, divorced him, and laid claim to all of his money and property. Kells opposed his mother's actions, and in 1936, with the help of Politte's brother, Charles P. Elvins in California, Kells obtained Politte's release from the hospital along with an official document declaring him sane. Politte was hardly sane, though, no matter what the certificate said, and Kells had to watch over him.[4]

It's not clear why Politte moved to the Valley in 1936. Land developers in Pharr were targeting Midwesterners in the 1930s, and perhaps Politte was lured by an advertising campaign emphasizing the cheap land and year-round warm climate in Pharr. However, it's also likely Kells recognized that the Valley was the perfect place to settle his mentally unstable father: No one knew Politte there, help was cheap, and eccentric gringos with money were easily tolerated. Ostensibly, Politte was a "citrus grower" in the Valley from 1936 to 1943.[5]

Burroughs remembered Politte as an "evil old man": It was Politte who famously described the young neighbor boy Billy Burroughs as looking like "a sheep killing dog."[6] Burroughs returned the compliment, featuring unflattering portraits of Politte in several works, including "Twilight's Last Gleamings" (coauthored by Kells), in which the Politte-inspired character cuts off the fingers of shipwrecked passengers attempting to climb aboard a lifeboat. He is also Dale's father in Jack Kerouac's novel *On The Road*. In the following passage from *Road*, Old Bull Lee (Burroughs) describes the house Politte built in Pharr in the late 1930s, a house still standing at the corner of Cherokee and Avenue D: "'Say, did I ever tell you about Dale's father? He was the funniest old man you ever saw in your life. He had paresis, which eats away the forepart of the brain and you get so's you're not responsible for anything that comes into your mind. He had a house in Texas and had carpenters working twenty-four hours a day putting on new wings. He'd leap up in the middle of the night and say, "I don't want that goddamn wing; put it over there." The carpenters had to take everything down and start over again. . . . Oh, he was horrible. I could tell you stories about him all day.'"[7]

If this portrait of Politte is only half true (and it was undoubtedly based on conversations Kerouac had with Burroughs), Kells obviously needed help managing his father, and that's how Danny Lohr came to know the elder Elvins quite well. Lohr, now in his late eighties, has lived his entire life in the Valley. He met Kells in 1936 on the golf course in McAllen. Soon thereafter, Kells asked him whether he would like a job helping Kells take care of his mentally impaired father. At one point, Lohr traveled with Politte to Mexico City, a trip somehow connected to Politte's plan to run for the

Texas Senate. Politte actually placed ninth in a field of twelve candidates — a fact that makes you wonder about the relative sanity of Texas politicians.[8] Lohr says that Politte had a reputation for being somewhat crazy, and he remembers Politte publishing eccentric editorials in the local newspapers. He also recalls a much younger woman whom Politte presented as his wife.

Ninety-three-year-old Anna Mae Kelly, who is related by marriage to the founders of Pharr, Texas, recalled a story from the 1930s about Politte's young wife, Margaret Faucelle Elvins, and a fur coat he had given her. They were set to go on a trip by airplane, but for some reason, as they left their house on Cherokee Avenue in Pharr, Politte became angry with Margaret and punished her on the spot by making her stand under a shower in fur, dress, and heels. Her clothes were ruined. Kelly doesn't recall the source of this argument, but she did say that the young men in town paid quite a bit of attention to Politte's wife, who could easily have been mistaken for his daughter.

It was probably this woman who finally took Politte off Kells's hands. Someone had to: Kells's friend Pat Lohr Paris recalls that the first time she went to Kells's house in Pharr, she saw bars on all of the windows. "Who are you trying to keep out?" she asked Kells, and he replied enigmatically, "They're to keep someone in." Clearly Kells had to make arrangements for his father's care, and Margaret struck some kind of deal with him. (Later she would sue Politte's estate for the rights to some of the St. Joseph Lead Company stock Elvins had given to her; in the litigation that followed, she was unable to provide proof of their marriage in Monterrey, Mexico, which she said had occurred on August 15, 1938. She did retain the stock, however.)[9]

With Margaret taking care of Politte, Kells left his father and was out of the Valley and back in school studying psychology at Harvard in 1938, the year he and Burroughs collaborated on the short story "Twilight's Last Gleaming." He was a psychiatrist in residence at the Huntsville State Penitentiary in Huntsville, Texas, in 1939, when Burroughs visited him for the first time in the Lone Star State. Kells received his master's degree in psychology at the University of Texas–Austin in 1941, writing a thesis titled "Forty-four Incestuous Fathers of Texas," a subject that evidently displeased the Texas fathers and led to his dismissal at Huntsville.[10] Subsequently he enlisted as a marine during World War II and was awarded a Purple Heart for wounds sustained in combat.

Politte's death brought him back to the Valley in January of 1943: His father, whom Jack Kerouac describes in *On the Road* as recklessly speeding around Texas, had been involved in an auto crash on New Year's eve. He died two weeks later from complications. Peter Elvins recalls seeing his father hear this news: "Kells was in his Marine uniform, jumped up, packed his things, and said: 'If my father is dying, I am going to Texas right now.'" Peter doesn't know whether Kells made it to McAllen before his father's death.[11] From 1943 to 1951, the Valley area phone book listed the owner of the farm that lay a quarter mile out on South Jackson Road as Kells Elvins.

Pat Lohr Paris and her sister Betty met Kells in 1945. Pictures from these years show that Pat was a lovely blonde, tall and slim, and her sister a delicate beauty. At twenty-two years of age, Pat was a war widow, her husband having gone missing in action in 1943; his body was recovered in northern France two years later. When she was introduced to Kells in 1945, he was still suffering from a touch of malaria contracted during the war, but Pat remembers being impressed by him: He was one of the best-looking and most intelligent men she had ever met. His eyes were black and fathomless, she says, his hair curly and brown, and he dressed very stylishly for the valley.

Pat dated Kells for a while ("never seriously," she says; they were "friends") and remained good friends with him until his death in 1961. Both were charter members of the McAllen Country Club, founded in 1946, and they were frequent golf and tennis partners. One day Pat told Kells she was too tired to play another game of tennis, and he offered her a pill to restore her energy. She perked right up, she told me. Only years later did she realize Kells had handed her some Benzedrine. After Kells began living with Obie Dobbs, a striking and sexy young woman from Mission, Pat became Kells's "official" girl on occasions when his nosy and strict mother came to visit him in the Valley. "She [Kells's mother] controlled the purse strings," Pat told me.

Kells was a marvelous raconteur and host at his modest house on South Jackson. Jazz was always playing, Pat recalled, especially one of Kells's favorite songs by Nellie Lutcher, "Fine Brown Frame." At one of these parties, a married woman found her way outside into Kells's orange grove with a man who was not her husband. It was an extremely windy night. A half hour later she sneaked back in wearing the man's coat — because her clothes had blown away.[12] Everyone remembers lots of drinking at these parties. Anna Mae Kelly recalls going to Kells's house for cocktails and being served by a woman in the kitchen who was never introduced — probably Obie Dobbs. When she asked why no one introduced Kells's live-in, she was told, "Well, Kells just assumes you wouldn't want to know a woman like that."

Pat became friends with one of Kells's friends, Ted Marak, when they found themselves sharing cab rides around town. She dated Ted a few times, and later Ted dated her sister Betty. Pat and Ted both still have copies of a picture taken in Reynosa from that period (around 1946), with Ted and Betty one couple; Pat and her future husband, Andy Paris, another; and Danny Lohr, brother of Betty and Pat, the fifth person in the picture.

Ted Marak's life story is truly a Beat one. Born in 1920, he was raised by a succession of desperately poor relatives in Depression-era Oklahoma. For a while he helped his grandparents make ends meet by delivering bootleg whisky for a neighbor with a still. When he was fourteen, Marak left home, hopping the first train that came through town. He didn't know where it was going but ended up out West. Eventually he made his way into the air force during World War II and was stationed outside of Las Vegas. That led to a job in one of Vegas's first casinos, owned by Guy McAfee, a former Los Angeles police captain who was fired for skimming money kicked back to the LAPD by gambling boat operators in Long Beach. Marak learned to be a dealer in McAfee's casino by studying with the best con men, cardsharps, and grifters in the United States. You had to know how to cheat if you wanted to catch someone else at it. One night he and a buddy made the rounds of the casinos, trying out some of the techniques they had learned for beating the house. At the Flamingo, Bugsy Siegel himself confronted Marak but couldn't catch him cheating outright. He offered Ted a job, which he declined: Bugsy was "crazy," he said.

Ted came to the Valley (where he had relatives) in 1946, when he was fired from his job in Las Vegas. "About that time I was working the cage as well as the floor," he told me, "and we had a sonofabitch named Ted Jorey. He was a crossroads hustler, and Guy McAfee had lost a bankroll and hired this Ted Jorey, and I was working the cage."

During the count every night, Jorey was setting aside five or six hundred dollars. Ted caught him at it, and Jorey said it was none of his business. Marak said it was, drew a gun on him, and made Jorey replace the money. Later Jorey made up a story that Marak was the one skimming, and McAfee believed him. Ted told McAfee, "'If you want to believe this lying son of a bitch, this thieving prick, well, that's your business. But as far as I'm concerned, you can take this job and stick it in your ass.' And I packed up and went to the Valley." Concerned for his safety that final night in Vegas, Ted slept on the floor of his hotel room. Sure enough, someone came by in a car and shot out the windows.

Ted doesn't remember how he first met his friend Kells Elvins, but it was probably because he wanted to meet Kells's live-in, Obie Dobbs, who must have been a stunning woman. I have talked with several septuagenarian and octogenarian males who, when I mention Obie Dobbs, suddenly come alive. She was "one good-looking heifer," "a fine specimen," "the best-looking woman I ever saw." Women tell a slightly different story — not that they didn't like her, she was "sweet" — and say she wasn't so much beautiful (there were more beautiful women in the Valley) as she was extremely sexy and very good at advertising her assets by the way she dressed and walked. Dobbs was raised in Mission, Texas, in the 1930s by a single-parent mother who had a drinking problem and was, by several accounts, oversexed. One man who knew Obie well told me Obie's mother, Ethel, was known as the "fucking machine" in Mission. Friends would help Obie haul her mother into the house after she had been left, drunk and unconscious, on the front lawn of their house.

Obie was cursed with sex appeal and great looks and apparently made her way through life on that basis. She was Kells's live-in from around 1946 to 1948. They had a real love affair, but it sometimes turned violent. Stories vary about what happened to Obie after she and Kells broke up. One man told me she became the mistress of the brother of the president of Mexico; Ted Marak says her sister told him she had married a doctor; one of her high school boyfriends says he heard from Anna Mae Kelly's sister that Obie had been spotted in Hollywood at the racetrack — sitting next to Lana Turner. Obie did in fact like to advertise that she had the perfect Hollywood figure, except that her ankle was a quarter inch too small. In the mid-1950s she called up an old boyfriend at the Circle Inn Bar in McAllen — where he was known to be in those days — and told him she was in Hollywood and wanted to know what kind of car she should buy. They chatted, and she gave him a Los Angeles phone number. He called the number later, but the man who answered told him never to call back. That was the last time her old boyfriend (or anyone I've found) ever heard of Obie Dobbs.[13]

Obie was probably the lure that brought Eugene Terry, another of the South Texas Beats, into Kells's crowd. Gene Terry's best friend from high school in Corsicana, Texas, John Taylor, described him to me as a "happy-go-lucky hell-raiser." Ted Marak took a more extreme view of him: "He was crazy, he really was," Ted told me. One time while Ted, Terry, and Kells were riding in Terry's truck, Terry stopped the truck with no warning, leaped out, jumped on top of a barbed-wire fence, and performed a perilous low-wire act. "He could have nutted himself doing that," Ted told me, still incredulous. Sometimes his lunacy was inspired, though, and Terry brought some ideas to this group that led to notable experiments, such as the orgone accumulator Kells built behind his house. His best ideas came to him, evidently, when he was high on psilocybin mushrooms, which he frequently was. Burroughs was so taken with Terry that he wrote a short story about him and the bizarre circumstances of his violent death.

Although Burroughs wrote a story about Terry, he never wrote about Ted or Obie or Pat (although she is an unnamed character in one of his Valley stories), and, in fact, he doesn't even mention them in interviews. But they remember him. Ted Marak, fifty-six years after the fact, recalled Burroughs's first night in the Valley for me when I interviewed him over the phone in the summer of 2002:

> I remember the night he came to the Valley. Elvins and I and Obie, and I had a date — she was blonde and blue eyed and oversexed — we were all drunk and naked and lying on the verandah in front of Kells's house. When he [Kells] was thinking, he always twisted the hair behind his ear. "I have a friend coming today," he says, twisting his hair. It's raining, it's pouring down rain. Fifteen minutes later two car lights coming down this drive drove up, a GI surplus Jeep, and a character sitting at the wheel: a fedora hat, he's got on a suit and tie, and his damn tie has become so saturated it was pulled out at the bias and was hanging down to his crotch. He got out, comes to the screen door. Elvins says, "Come on in, Billy." Nobody stirred, we were drunk, and he comes in pouring water. "You better get out of those wet clothes," Kells says. Billy proceeded to strip naked, put his clothes in a pile.
>
> I was introduced to Billy. We were to have lunch in McAllen at a little restaurant on Main Street. Here comes Billy wearing that suit. It had dried lying down, and his tie was still hanging down past his crotch. Joan arrived. Joan always wore one style of dress, buttoned all the way down the front, and they were always too small, and she never wore undergarments. She had "gapsies" in her dress that I had trouble not looking at. And that poor girl, she'd eat two, maybe three Benzedrine inhalers a day. Never heard her speak a word. I didn't have an occasion to speak to her.

Pat Paris also met Billy, Joan, and Joan's daughter, Julie, around the same time. In an interview in 2002 she told me that "she [Joan] was very nice, and they had a little child. And they lived in a broken-down hotel that you would not believe in McAllen. . . . Probably the worst, shacky motel around. It's not there now. It was just off Tenth Street on Ash. I remember Kells, and I went over to pick her up or pick both of them up, and they brought the baby [Julie] with them, and we went back to Kells's house [on South Jackson] and spent the afternoon." Julie, she recalls, had on "no underpants . . . [and was] dirty, barefoot." I showed her a picture of Julie standing on the rickety front porch of Burroughs's East Texas farm. She looks like a child in a Walker Evans photograph. "You see what I mean," Pat said.

Pat has several other distinct memories of Billy Burroughs. One day, she told me, she and Kells and Billy went golfing at a course in Edinburg now located next to the Echo Hotel: "We went golfing in Edinburg and then went swimming, me and Kells and Billy — Joan wasn't here, or if she was, she wasn't with us. It was around noon, and we were swimming, and we just kept on our suits, and we got in the car and started down this little narrow road at the time . . . and that's when one of them spied that snake, so we just got the golf clubs out and went over and tried to kill it, and I guess we did. I kept thinking afterwards that we were just burned, blistered, out there in our swimsuits [killing a rattlesnake]. Well, it was fun. You know, he [Burroughs] could get with it, but conversation was lacking, not much conversation."

Burroughs recalls this scene (minus Pat and Kells) in several places in his work, most prominently in *Interzone*'s "Lee and the Boys." He connects the rattlesnake incident to his days rolling drunks in the New York subway, which he had been doing just two years before he landed in the Valley: "In the Rio Grande Valley of South Texas, he had killed a rattlesnake with a golf club. The impact of metal on the live flesh of the snake sent an electric shiver through him. In New York, when he was rolling lushes on the subway with Roy, at the end of the line in Brooklyn a drunk grabbed Roy and started yelling for the law. Lee hit the drunk in the face and knocked him to his knees, then kicked him in the side. A rib snapped. Lee felt a shudder of nausea."[14] Today Pat says she's not sure it was a rattlesnake at all and says Burroughs was probably using his authorial license in the retelling.

Pat's husband, Andy, also shows up in *Interzone,* a book Burroughs wrote just a few years after leaving the Valley and one rich in references to his South Texas days — if you know what to look for. During World War II,

Andy Paris made a small fortune by cornering the market on Mexican "chicle," or gum, and he became known as the "bubble gum king." Burroughs incorporated this story into a routine in *Interzone*'s "Word." He is telling the history of a left-wing magazine called the *Sundial* and says, "You recall the rag folded when their angel, an Albanian condom tycoon who came on like an English gentleman — the famous Merchant of Sex, who scandalized the International Set when he appeared at the Duc du Ventre's costume ball as a walking prick covered by a huge condom — went broke and shot himself during World War II. He couldn't get rubber, and Alcibiades Linton, the Houston Bubble Gum King, beat him out on Mexican chicle."[15]

I was a bit hesitant to read this ribald story to Pat Paris, but she found it quite funny and said that her late husband had a great sense of humor and would have enjoyed it, too. However, she reminded me, Andy did not know Burroughs and would not have associated with people like him in the Valley. (Pat had split with Kells's crowd by the time she met Andy Paris.)

Overall, Pat was unimpressed by Billy and was extremely surprised in 1959 to see his picture in *Life* magazine as the author of *Naked Lunch*.[16] Back when she knew him in the late 1940s, he was simply a nonpresence even when present, she says, and his intellect was definitely suspect. Her impression of him at dinner one night in Reynosa in 1946 or 1947 is typical of many people's memory of El Hombre Invisible during these years. Pat, Kells, Obie, Billy, and possibly Ted dined that night in Reynosa at Sam's American Restaurant, across the street from Joe's Place, where Kells and the gang would go to drink until late at night. Pat does not remember much about Burroughs at the dinner party except that he was incapable of joining in the conversation: He seemed to have no social skills. Some time later Kells phoned Pat and asked if she would like to join them on another dinner party to Mexico, saying she could accompany Billy. Pat replied, "Why would I want to go out with an idiot like that?"

Ted Marak knew Billy Burroughs about as well as Pat Paris did — meaning that Burroughs was more Kells's friend than he was theirs — and he had a similar impression of Billy Burroughs's mental capacity: "I actually thought he was a little slow witted. He always talked like he had a wad of snuff in his mouth. His lip kind of hung out in front." He remembers Billy as quiet, too, but capable of great bursts of enthusiasm. One incident stands out in his memory. After Billy and Joan moved out of the run-down motel, they lived in a run-down house on the north side of Kells's South Jackson orange groves. Billy had been fixing it up, and when it was presentable, he held a dinner party. Joan cooked. The furnishings of the house, Ted says, were unusual to say the least: Billy had built side tables and a dining table out of railroad ties held together with rebar and bolts. During dinner Billy said almost nothing, which was pretty normal for him; however, says Marak, "In the middle of dinner, Billy jumps up on the table right in the middle of the food and dishes. 'Now, by God, this is functional!' he says."[17] Ted had no idea why Burroughs felt the need to demonstrate the sturdiness of his odd dinner table that night.

A few years later, Jack Kerouac witnessed a similar scene. In *On the Road,* he describes Old Bull Lee's exclamations about a bookshelf he plans to make, which, like the South Texas railroad-tie table, will be ridiculously overengineered: "'When I get all these nails out of this I'm going to build me a shelf that'll last a *thousand years!'* said Bull, every bone shuddering with boyish excitement. 'Why, Sal, do you realize the shelves they build these days crack under the weight of knickknacks after six months or generally collapse? Same with houses, same with clothes. These bastards have invented plastics by which they could make houses that last *forever.* And tires.'"[18]

Allen Ginsberg also recalled that in New York in the mid-1940s Burroughs proposed the idea of building houses out of cast concrete so they would last for a thousand years. Burroughs didn't see why things in the United States weren't built to last — except to rip people off by selling them substandard crap. That wasn't what U.S. industry should be, Burroughs believed. That night in the Valley, he showed everyone that, by God, he had built an indestructible dinner table.

Ted recalls an even more significant and unfortunately characteristic scene with Burroughs in it. Billy, he says, was an expert shot. Ted knew this for a fact because he himself qualified as an expert marksman during his time as a member of the army cavalry in the late 1930s. Billy, he says, would show off by having Ted or Kells throw grapefruit or oranges into the air. Billy would draw a bead on them and hit them on the fly nearly every time. However, he didn't limit himself to shooting fruit tossed into the air. Joan, Ted says, would place fruit on her head for Billy to shoot in a reenactment of the William Tell scene, an act that would have tragic consequences a few years later.

Ted told me many stories of his Valley days, and quite often his accounts corroborated Burroughs's tales in *Junky,* although when I first interviewed Ted he had no knowledge of *Junky.* Both Burroughs and Marak remembered that most of the evening drinking and partying took place on Kells's front porch. As Ted told me, "We were a bunch of drunks. Our head man would go over to Mexico and get the makings for gin. Buy five gallons of sugarcane alcohol, mix half and half with Ozark water. Make ten gallons of gin. Whether it was my place or his, the gang always met." It wasn't just the gin, though, that kept the party going: "Well, we were always high on bennies. That was what sustained us: gin, bennies, pot. I was taking the pills." Joan, as she had been doing since New York in the mid-1940s, would get high off Benzedrine extracted from asthma inhalers. "Only Billy's wife needed enough to eat one of the inhalers," Ted says. The pot they smoked was Kells's crop — "nice pot," according to Ted — grown in a tin barn on his property. Billy, Kells, T. L. Reed, and Gene Terry would also eat hallucinogenic mushrooms, Ted says, but he himself "didn't care for it."

Apparently, they thought quite a lot about how to solve the world's problems during these all-night drug and drinking sessions. Marak doesn't specifically recall Burroughs being in on many of these gatherings, but the ideas and schemes they came up with are characteristic of Burroughs, including building a "life essence" machine called an orgone accumulator, which the eccentric psychoanalyst Wilhelm Reich designed in the 1940s.[19] Burroughs wrote about his own South Texas orgone accumulator at length in the recently restored chapter 28 of *Junky*, but that account is quite technical and not nearly as amusing as Ted Marak's: "We first decided to build an orgone accumulator. We had a speckled rooster. Well, we saw no speckled chicks, so Elvins and I, we came to the conclusion that we'd put this rooster in the orgone accumulator, and after three months, the chicks started coming out speckled — proof positive to our gin-soaked brains that the thing worked. Obie [Dobbs] hated it. It was solid lead and open to the top. It bred the largest damn mosquitoes in South Texas. 'You bunch of brains,' said Obie."

The orgone accumulator didn't just breed speckled chicks and Texas-size mosquitoes. Later, Ted told me, they put a mare that wouldn't foal into the orgone accumulator for treatment. Soon thereafter, she foaled. I told him I didn't realize it was big enough to accommodate a horse, but he assured me it was. (When I told Pat Paris the story of the horse in the orgone accumulator, she asked me, skeptically, "What part of the horse [fit in]?") I also asked Ted whether the orgone accumulator had the same effect on him that it did on Burroughs: In *The Adding Machine*, Burroughs says he built a portable orgone accumulator in "an orange grove in Pharr, Texas, and no hands achieved spontaneous orgasm age 37 years old."[20] "Shit," Ted told me after hearing of this feat, "back then, I had a hard-on all the time anyway."

This was not the only scheme hatched by the gin-soaked brains participating in the nightly think tanks ("The Think Tank" is the title of Marak's short story about this group). As Ted told me in my 2002 interview with him,

> I'm writing a little book. In our think tank, we come up with the idea of raising cockroaches on a farm. Billy didn't have much to do with this. Tiger Terry was telling us about a border patrolman conning him, trying to find some [magic] mushrooms. This guy brought up cockroaches as ideal food on hoof for chickens. You didn't have to give them anything for a craw if they ate them, too. We got off on that. We were millionaires in our minds for starting to raise those things. Kells had some hydroponic tanks, and we thought that would make good bedding for the cockroaches. The feed was pectin, orange peels, molasses, and calf corn. We even pelletized them: We took an old sausage grinder and put larger holes in it and would push the cockroaches through it in a long piece and we'd whack it off at half an inch, and we'd let it dry on some paper. Some guy let the cat out of the bag, and the McAllen health department got wind of it. The FDA people came out and said it's great food, and you can feed it to chickens, but if you sell the chickens, you have to stamp on them, "Not fit for human consumption."

Ted described another project right out of the 1951 film *The Man in the White Suit* by Alec Guinness (a film about a man who invents an indestructible fabric) that was also scuttled by the powers that be: "Then we started the 'ramie project.' Ramie was a plant Egyptians used to make a cloth they put around their mummies. Elvins went someplace and got some shoots of this plant. We had a piece of ground that was really salty along the canal bank, and we planted it [ramie] and couldn't kill it because it made a root network underground. Burlington Mills made 5–10 yards of cloth out of it for us. We made a shirt from it that was indestructible. You couldn't even burn it. Beat Nylon 10 to 1. But Dupont got wind of it. That shut that down. Legislation was passed saying, 'This plant was not to be brought into the United States.'"

Ted doesn't recall Burroughs being involved with either the cockroach farm or Project Ramie, but a section of *Interzone* shows that Burroughs knew about ramie and any number of offbeat money-making schemes in the 1940s and 1950s: "Chris, the English Public School man, is the type who gets involved in fur farming, projects to raise ramie, frogs, cultured pearls."[21]

Clearly, these people in South Texas were as eccentric, intelligent, and wild as the types Burroughs knew back in New York City before he was forced to leave there, eventually ending up in South Texas. Once again he found a group of very interesting, more or less likeminded misfit souls. Ted Marak tells outrageous stories about the exploits of Kells, Gene Terry, Obie Dobbs, and Ted himself, some of which I can't publish because the principal characters are still alive: "Did you ever hear about the time that Elvins somehow got control — political control — of the Citrus Exchange? We could get by with anything at the McAllen Country Club. The first thing we did, well, they [the members of the country club] were hard-nosed Baptists. Ladies weren't allowed to wear shorts and had to wear one-piece bathing suits. We decked Obie out in a body sock that was the same color as her skin — it looked like she was naked — and would take her to the pool. Did that once or twice when we'd been up forty-eight hours on bennies and were drunk." They had gone to San Antonio, he told me, to have the body sock specially made from one of the new synthetic materials that was appearing on the market. They also put Obie Dobbs in this flesh-colored suit and had her ride on the back of one of the McAllen fire department's trucks during a Fourth of July parade, causing quite a controversy.

Not all of their stunts were tolerated, however. One Saturday night, drunk and high, they went to the country club dressed in jeans and T-shirts — hardly the required uniform for a Saturday-night formal dinner and dance at the club. Even worse, Kells brought along his dog, Bopper. "We ordered T-bone steaks and ate them with our hands," Ted says. "Then we'd throw the bones onto the dance floor for Bopper to fetch."[22] Bopper would oblige, upsetting the crowd of formally dressed dance couples. Of course, the club threatened to call the police on them, and they had to leave. All in all, Ted recalls, "That was a pretty good night. Don't you agree?" he asked me, and I said I did, heartily, and I'd like to believe that I would have been there with them, eating steak with my hands, too — but I'm pretty sure I wouldn't have had the nerve.

That's an important part of the story: There were lots of real characters in the Valley, and they were mostly tolerated, but Kells's group of collected characters alienated the more reasonable people who knew them with their self-destructive and dangerous behavior. Pat Paris recalls the night she decided she should no longer see Kells's and Billy's crowd socially: "I remember this one girl, Obie. It was right after this I began thinking that some day there's going to be a disaster. We were at a dinner party at Kells's house. They were drunk, and Obie picked up a roast and threw it at Kells and hit him right here [points to her temple] and hit a vein, and the blood just . . . and so a doctor lived down the street, and they went and got him. Now [that night], I was with his friend Ted [Marak], very nice, conservative man, and Obie threw that roast and slit his head, right here, where it would bleed profusely, so I said to myself, all this drinking . . . gin . . . I'm out of here. Something terrible's going to happen."[23]

And it did. Within three years, Tiger Terry and Joan, both in their twenties, were dead. Ted Marak also had forebodings of disaster while hanging around with Kells and his gang in the Valley. After a while, he told me, he had to "get off the gin" because the wild life had become too wild. He sobered up, he says, and began working as a window dresser at the McAllen J. C. Penney, where his displays eventually set national trends and were published in trade journals. Some of Kells's associates, such as Eugene Terry, he says, were just plain crazy.

The same had been true back in New York City among Burroughs's friends. In New York, Bill Cannastra died when he stuck his head out of a subway window and smashed it on a pillar; Dave Kammerer was knifed to death by Lucien Carr; and Phil White, a convicted murderer, hanged himself in "the tombs." In South Texas, Walter Benson was shot by his father-in-law in his front yard in Pharr, Texas, and Tiger Terry died in the jaws of a pet lion at Joe's Place in Reynosa. Finally, in Mexico a few years later, Billy fatally shot Joan Burroughs during their William Tell routine. The early deaths of all of these people came as no surprise to those who knew them.

Those were the kind of extreme, self-destructive characters Kells "collected" in South Texas. Kells died young, too, in 1961 in New York City, but he was buried in McAllen. The Valley got him back, just as Burroughs describes all of the ill-fated people who tried to leave the Valley in *Junky*: It reels them back in.

TIGER IN THE VALLEY

Get away from here, oh father of mine,
Because I am more fierce than a lion.
Let it not be that I draw my sword
And split your heart.
— "El Hijo Desobediente"

William S. Burroughs came to the Valley, as did many of the Anglos he knew there, because it was, for them, the end of the line, the bottom of America, the place of dead roads. "All the worst features of America have drained down to the Valley and concentrated there," Burroughs writes in *Junky*. The Valley, he believed, was a place where you came to die, not to live, a great elephant graveyard: "[T]he dying cell gravitates to the Valley," he says in *Junky*.[1] Like eels drawn to the Sargasso Sea, where they mate and die in self-destructive frenzy (a scene that fascinated Burroughs), the Valley draws those whose biology of doom predetermines their fate.[2]

Several of Burroughs's Valley acquaintances seem to have been victims of the Valley's deadly gravity — how Burroughs himself escaped is a good question — but none fits this picture of a dying cell that gravitated there more than Burroughs's "young friend" Eugene "Tiger" Terry. His death in the jaws of an African lion that was a pet in a border restaurant is perhaps the most bizarre fate of any of Burroughs's friends, with the exception of Joan Vollmer. It certainly stuck with Burroughs: James Grauerholz says that the story of the death of Tiger Terry was one of Bill's favorite conversation pieces.

Eugene Terry was born in 1928 and raised in Corsicana, Texas, south of Dallas. A woman who knew him in his teens described him as "suave" and a sharp dresser. "All of us girls were in love with him," she said. In high school he was popular enough to be in the exclusive "Skulls" club, which explains his 1944 high school yearbook photo, showing him with a human skull balanced on his shoulder — an eerie harbinger of his early death.[3] After high school, near the end of World War II, Terry joined the navy as a medic. He undoubtedly served bravely in this capacity, but unfortunately he didn't limit himself to medicating injured soldiers. According to Ted Marak — who heard it from Kells Elvins — Terry "fell in love with morphine kits. Everybody had a morphine kit, and he went around stealing them. Kells said that's what messed up his brain. His brain was like scrambled eggs. He was really squirrelly." After the war, Terry and his buddies from Corsicana went to college, some to Texas A&M, and others to the University of Texas (UT) at Austin. Terry went to Austin but flunked out his first semester: He partied too much to make the necessary grades.

That was how he ended up in the Valley. Terry's best buddy from high school, John Taylor, told me that Terry's father and several other men owned citrus groves in San Juan, near Pharr, and after Terry flunked out of UT, his father sent him to South Texas to oversee the orchards. Terry's father hoped he would learn the business and settle down, or perhaps he reasoned that in the Valley Terry would at least have some room to sow his wild oats, both in the United States and Mexico. Terry evidently did a little farming, knocked around in the oil fields, and sowed a lot of wild oats.[4]

Inevitably, living in the small town of San Juan, Terry found his way into the company of Kells Elvins, another black sheep of the family, living in neighboring Pharr. John Taylor visited Gene during spring break of 1948, and they went out to a farm on Jackson Road to see a man named Kells, who was living with a woman Taylor still recalls as being "one fine-looking specimen" — undoubtedly Obie Dobbs. The visit was brief, just a couple of beers as they stood outside a trailer home on Kells's farm. On another afternoon, Taylor and Terry visited a border restaurant in Reynosa, and it was apparent that the owner knew Gene very well. The restaurant had a large interior courtyard, and to Taylor's surprise, the owner let loose several African lion cubs and allowed them to roam freely on the patio. The cubs would nip at Taylor's and Terry's heels, playfully but dangerously. Gene and his buddies took pictures of each other with the lions, but unfortunately Taylor misplaced them over the years.

When I asked Taylor why Gene was hanging around with guys such as Elvins and Burroughs, he said, in response to an essay I had published on Burroughs in South Texas, "Well, it wasn't because of what is in your article. He wasn't a junky, and he wasn't a queer."[5] Still, Taylor recalls he was a little suspicious of Elvins's friendship with the younger man. In Taylor's opinion, Kells "was using Gene to pick up the tab on everything. Gene was a free spender, and if he had it, he spent it." (In fact, say Ted Marak and Pat

Paris, the reverse was true: Kells never mooched off anyone, but plenty of his hangers-on mooched off him.)

At any rate, Gene Terry was a regular partier and hanger-on at Kells's place during those years (1946–1950), and his addled mind came up with some fertile ideas, including the plan to make chicken feed from cockroaches. Ted Marak has written a short story (currently unpublished) about Gene Terry, Kells, and Obie that captures the interaction among these three characters:

> Six o'clock was drinking time. Hard and fast rule. . . . As the minute hand slowly approached its zenith on the Ingersoll clock, you could have heard a gnat fart except for the dripping of the condensation on the glasses. "That damn thing stop?" asked Elvins. "Oh shut up," said Obie, as she moved the glass closer to her mouth. "You never heard of an Ingersoll that just stopped. They just slowed down and died, according to my Mother." "Oh can't you talk about anything but your family?". . . Terry let out an acceptable burp saying that the five-gallon bottle of Ozark gin water was getting low. Kells said he'd send Eusabio across the river tomorrow for his usual five-gallon purchase. That to Terry seemed a major decision. He smiled and felt a little more secure, since gin and quinine water along with a little pot were the sustaining factor for this present group.
>
> Suddenly Terry's brain clicked and went into high gear, and he asked Kells what he thought about raising cockroaches. Now cockroaches was about as bad a word as clap in a whorehouse. Three of the "brains" went into shock at the sound of the word. Bopper's [the dog's] ears even went up; before they went down, Terry was explaining how he was trying to find out from an off-duty border patrolman how to get a line on some mushrooms. Well one thing led to another. Dickie Dean had mentioned that cockroaches were on-hoof chicken feed. Then, after guzzling most of his drink, how easy it was to grow them and dry them and make them into pellets. "You're out of your mind, Terry," hollered Obie. "You been on the mushrooms again?" "Naw, I'm off that shit," replied Terry indignantly. "Kells, can't you get that gal off me? She's always downing me like I'm some kind of embryo." "Embryo? You mean imbecile, Terry," Obie chirped. "I mean you treat me like I'm so dumb I wasn't even born yet," [said Terry]. "Naw," said Kells. "You know Obie's all bark. Besides," he said, addressing Obie, "it was Terry who came up with the orgone accumulator." "Yeah, yeah," said Obie. "Spotted chickens and a bunch of

> hardons. Can't you guys come up with some logic, or at least make some money?" "It would have made money if it hadn't been for those members of the White Legged Breeders Association accusing us of having mutilated the breed," [said Terry]. "Not mutilated," said Obie, shaking her head. "Mutation was the reason why, Terry." "Well, whatever I had in mind didn't mean killing the sonsofbitches. Besides, you had to admit that these longhorns were a damn site prettier with spots on them. On top of that, it would be commercially enviable if you had meat that winked." "Oh, Terry."

In this story, Kells is like a parent trying to separate fighting children; Obie Dobbs is exasperated by both men's stupidity from her commonsense point of view; and Terry is the brunt of Obie's sharp wit because of his frequent, addle-headed malapropisms.

Burroughs isn't in Ted's short story, although in the original manuscript Ted called the Terry character "Billy," perhaps because he remembered Billy's name fifty years later but had forgotten Terry's. Still, Burroughs was part of this gang (when he was in the Valley) and knew Terry well enough to call him his "young friend" in interviews. They partied together on Kells's porch as part of the think tank, and they made weekend jaunts up the coast to Corpus Christi. Most of Burroughs's memories of Terry are ominous, though. In *Interzone,* he recalls the detail that Terry drove a 1936 black Ford pickup (the one Ted saw Terry hop out of to perform a tightrope act on a barbed-wire fence) nicknamed the "Black Death." This was typical of Burroughs's selective memory: One of his favorite writers was Denton Welch, and, like Welch, Burroughs often searched for portents of impending disaster in his retellings of tragic histories. The Black Death was such a portent, but even more inauspicious was Terry's nickname, "Tiger," which Eugene picked up while partying with Burroughs at a waterfront bar in Corpus Christi.

Burroughs tells the Corpus Christi story and the one of the bizarre death of twenty-three-year-old Terry in two places in the *Interzone* manuscript and also mentions it in interviews. The longest version in print is the following one from Victor Bockris's *With William Burroughs: A Report from the Bunker* (1981). In 1980 Andy Warhol was giving Burroughs a tour of the "Factory" (Warhol's studio), and Burroughs was reminded of his South Texas friend Eugene Terry when he saw a stuffed lion an artist had given Warhol as a birthday present:

> Look at this lion! I had a friend who was killed by a lion in a nightclub. The lion was asleep in a cage and Terry went into the cage and threw a flashlight in the lion's face and it leapt on him. He was DOA at the Reynosa, Mexico, Red Cross. He had a crushed chest, a broken neck, and a fractured skull. It just jumped on him and killed him. Can you imagine anyone waking up a sleeping lion with a flashlight? The Mexican waiter went into the cage and tried to get it off him with a chair and he couldn't. The lion dragged Terry into a corner. At this point the bartender came vaulting over the bar with a .45 and he went in and killed the lion, but Terry was dead. It's a funny thing. About a month before Terry annoyed the lion we [Burroughs, Kells, and Terry] were in Corpus Christi and we built Terry up as Tiger Terry, this punch-drunk fighter, and Terry goes into a spit-and-shuffle act. Yeah, *Tiger* Terry.[6]

The emphasis on the "coincidence" between Terry's new nickname and the manner of his death in a Reynosa restaurant indicates that this was no coincidence at all. In the Valley, death is not a fluke; for Burroughs, it is why you are there.

Reynosa, where Terry was killed, is the Mexican border town about eight miles from McAllen-Pharr. In a version of the Tiger Terry story told in "Word" (Burroughs's rough draft of *Naked Lunch*), the restaurant with the lions is identified as "Joe's."[7] Today, there is no Joe's restaurant in Reynosa, but several elderly Valley residents told me that "Joe" was José Ortega, owner of Joe's Place in Reynosa, a border restaurant that was popular well into the 1960s, although Joe died in the mid-1950s. Joe's niece and former executive director of the Hidalgo County Historical Museum, Fran Alger, shared with me her memories of her uncle's fabulous border establishment and what she remembered about the night Eugene Terry was killed there:

> I grew up with Joe's Place. Joe's was a nightclub and restaurant. At ten [o'clock] you had your first show, and you could eat there with your family and see the show. But the midnight show was an adult show that always ended with a stripper. And there was a two o'clock show, and I don't know what after that. It had two huge fireplaces in the dining area, and they were tall enough for people to stand in them. When it was cold, they would build big fires and roast potatoes. My uncle liked animals, and one of them was a bear he kept behind the bar. The bear would drink scotch. My uncle's favorite trick was to bring the bear out, and he'd say, "I betcha I can get a bear to drink scotch. I betcha can't drink more than

> my bear can." Another was a lion, and he used to walk through the restaurant with it. So many of the guests would enjoy going because they would get the chance to pet him. The lion was in a pit with a steep incline so that the lion couldn't get out, like a zoo. And it was on a huge chain. It made an impact to go to a restaurant and see these animals. [Terry] did get very drunk, and he was boasting to a friend that he could get the lion to eat out of his hand; what he did was he went down in there and flashed him with a flashlight, and the lion did what was natural and stood up on his hind legs and hit him with his paw and broke his neck. Terry had been told not to go out there. It was very late at night. Joe knew this man well, and they were good friends.[8]

I asked Fran how the incident affected business, and she said business doubled afterward: People wanted to see where the man was killed by a lion.

With Fran's help, I contacted a number of other Valley residents who could add to the story, including Jim McKone, a local journalist (now a public relations officer for the Hidalgo County Historical Museum) who was a teenager working as a cub reporter for the *Valley Evening Monitor* when the story broke. "It was the most bizarre story I was ever around in my fifty years covering news," he told me. His friend Bryce Armstrong wrote the front-page *Monitor* story headlined "Lion Kills San Juan Man at Night Club in Reynosa." McKone says the reporters at the time were a hard-boiled, cynical bunch that joked about trying to stage a picture of the lion with a piece of Terry's body still in its mouth — a type of dark humor also found in Burroughs's retelling of the story.[9]

The newspaper accounts have all the elements for a story that would interest Burroughs — death, handsome young men, exotic locations, and wild animals. According to the *Monitor* story, around 12:30 A.M. on November 9, 1950, Terry was out partying with two other young men in McAllen and decided he wanted to go to Mexico and "pet the cats" at Joe's Place. Terry's friends had never been to Joe's and didn't believe Terry's stories about petting lions. They crossed the border at Reynosa, Terry bought some cigarettes, and they hit a couple of bars before arriving at Joe's around 1:30 A.M. At Joe's, Terry took them to the lion's cage, and despite the pleas of his terrified friends, he entered the cage. Provoked by Terry's sudden intrusion, the lion attacked him and dragged him into its lair underneath the nightclub. The screams were "terrifying," according to one eyewitness (not named in the newspaper). Roberto Perez — *el domador,* the lion's trainer —

and Joe Ortega were asleep at the time and arrived on the scene still wearing their shorts. Joe broke a chair and glass over the lion's head, trying to get it away from Terry. Finally, the domador shot the lion, and Terry was rescued, but he was mortally wounded. On the floor of the cage was the unopened pack of cigarettes Terry had bought. According to the news account, Joe was good friends with Terry and had warned him not to pet the lions, one of which had deeply scratched Terry before. "He was a helluva nice kid. That's not a pretty way to die," Joe said, then added thoughtfully, "At least they didn't chew on him."[10]

Five years later Burroughs turned Terry's death into a short story as part of a manuscript titled *Interzone*. James Grauerholz, Burroughs's literary executor, has confirmed for me that this story has yet to be located in Burroughs's papers or in a private collection — thus making it Burroughs's most famous "lost" story. However, we do have good information about the story in Burroughs's letters to Allen Ginsberg and Jack Kerouac in 1955. As Burroughs told Ginsberg, "I enclose the story I wrote about Terry who was killed by the lion. I don't like it too much. I am not cut out to write anything so separate from myself. . . . Possible titles for story: Death in Another Country; 'You Gotta Have Something Special'; Tiger Ted."[11]

Burroughs does not like the story because it is "so separate from myself," confirming that he was not in the restaurant himself that night. In fact, when Terry was killed, Burroughs was already living in Mexico City and probably created the story from the newspaper accounts or from Kells Elvins's re-creation of the events.[12] Burroughs saw a lot in his life, but if he had seen Terry killed by a lion, I think the story would be a bit more personal and not "separate" from him. By contrast, a story written about the same time and mentioned in this same letter to Ginsberg — "The Finger" — is a straightforward, hardboiled account of Burroughs cutting off part of his finger with poultry shears in order to impress a young man he was in love with, material obviously quite close to Burroughs. The playing around with the titles is also interesting. He begins with a Hemingway-esque title ("Death in Another Country") and also offers a quotation as a title ("You Gotta Have Something Special"), which old-time Reynosans tell me summed up José Ortega's business philosophy, meaning "You gotta have something to bring in the customers": a lion, a scotch-drinking bear, strip shows after hours.

A second letter from this same time relates to the titling of the story. Burroughs discusses how eels are irresistibly drawn to the Sargasso Sea, where they mate and then die. He then tells another story from the animal kingdom about sex and death — lampreys that mate and tear each other up in the process. Following this chain of thought, he remembers the still untitled Terry story and suggests Sargasso Sea titles: "What I want to convey, though, is the *inner* pull towards Sargasso: Sargasso Yen, Sargasso Time, Sargasso Kicks, The Sargasso Blues. I can't get it. This is all trivial, doesn't convey those eels wiggling across fields at night in the wet grass to find the next pond or stream, thousands dying on the way. . . . Do you know about lampreys? When they mate they tear each other with their suction cups so that they always die afterwards. . . . 'See you in Sargasso.'. . . One of the Sargasso titles might do for my story about Tiger Ted."[13]

I don't think this is a meaningless series of associations. Burroughs felt that the Valley was a place where people came to die, as he says in *Junky,* almost as if a force drags people here — and did him, too. The journey to mating and death by the eels bound for the Sargasso thus has a parallel. There is more, though. In other versions of the story, the lion is a "lioness": In "Word," Burroughs writes, "Young friend of mine name of Terry have this 1936 Ford he call the Black Death. One night he get in the Black Death and cross the Rio Grande to Reynosa, where a *mangy old lioness* [emphasis added] stood in a cage in Joe's patio. So Terry goes in the cage, throw a flashlight in the lioness' face, who leaps on him and break his neck, and the bartender vault over the bar with a forty-five blast the lioness. But Mr. Terry, he dead."[14]

In the context of the stories Burroughs tells of the eels and lampreys, Terry appears to have been killed while mating — in a sense — with the lion. In *Naked Lunch,* another association is relevant here: In the story of the "elegant faggot" from Texas who comes to New York and is immediately "taken up" by an older woman who collects fags, the woman is described as an "old moth-eaten tigress shit sure turn into a fag eater."[15] (Ironically, the fags literally eat *her.*) Females are often threatening — and even deadly — in Burroughs's work, and the Tiger Terry story is no exception. Joan Vollmer, by the way, was described by Burroughs's mother as a "tigress."[16]

A more obvious reference in the *Interzone* account of Tiger Terry, however, is to Joseph Conrad's *Heart of Darkness* ("Mr. Terry, he dead"), another story about the death of a white man in a foreign country. Conrad was one of Burroughs's favorite writers, and he often adapted Conrad's works for his own purposes (see, for example, "The Examination" in *Naked Lunch*). In the context of Conrad's *Heart of Darkness,* Terry's fate raises an interesting question: Was death (in the form of a pet lion) waiting for Terry when he crossed into Mexico, or did Terry bring his own death with him? In *The*

Place of Dead Roads, Burroughs further connected Tiger Terry to Conrad's Lord Jim by placing the character of "the punch-drunk fighter who comes up off the floor to win by a knockout" in the company of Lord Jim, the Great Gatsby, and Comus Bassington. Such men, he says, "are the flawed doomed but undefeated radiant heroes who attempted the impossible." Regardless of whether Burroughs had Tiger Terry in mind when he placed the character of the punch-drunk fighter on this list of distinguished, noble failures, it is worth noting that Burroughs's description of these men could well stand in for a definition of the archetypal Beat characters ("doomed but undefeated"), linking Terry to men such as Bill Cannastra and Dave Kammerer.[17]

There are other levels of this story that could explain Burroughs's lifelong interest in it. James Grauerholz has pointed out to me that it must be more than coincidence that the name of the straight young man in *Queer* who is seduced by Burroughs's alter ego, Lee, is named *Eugene* Allerton. This is the only Eugene in Burroughs's fiction, and Burroughs may well have been writing *Queer* when he heard that Eugene Tiger Terry had been killed. Burroughs did indeed attempt (mostly unsuccessfully) to seduce straight young men, and although there is no evidence that Gene Terry was the object of such a seduction — nor that Gene was anything but straight — Burroughs's use of Eugene's name is provocative in light of Burroughs's subsequent behavior in Mexico City.

Burroughs left one more important clue as to the content of "Tiger in the Valley." He was one of those writers who considered all fiction autobiographical, and I believe his Tiger Terry story is no exception — even though he considered it "separate" from himself. In the final analysis, "Tiger in the Valley" could have been written as a cover story for what was his ur-story in many ways, the accidental death of Joan Vollmer. The connection between Joan's death and the Tiger Terry story shows up in a February 7, 1955 letter to Allen Ginsberg: "May yet attempt a story or some account of Joan's death. I suspect my reluctance is not at all because I think it would be in bad taste to write about it. I think I am afraid. Not exactly to uncover the unconscious intent, it's more complex, more basic, and more horrible, as if the brain drew the bullet toward it. . . . To summarize, I pass along one of my specialized bits of wisdom, like 'Always use poultry shears to cut off fingers': Never participate in [an] active or passive role in any shooting things off of, or near one, or knife throwing or anything similar, and, if [you are] a bystander, always try to stop it."[18]

As it relates to Burroughs's experiences in South Texas, this letter is important because of his expressed desire to write "a story or some account of Joan's death." In *Queer,* he had done so by pointedly *not* telling the story of Joan's death (as he illuminates in his 1985 "foreword" to *Queer*).[19] Could he have written other stories in which the death of Joan was the underlying text of the story? Perhaps Burroughs is providing a clue when he tells Ginsberg that the bitter lesson he learned from accidentally shooting Joan was that if you ever see someone about to do something stupid with a gun or a knife "or anything similar," stop them: You are not an innocent bystander at that point and cannot be passive. What could be something "similar"? We know Burroughs sent a copy of the "Tiger Terry" story to Ginsberg and Kerouac just a few months after he wrote this letter to Ginsberg;[20] therefore, something similar to a bunch of people watching a drunken man shoot a glass off his wife's head might well be watching your drunken friend climb into a lion cage. Everyone who knew Terry in Mexico recalled that numerous people had warned him to stay away from the lion; the newspaper accounts said the waiters had kept him away from the cage that very night, but he "got away from them."

In the end, no one, including his friends, stopped him, and they had thus participated in a "passive role" in Terry's death. When read in this light, "Tiger in the Valley" certainly seems to be one of those stories that retells the death of Joan Burroughs but does so by describing what appears to be an unrelated account of another "accidental" death. Yet how accidental was it? Like those eels drawn by some "inner pull" to the Sargasso Sea or Eugene Terry drawn to his death in the jaws of a lion in Mexico, Joan, too, "drew" the bullet to her brain, as Burroughs told Ginsberg — a version of the "accident" Burroughs would maintain for many years.

After struggling with a title for the story, Burroughs finally settled on "Tiger in the Valley," a fact we know from a letter Jack Kerouac sent to his agent, Sterling Lord, asking him whether he could sell the story for Burroughs. Kerouac described the story as "exquisite and macabre."[21] If you want to know what Kerouac meant by this, the best place to look is "The Finger," which Burroughs mailed to Kerouac with the Tiger Terry story. In "The Finger," "exquisite and macabre" may describe a passage such as the following: "Finally he saw what he was looking for: poultry shears like the ones his Father used to cut through the joints when he carved the turkey at Grandmother's Thanksgiving dinners. There they were, glittering and stainless, one blade smooth and sharp, the other with teeth like a saw to hold the meat in place for cutting."[22] You can imagine, then, what Burroughs might have written about a *lion's* teeth holding a man by the neck.

That's the literary history of "Tiger in the Valley," which was by no means the end of the story as it relates to Burroughs and his experiences in South Texas and Mexico. What I was missing was the Mexican side of the story. Mexico is more than just the setting of "Tiger." Tiger Terry's tragedy, it seems in retrospect, could have taken place only in the world that was Reynosa's Zona Rosa, there at the intersection of Miguel Alemán and Paseo de los Pirreyes, and at the most fabulous of Texas' border nightclubs, the tourist-friendly-sounding Joe's Place, owned by entrepreneur José Ortega. I needed to know this side of the story, but I encountered several problems in uncovering it: It had been fifty years, Joe's Place no longer existed (although the building was intact), I didn't speak Spanish, and I knew no one in the Zona. I needed a guide. Fortunately, he found me.

Juan Ochoa is one of my graduate students, but he is also a licensed Mexican lawyer. He spent his teenage years in Reynosa, where his father was a man of considerable underworld influence. When Ochoa heard I was trying to dig up information about junkies, queers, and a gringo killed by a lion in a Reynosa restaurant, he knew he was the man to help me out. He tells this story in a fine essay called "Desportando Leones" [Sleeping Lions]: "It may have been . . . the excitement I felt knowing that someone like Burroughs walked the same streets of my reckless youth that inspired me to volunteer to investigate the death of Eugene Terry in a Reynosa bar. But what really lured me into this research was the chance to revisit my old stomping grounds, Reynosa's *Zona Rosa*."

At first, Ochoa walked around Reynosa, stopping all of the old men on the street he met, asking them whether they remembered the story of the gringo who was killed by a lion at Joe's Place half a century ago. "Why do you want to know?" they asked him suspiciously. "Is this about a lawsuit?" He would then explain to them that the man was a friend of a very famous author, William S. Burroughs, who wrote a short story about the incident, as well as masterpieces such as *Junky, Queer,* and *Naked Lunch*. "If you're looking for a queer, try the Gato Negro down the street there. You can't miss," Ochoa says he was told, and "Stay away from the *mugre* [junk], *hijo* [sonny], you have your whole life ahead of you." He wasn't getting very far, and for good reason: "It was only natural for men who had worked the

Zona's angles for more years than I had been alive to be suspicious of a man asking about such flamboyant characters as were Tiger Terry and William S. Burroughs."

Eventually Ochoa felt defeated and decided to lift his spirits with a shave in his uncle's barber shop in the Zona Rosa. While his uncle shaved him, Ochoa told him about his frustrating search: "My Uncle — who had been silent throughout most of my tale — proceeded to sell me a number that runs on the fringe of Mexico's 'official' lottery and then meekly inquired if I would still be interested in speaking with anyone from the Zona that might remember Joe's Place or the dead Gringo. I laughed and gave my Uncle a playful hug. 'Why, you old gossip,' I said facetiously, 'I'm a trained researcher. What makes you think a number-running barber like you can get any further with these untrusting old coots?' La Borrega (so named for his lamblike curls) shrugged and stifled a giggle and said, 'Let me see what I can do,' while he wrote and initialed the ticket."

Of course, Ochoa came to realize — kicking himself because of its obviousness — that, in Mexico, if you want to find someone, you don't hire a private investigator or a lawyer; you talk to the local barber, in whose chair every man eventually sits and talks. Through his *tío* [uncle], la Borrega, he eventually met and interviewed the bouncer at Joe's Place, a dancer who performed there during those years, the cook at Joe's Place, a taxi cab driver who was not only working the night of Terry's death but also knew Burroughs firsthand, and, finally, a mariachi musician who was an eyewitness to Terry's death. I accompanied Ochoa on these interviews and was humored by the interviewees as the non-Spanish–speaking professor from the American university who was writing a book but whose real work was being done for him by this son of Reynosa. I was dubbed "El Muchacho Profesor" [the boy professor].

One of the best of these interviews was one in February 2002 with the cook at Joe's Place, Berto Guajardo, who was known (for his girth) as "El Soplado" [the blown up, as in "inflated"]. El Soplado worked at Joe's place in the forties and fifties, and we talked with him at his home in a middle-class suburb of Reynosa. His daughter brought us diet Cokes to drink and listened to her father tell stories about the heyday of Joe's Place. He said that back then there were a lot more tourists on the border than today. The place was wide open, he said. No one cared if you took off your clothes and danced on the tables and did whatever you wanted. He wasn't sure when (or why) the license for that kind of behavior in Mexico had expired.

Joe's was where the more adventurous crowd went, although once you hit one bar over there, you just kept moving along — to El Patio, the Singapore, El Trópico, the Flamingo, and Sam's American Restaurant. After the gringos would have a drink at Joe's and meet the scotch-drinking bear, they expected every place in Reynosa to have a bear behind the bar. A joke went around that some tourists went into Sam's Place and asked "Where is the bear?" and the Mexican bartender said it was in the cooler, thinking they were asking, "Where is the beer?"

El Soplado said Joe was an adventurous man who had traveled throughout the United States. After a stint as a bartender in LA and Tijuana, he finally settled in the Valley and opened his own bar. The original Joe's Place was in Río Rico, situated on a spit of land in the Rio Grande that was claimed by neither Mexico nor the United States — a no-man's-land that was destroyed by a flood in 1941. Joe had a good head for knowing what the tourists wanted. At the Río Rico location, he had a greyhound track running all the way around the restaurant. At the Reynosa location, he stocked the place with exotic pets such as lions, peacocks, and coyotes: "He knew if he filled his bar with savage animals, the tourists would come." One of the coyotes attacked the cook, who showed us the scar on his left arm. He never went near the lions, though. Joe himself would venture in their cage, El Soplado said, but he wouldn't do anything stupid around them — and that was saying a lot because he was always drunk. Joe drank about a quart of whiskey a day.

Of Gene Terry, the cook said, "Terry must have been one of those fools who think the moon is made of cheese." After Terry's death, he said, the sentiment was more "poor lions!" than "poor Terry!" Everyone knew Terry was reckless and headed to destruction, but the lion, which was subsequently destroyed, was only acting in defense of its cubs.[23] The cook was not there at the time Terry was killed — the kitchen closed at 1:00 A.M. — but he heard about it the next day. Joe had spent the night in jail, and the employees were all afraid of him, so they could discuss the incident only in whispers — and never around the boss. Joe must have paid a lot of money to hush up the incident, the cook said, because the newspaper articles in Mexico were brief, and there were no follow-up stories — in contrast to the front-page articles on the American side. However, the tourists flocked to see the place once the story got out in the States.

El Soplado revealed a darker side of Joe that would especially have interested Burroughs, who almost certainly talked and drank with the gregarious restaurateur. Joe was known to have strong ties to the underworld, and it was rumored that his restaurant had been bankrolled by Al Capone, who, at one point during Prohibition, was using Reynosa and the border as a base for smuggling liquor. "Joe liked to walk the shady side of the street," El Soplado said, and the same can be said of Burroughs. As Juan Ochoa speculates, Burroughs, who was thinking about opening his own bar on the border, would have picked up a lot of information from Joe about the system of *mordidas,* or bribes, in Mexico, that allowed you to run a business without running afoul of either the law or politicians.[24] In *Queer,* Burroughs's knowledge of the mordida is as accurate as the description of this system by any Mexico City native — and "very hip," Juan Ochoa told me.

The cook was not an eyewitness to Terry's death, but there are two living observers, one of whom is seventy-five years old and currently in jail for trafficking cocaine; the other is a musician named Luís Alejos. Luís had heard about Juan and me and left word with a waiter that he wanted to meet us at Sam's Restaurant, where Burroughs himself used to dine and where Juan and I would end our day of research with some Carta Blancas. Among the Rashomon-like, varied accounts of this incident — the newspaper accounts, the rumors on the street, Burroughs's story as told to Andy Warhol, and other versions I have come across — I consider this version (translated by Juan Ochoa) the most reliable. Luís started his story by describing the actual cage where the lions were kept:

> It was more like a hallway than a cage. The door had allowances for a padlock to be placed on it, but the main lock was a large wooden beam. . . . Because the beam was so big and heavy, the lock kind of became unnecessary. I guess they never figured anyone would be crazy enough to enter the cage. I was one of the few who dared to go around the lions and the bears in the company of Roberto Perez, the trainer and the keeper. Under reasonable circumstances, the animals were tame. Terry had seen me and Roberto feeding and handling the lions, and he wanted to do it, too, only he would take it a step further and roughhouse with the animals. Terry figured the lions were tame enough — they're just big cats, he thought — to be able to take a couple of slaps across the face. The lions were obviously not of the same opinion and jumped Terry from behind when Terry turned his back to the she-lion, proudly grinning at me and Roberto. The lioness swatted Terry across the back around the shoulder area, producing some pretty bad gashes. Terry tried to play down the incident, but the wounds were bad enough to be reported to Joe. Tina,

Joe's wife, tended to Terry's wounds. Terry's body was said to have been scarred with claw marks. Joe scolded me and Roberto and held us responsible for Terry's recklessness. I was weary of Terry after that.

On the night of his death, Terry entered Joe's boasting to his friends that he could "pet the cats." After seeing Terry order a round of drinks, I lost track of him — until I heard screams and saw two gringos [Mickey Whilley and George Cameron] running away from the cage. My brother José, Roberto Perez, and I ran back toward the lion's den. When we arrived, we found the big wooden door barred by the beam, and I could hear Terry's screams coming from the top of the doorway. The lion's growl seemed much closer. Terry was obviously trying to escape the lions by climbing to the top of the door since the main artery in his leg had been sliced in a downward slash. I believe Terry entered the cage with his two friends, but when the lions started to rise up, his friends ran out before Terry, closing the door behind them. As the door slammed shut, the beam fell, locking Terry inside.

When we opened the door, José Ortega was on the scene. We saw Terry's limp body being jostled by the lioness as she clamped her jaws down around the neck and shoulder area. Joe Ortega ordered the men to "get that kid out of there — *saquen ese muchacho*." By this time, more people had arrived. Among them were the night watchman, who had come armed with a .45 Colt, and Jaime Torres, and the bartender. This group of men, including me, rushed into the den at Joe's command, hurling whisky glasses and chairs, beer bottles, anything we could get our hands on, at the lions. The lioness dropped Terry's body and hovered over for it a moment. The rest of the lions scattered. Roberto took the gun from the night watchman and started to hold the lioness back with a chair that he held in one hand while he aimed the .45 with the other. He kept the beast at bay with the chair until he was able to get off one fatal shot at the lioness, hitting her square in the chest.

While this was happening, I and a group of others were dragging Terry's body away from the lioness. I was now able to check for vital signs; I found none. Joe ordered the body into his Cadillac and told Jaime to take him to the Red Cross in Reynosa, but [Joe's wife] Tina said he would be better off in McAllen for medical treatment. We now know that Mexican officials prevented Jaime from crossing into the American side, forcing him to take Terry to the Mexican Red Cross, where he was pronounced dead. The fate of Terry was kept from Tina until the comandante arrived. Tina is said to have asked, "How's the boy doing?" To which the comandante replied, "You mean the dead one?"[25]

In this account, Terry's foolishness is evident throughout, and Luís (like El Soplado) was irritated that he was somehow supposed to protect Terry from his own recklessness. Even after he had been clawed by the lions in a previous incident, Terry was crazy enough to enter the cage again — this time without Roberto Perez or anyone else trained to handle the lions. What follows is truly horrible: Terry trying to climb beyond the reach of the lioness, the main artery in his left leg ripped open, and finally being dragged down by his neck. (In an earlier interview, Luís told us that he can hear Terry's screams to this day.) The rescue party was faced with this awful scene, and you can see just how powerful José Ortega was: When he orders the men into the cage to rescue Terry, they unhesitatingly do so, armed only with bottles and chairs. (The newspaper account in McAllen, by the way, attributed the rescue heroics to Joe himself.)

With no rehearsal and on camera, Luís rendered this version of Terry's death for a documentary film, and he told it perfectly. Kerouac described Burroughs's short story "Tiger in the Valley" as "macabre," but I doubt that Burroughs's tale could be as macabre as Luís's retelling of the event: "You mean the dead one?" asks the comandante rhetorically.

Today, the old Zona Rosa is in decay, and its present atmosphere hardly compares to what it was in the 1940s and 1950s, when Burroughs was there. The shell of Joe's Place is now a disco called the "1040," and Juan and I have tried to interest the bartender there in concocting an original drink called the "Tiger Terry." Maybe that will enliven things. However, among the older denizens of the Zona Rosa, our interest in the story of Tiger Terry's death has had a revivifying effect. They have taken to calling themselves "the Lion Gang" and once again are able to tell tales about the heyday in Reynosa, the best years of their lives.

You can clearly become too fascinated with this story, as Juan and I have. Juan keeps looking for a "keyhole" to see it through, he tells me. For example, he points out that the story obviates a common misperception about Burroughs — that he was self-destructive. In fact, says Juan, Burroughs was "running around Mexico and South America looking for ways to live forever" — a reference to Burroughs's and Kells's trip to Mexico to be injected with Dr. Bogomoletz's "fountain of youth" serum. Therefore, when he says, "Can you imagine someone doing something as suicidal as shining a flashlight in a lion's face?" he means that he *can't* imagine it. Perhaps that's why Burroughs felt the story was so "separate" from himself. For Juan, the moral of the story is contained in the title of his essay on Terry: "Desportando Leones" — don't wake sleeping lions.

Or perhaps the key to Terry's story is in his nickname. In Spanish, "El Tigre" is the nickname given to men who are especially virile: They are tigers. Terry wasn't especially virile — he was a small man, about five foot six at most — so the title was no doubt meant ironically. The nickname probably had nothing to do with his fascination with Joe's lions in Reynosa, but there is a tie-in. Just as underworld figures and drug dealers in Mexico to this day showcase their virility and power by owning dangerous animals such as tigers, wolves, and lions, so too did José Ortega like to prove his manhood by standing amid his uncaged lions. A picture taken in 1952 shows Joe and several of his employees on the back patio of Joe's Place, where the lions are being fed. One of the larger lions glares at the photographer over his bowl of raw meat. Joe is in the center of the picture — smiling, relaxed, and smoking a cigar. In the left corner is Roberto Perez, who also appears nonchalant. Several other men appear considerably less at ease. Eugene Terry, no doubt, was out to prove something about his courage by repeatedly putting himself in dangerous situations around the lions. That must have been part of his boast to his two disbelieving friends that night: "Sure, you're going to feed the lions," his companions must have dared him, and in they went.

In South Texas and northern Mexico there is a famous border ballad about machismo titled "El Hijo Desobediente" [The Disobedient Son]. It is the story of a young man whose father cautions him against fighting. The son responds,

> Get away from here, oh father of mine,
> Because I am more fierce than a lion.
> Let it not be that I draw my sword
> And split your heart.
>
> Son of my heart,
> For this that you have spoken,
> Before the coming of the first rays of the sun,
> Your life will be taken.
> — Translated by Juan Ochoa

Of course, the young man is fatally stabbed but lives long enough to sing a few plaintive, repentant verses. It is the most famous of all border ballads, rich in significance for the Mexican culture, one that celebrates machismo but at the same time recognizes the cost of such foolish pride and of feeling "more fierce than a lion."

The story of Gene Terry is worthy of a ballad, and, in fact, with the resurrection of his story, a song is being composed. The moral: probably something like that of "El Hijo Desobediente": You don't have to climb into a lion cage to prove anything.

There is, finally, a coda to this story, which I discovered while interviewing Kells Elvins's second wife, Marianne Woolfe, who met Kells in McAllen in the spring of 1950. Offhand and not expecting much, I asked Marianne whether she remembered Eugene Terry, the man who was killed by the lion. "I dated him," she told me. In fact, it turns out she met Kells through Gene Terry but eventually found Kells more to her liking. Against the advice of her mother's bridge club members, who considered Kells a "rake and roué," they married in July of 1950. "I'm not sure how long after this [it was] when Terry's tragic death occurred," she wrote to me. When Terry was killed, she said, Terry's father contacted Kells first because he was Terry's best friend in the Valley. Wrote Woolfe, "His father came down, of course, and in a sorrowful visit with us, mentioned that Terry had told him, 'My best girl married my best friend.'"

It was the end of an era for Kells in the Valley. Billy was gone, Ted Marak had returned to Las Vegas, and Terry was dead. To top it off, the Valley was hit by a devastating freeze in 1950 and 1951. Marianne remembers watching Kells's orange groves being cut down. "This [Terry's death] plus the sight of the orchard being destroyed tree by tree made the Valley almost untenable," she recalled.[26]

Gene Terry was buried in Corsicana, and his high school buddy John Taylor was one of the pallbearers. He kept Gene's truck, the Black Death, around for a while but eventually sold it. Gene is still remembered in Corsicana by old-timers who went to junior high and high school with him. They refer to him as "that poor boy who got killed by the lion."

THE WETBACK DEAL

After leaving New York in 1946 and up to the writing of *Junky* and *Queer* (1950–1951), William S. Burroughs had a standard reply when asked what his occupation was: He was a farmer. Not a writer, a farmer. For example, in *Junky,* the following exchange takes place between Burroughs and two New Orleans cops who have arrested him for possession of illegal drugs:

> "What is it that you do, Mr. Lee?" he [the cop] politely asked, in the accents of an educated man.
>
> "Farm," I answered.
>
> The man with the pipe laughed.
>
> "Corn with weed between the rows, eh?" he said. (73–74)

Two years later, while attending Mexico City College in 1950, Burroughs was interviewed by the college newspaper (the *Collegian*) as an "interesting" student, and he told the reporter that "after the War he decided to raise cotton in the Rio Grande Valley." In September of 1951, following Joan Vollmer's accidental death, he once again had to describe his occupation, and the *New York Daily News* identified him as a "wealthy cotton farmer from Pharr, Texas."[1]

Of course, when asked, he could legitimately have said he was a junky rather than a farmer or that he had become a farmer only by default after he had taken a fall in New York City and was forced to find another line of work. And he could have said that two of the "crops" on his "ranch" in East Texas had in fact been marijuana and opium poppies. Still, in South Texas at least, he truly was a farmer, even if in some ways being a junky and being a farmer were the same thing to him. Burroughs became addicted to junk to find out what it was to be an addict. He initially became a farmer to have a legitimate cover for his undercover activities and to make a little money, but because he was William S. Burroughs, a man both cursed and blessed with a Faustian need to understand how everything works, he started to study farming. That's how a long digression on farming showed up in a book called *Junky.*

It was the most basic and essential of all needs: food. But who controlled the farming game? Who were the Big Holders, and who was left holding? Where was the mark inside? He had asked these questions about addictive drugs, too, and now he applied them to farming. Moreover, these were not questions he asked in the 1940s and left behind. In the 1960s, for example, he lectured would-be revolutionaries, such as Abbie Hoffman, by posing a very good question: "How are you going to feed everyone in this new world of yours?"[2]

However, it is also reasonable to ask why William S. Burroughs, whose famous grandfather had perfected the first workable version of the adding machine, would ever consider being a farmer at all. Herbert Huncke was certainly suspicious of Burroughs's motives. In his description of Burroughs on the New Waverly farm, he styles Burroughs a "country gentleman" who expected to "find his way into a wealthy crowd."[3] In a 1951 letter to Allen Ginsberg in which he discusses plans to buy a ranch in South America, Burroughs also reveals this colonial side of his personality: "And you live like a king on a ranch [in South America] while you are making the $. Hunting and fishing, and a hacienda full of servants."[4] In 1946 he probably saw a similar setup as being possible in South Texas. As he wrote to Allen Ginsberg in October of that year, "Money to be made here [South Texas] like picking fruit off the trees" — not that he would be doing the picking himself, of course.[5]

There most certainly was a colonial side to Burroughs's 1940s-era personality, but a more dominant aspect of his character is also revealed in his farm ventures: Burroughs as American pioneer and radical individualist (the side Ted Morgan emphasizes in his biography of Burroughs, *Literary Outlaw*).[6] This pure American desire to be self-reliant and live beyond the constraints of society no doubt began in his childhood. Growing up in St. Louis, the "Gateway to the West," through which passed generations of American pioneers and fortune seekers, Burroughs must have felt connected to the country's frontier past. As a boy, he read books about outlaws such as Billy the Kid and Jack Black and wrote a story about a grizzly bear.

This "Wild West" pioneer ethos was strengthened during his teenage years, which he spent at a "ranch school" in Los Alamos, New Mexico, where the boys learned basic camping and survival skills. They also learned to shoot guns, and Burroughs developed a passion for guns that lasted throughout his life.[7] It is no surprise, then, that in his letters and books Burroughs writes of wanting to get some land where he could fish, hunt, and farm, thus maintaining an independence from all authority and control. This fantasy was particularly alive for him during the years he lived in Texas and Mexico. As he wrote to Allen Ginsberg in 1950, living on his own ranch in Mexico would provide "unlimited opportunities and any kind of life you want to live you can find."[8]

In a world increasingly controlled by government bureaucrats and cops, it was hard for a man to live freely, and, for Burroughs, that was what being a man was all about. Kells Elvins's son, Peter, told me he thought his father and Burroughs both wanted to be farmers because it was an appropriate "masculine" role in life: "Kells very much liked to do macho things — he admitted that he joined the Marines instead of the Army because he wanted to prove himself a man — and maybe farming fell into that category, too. Perhaps Burroughs might have had similar reasons for being attracted to farming."[9] I think he did, and Burroughs therefore jumped at Kells's invitation to be a farmer.

The setup was ready made: By 1946, when Burroughs joined Kells in South Texas, Kells's farming operations were already extensive. According to Ted Marak, "Elvins had so much goddamn property down there [in the Valley]." In fact, Elvins had land spread out from the lower lift (the first irrigation "lift," or pumping station, on the Rio Grande) all the way up to the Redlands, north of Edinburg. In an interview with Ted Morgan in the mid-1980s, Burroughs described Elvins's headquarters for this farming operation, a quarter mile out on South Jackson Road (now at the corner of Kelly and South Jackson): "Kells had a citrus orchard. It had Ruby Reds and it had limes as well. . . . Ruby Reds are esteemed above Foster Pinks in grapefruit. He had a grove of those, about 20 acres, so it was doing pretty good. . . . He had a house that he'd bought for practically nothing — during the Depression his father bought — for $5,000, with ten acres of citrus, which at that time would be worth $50–60,000 easy."[10]

According to land records, Elvins's property on South Jackson stretched all the way up to what is now the expressway in McAllen, significantly more than the twenty acres Burroughs describes. An indication of just how much land he had is that, when the crops needed picking, Kells had to set up a camp to house more than two hundred workers.

Even by local standards, which would require one thousand acres or more for someone to be called a real farmer, Kells was one, or close to one. Burroughs and Marak, on the other hand, were basically sharecroppers on Kells's land. The deal, according to Ted Marak, was that Kells "used to furnish the tractors, the equipment, the land and I was to furnish the payroll [for workers] and to pay for the water." Burroughs would have been in on the same kind of deal with Elvins.

But Burroughs owned some land of his own, too, now located at Monte Cristo and César Chávez in Edinburg. He was proud of this land and described it as "50 acres of the finest land in the Valley."[11] He grew carrots, peas, lettuce, and cotton and dutifully reported the rise and fall of his farming fortunes to city slickers such as Allen Ginsberg back in New York. There was success — "Peas. We should gross about $5000 on this deal. Lettuce and carrots are coming along" — and failure — "My first crop of peas froze 5 days before harvest."[12] He also took care of the Mexican laborers, seeing to it that they had medical care, clothing, and enough food, and he paid for these expenses out of his own pocket. As a South Texas farmer, Burroughs thus took on the traditional role of the Spanish-style patrón, who is ultimately responsible for both the success of his operations and the welfare of the workers.

Peter Elvins believes that Kells and Burroughs worked very hard at farming, but by the standards of local farmers, they were "gentlemen farmers" at best. As Burroughs admits in the Valley section of *Junky,* "The farmer did all the actual work."[13] Kells's McAllen wife, Marianne (Elvins) Woolfe, scoffed at the idea that Kells rose at dawn and worked until sunset as a farmer, telling me that Kells's life was very much that of the leisure class. Ted Marak also admitted, "I knew shit about farming. But I had Eusebio. Eusebio was a good farmer." In an unpublished short story, Marak comically described their daily routine as "farmers": "To keep everyone from being either stoned or drunk during working hours on the farm, a turn-on time of 6 PM and a turn-off time of 4 AM was established. Except for Sat and Sun; they were over at 6 AM. Anyone who couldn't eat and sober up in two hours wasn't trying. It worked out OK since about all there was to do was get the wetbacks in the field and caution the tractor driver not to play Grand Prix while cultivating. Then you could settle down for a snooze by the canal bank until noon."

Snoozing by the canal bank and drinking until sunrise did not earn these Midwesterners much respect from the local farmers. The following story reveals just how much Burroughs and Kells appeared to know about farming. It was told to me by John Snider, who was a cash buyer of cotton and vegetables in the late 1940s and later managed the San Pat Vegetable Shed in Pharr:

> The reason I know him [Kells Elvins], I was buying cotton for a cotton broker in Memphis, in 1948 or 1949. We'd wait until the cotton got so high in the field, and we'd go out and look at it and make 'em an offer and pay 'em right there. Well, I met him northwest of San Carlos, up there about where the prison is. He had a field of cotton up there, and I looked at it, and it wasn't even worth looking at. It was planted too late. It was dry-planted; you don't plant cotton dry, you got to have moisture to get it on up there. It was still down there in the furrow, and he was trying to kick dry dirt into it to cultivate it. Mexican didn't know what he was doing, and no one was telling him, and so I just pissed him off. Well, I called John [the buyer's boss], and he said to Kells, "Well, my man already looked at it," and Kells said, "Well, he don't know what the hell he's talking about," so John met us out there, and I just sat over there and said, "John, go look at it." John looked at it and said, "Well, my goodness, there's not enough cotton come out of there to wad a shotgun." Well, Kells just sit there, and he had somebody with him, but the guy never got out of the car — I didn't know who the hell he was, could have been Burroughs — and boy, he just got to raging, cussing, and all that: "It's a bumper crop!" You can't grow cotton up there anyway — the land was not cotton land. It's that old citrus land that they had bought. I don't know why they bought it.

From the point of view of the locals, Kells and Billy were just a couple of Valley suckers who had bought some untenable land and were frustrated when nothing grew on it.

Maybe Kells and Billy didn't know that much about farming, as they themselves admitted, but that didn't stop them. After all, they had Harvard educations and came from a line of successful, self-made men. Therefore, I wasn't too surprised to hear other stories about Kells and Billy showing how they approached farming with the same Yankee inventiveness and resourcefulness they brought to all of their money-making schemes, such as the dry-cleaning machine they worked on in St. Louis. Pat Paris's brother, Danny Lohr, remembers an unconventional scheme Kells had for growing papayas in winter: "Kells rigged up some gas furnaces to protect some papaya plants. Down there on South Jackson he rented some land and planted . . . two acres in papaya trees. A natural gas line came down the east side of Jackson road, where his property was, and Kells got them to connect up so he could heat his papaya plants in case of a freeze; they won't last in a heavy frost. He had one of these furnaces between each tree, and he was hoping there would be a freeze. Don't know if the freeze or the furnaces killed the papayas."[14]

Ted Marak remembers another scheme Burroughs and Kells thought up to maximize the productivity of their land. Much of the soil was ruined by salinity, the result of irrigating with contaminated water, and only salt grass would grow on it. Kells and Billy, however, figured out a novel plan to leach the salt out of the ground: They planted the land in radishes, grazed their hogs in the radish fields, and let the manure from the hogs fertilize the soil. Later they could slaughter the hogs or sell them. An efficient idea. After one or two seasons, they believed, the land would be restored. Ted says Billy and Kells had a great deal of land they planned to treat this way, but he was glad that he didn't get involved: "Thank God I wasn't in on that deal." It wasn't really such a crazy scheme, though: In *Rio Grande Wetbacks,* his memoir about farming the Valley in the 1940s, Carrol Norquest also describes a strategy to leach the salt out of his barren farmlands.[15]

In this sense — as an occupation that Burroughs set about to study — farming *was* a serious endeavor for him. But it was about more than clever ways to maximize production. As his letters to Allen Ginsberg and others show, Burroughs saw the farmer as the embodiment of American free enterprise and rugged individualism. There was, of course, a strong historical precedent for his views. In the late nineteenth century, Frederick Jackson Turner, in his famous "Frontier Thesis," extolled the agrarian philosophy that "natural" struggle defined the American character. However, as Henry Nash Smith pointed out in the 1940s, Turner failed to take into account the effects of the industrial revolution on the agrarian ideal, which he regarded as "an unfortunate and anomalous violation of the natural order of things."[16]

Burroughs's letters reflect Turner's agrarian myth of the nobility of "natural" struggle: He is proud of his occupation, self-righteously (and in part comically) referring to himself and his fellow farmers as "sons of the soil."[17] He sends Kerouac and Ginsberg regular reports on crop yields and commodity prices, and he enjoys lecturing his friends about farming, often making fun of their ignorance: "Mere lack of knowledge could not account for your staggering ignorance of agricultural operations," he wrote to Allen Ginsberg on February 7, 1949. "Ruined by *one freeze* in *January* in an area that makes two complete crops a year, three if need be? . . . Ruined when I own 50 acres of the finest land in the Valley?"[18] Such proud, defiant rhetoric reflects the Turner thesis of the self-reliant, individualistic American farmer, but, unlike Turner, Burroughs was well aware of the threat the small farmer faced due to industrialization, specifically the expensively mechanized "factory farms" that were overrunning modest operations such as his own.

Moreover, Burroughs added to this critique of the agrarian myth two factors that neither Turner nor Smith observed during their lifetime: on the national level, the controlling influence of government bureaucrats, and, on the local level in South Texas, the quagmire created by the use of illegal laborers in the South Texas fields. As a farmer in the Valley in the post–World War II period, Burroughs thus confronted many of the issues that he would later dramatize in his original indictment of the United States, *Junky*: government interference in the lives of citizens, the failure of U.S. capitalism and the concomitant need for a cooperative society, and the dependence of the police state on criminal activity.

More so than any other single issue related to farming, the so-called labor problem in the Valley forced Burroughs to confront the end of free enterprise in the United States and to give up on the notion of farmers as the last noble representatives of the old American spirit. As his letters to Jack Kerouac and Allen Ginsberg from 1948 to 1950 indicate, Burroughs tried to make an honest living as a farmer, but to do so he found he was compelled to hire *illegal* laborers from Mexico, who were willing to work for substandard wages: "[W]e farmers in the Rio Grande Valley," he wrote to Allen Ginsberg, "depend entirely on Mexican laborers who enter the Country illegally with our aid and connivance. . . . To get my tomatoes picked and delivered to the vegetable broker who buys them . . . the broker backs a truck up to the Rio Grande and loads it with Mexican 'Wetbacks' as they swim or wade across the border." The irony of the situation was certainly not lost on Burroughs, who, as a drug addict and sometimes drug dealer, was himself an "illegal." As he wrote to Allen Ginsberg on November 30, 1949, "In short, my ethical position, now that I am a respectable farmer, is probably shakier than when I was pushing junk. Now, as then, I violate the law, but my present violations are condoned by a corrupt government."[19]

Burroughs's fellow Edinburg farmer Carrol Norquest also recognized the hypocrisy of the system. In his memoir, *Rio Grande Wetbacks: Mexican Migrant Workers* (1972), Norquest says, "The laws would not allow us to use them honestly, so we all — wetbacks, farmers, lawmen, even *la chota* [Border Patrol] — became liars. Everybody made a flimsy show of being law-abiding."[20] In this context, junk and cotton do not seem so far apart, and that is how the "Valley section" came to be in *Junky*, although Burroughs's letters make this connection between cotton farming and pushing junk much more explicit than the published book does.

Burroughs's "labor troubles" (as he refers to them in letters) thus have a specific context worth knowing, for he happened to be farming in the Valley during an important chapter in the story of Mexican American labor.[21] Here is some history: Before World War II, when, for example, Politte Elvins first bought a number of citrus groves, Texas farmers had always been able to hire laborers directly from Mexico with no regulation or governmental oversight. During the war, the Mexican government used the labor shortage in the United States as leverage to institute a "braceros" program (the "arms" of Mexico), which would regulate and supervise Mexican labor for its neighbor to the north. Texas, however, was specifically excluded from the bracero agreement because the state had a long history of abusing Mexicans and Mexican laborers: Mexicans could thus work in Arkansas, Oklahoma, California, and anywhere else, but not in Texas. This exclusion was fine with many Texans, though, since it indirectly encouraged them to use — and in some cases abuse — *illegal* laborers, who worked more cheaply than legal braceros.

While Burroughs was hiring illegals to work his farms, labor troubles were starting in Texas. They began in October of 1948, when the Mexican government claimed that braceros working in Arkansas had been transported there in crowded and unsanitary trucks previously used to ship cattle. One man, thought to be asleep by his fellow workers, had reportedly died en route. There were also charges that the laborers had been forced to bathe in DDT before crossing from Reynosa into McAllen. In response, the Mexican government suspended the bracero agreement with the United States on October 4, 1948, just at a time when an unusually heavy cotton crop required harvesting.[22]

Throughout early October, workers hoping to enter the United States and harvest cotton continued to mass on the border. They slept in the streets of towns such as Juarez and Reynosa, just across the border from Burroughs's and Kells's land. On October 15, 1948, in what was described in the national press as an "invasion," border patrol agents turned a blind eye and allowed thousands of illegals to cross the border at El Paso and all along the Texas border.[23] However, as soon as enough workers had been hired to meet the farmers' needs, the fence went back up. The Mexican government was furious, again citing the threat of discrimination against its citizens working illegally in Texas. Texas officials, matching the Mexicans' rhetoric, claimed that, by cutting off the flow of laborers, the Mexican government was "pointing a pistol at the American farmer's head."[24]

Burroughs refers to this series of events — written up in national newsmagazines such as *Time* and *Newsweek* — in a December 2, 1948, letter to Allen Ginsberg: "Enclose article about Texas labor situation."[25] In the letter, he uses the labor situation to explain his precarious position as a farmer to Ginsberg, claiming that, if he lost the services of the illegal laborers or if he had to pay them a minimum wage, he would go broke. Similarly, he told Ginsberg, the threat of these laborers' forming a union was a "nightmare" to him. The only alternative to cheap labor, the letter says, is to eliminate "stoop" labor altogether and replace it with machine harvesting — but only the Big Holders had the money to buy the expensive machines. As for the mistreatment of these workers, Burroughs admitted to hearing stories of laborers being killed by a local foreman. In later letters to Ginsberg, however, he would soften this picture of the abuse of the illegal laborers, pointing out that he and many other farmers treated their workers well: They provided them housing and paid for their medical and legal expenses, the letter says. Still, in a 1974 interview with John Tytell, Burroughs recalled stories of the ill-treatment and even murder of these workers: "In the big ranches the wetbacks were herded all over the place. They had guards with machine guns. They tried to pull a strike once and all the guards shot three of them, so they all went back to work. They had no rights."[26]

The October 1948 "invasion" brought these issues related to the exploitation of Mexican laborers to the full attention of the federal government, and a commission was formed to investigate border "labor trouble." Titled *Study of the Spanish-Speaking People of Texas,* this report, released on June 12, 1949, was written by University of Texas (UT) faculty member George I. Sanchez. The report demanded "emergency legislation which would penalize the use of illegal alien labor. . . . In every piece of fruit, every vegetable, every product of any kind that is produced in areas of wetback concentrations there is a hidden cost that never appears in the retail dealers' price tags" — hidden costs that included unsanitary, disease-infested living conditions, unequal access to education, and the use of child labor. Most ominously for farmers such as Burroughs who relied on illegal labor, the study warned that the economy of Central, Western, and South Texas was "being founded upon most dangerous ground: the shifting quicksand that is the wetback — contraband labor. The cotton and citrus industries, vegetable farming and similar enterprises there, by the shortsighted dependence on wetback labor, are sowing the wind — and, as a result, the state and nation will long reap a whirlwind of social misery and unrest."[27]

The local response to this Washington-generated edict was mixed. The editor of the *Evening Monitor* in McAllen thought the report sounded mostly accurate, but he encouraged the paper's readers to gather the facts themselves by going out and talking to both farmers and laborers — a suggestion that would have pleased the "factualist" Burroughs.[28] A more conservative response, and one that Burroughs would echo in spirit in his letters to Ginsberg and Kerouac, was that the report was a lie and that it had been written, according to a local farmer named Allen M. Drury, by people with "Communistic leanings." Another local farmer, Ed Kornegay, told the *Monitor* reporter "he had been informed that a highly-financed propaganda machine had been organized to put out reports on alien labor conditions." The "propaganda machine" to which he refers may well have been the League of United Latin American Citizens (LULAC), the president of which had been a coauthor of the UT study.[29] At this time, such conspiracy theories were quite in line with the view Burroughs developed of the United States as a place "bogged down in the octopus of bureaucratic socialism."[30]

Propaganda or not, the study produced quick results, for within two weeks of its publication, Burroughs was complaining to Jack Kerouac that the Border Patrol had deported the field hands he had hired. Throughout June and July of 1949, local newspaper headlines reported that, on the Mexico side of the border, security had been tightened. "Mexico Adds 5000 to Patrol against Wetbacks, Smugglers," reads a July 24, 1949, *Monitor* headline. Although the Mexican government was no doubt motivated by its concern over the mistreatment of illegal Mexican immigrants in Texas, there were other reasons for closing its border: Mexican farmers wanted laborers to stay at home and harvest a large cotton crop in northern Mexico. Mexican workers, however, had other ideas and believed they could make more money by illegally harvesting crops in the United States. The field hands were clearly the losers here, caught in a tug-of-war between two governments.

Wetback "addicts" such as Burroughs suffered, too. Withdrawal meant watching their crops wilt and their farms slide closer to foreclosure. Once again, this time in the summer of 1949 (right when Burroughs was living in South Texas on a permanent basis and when his cotton needed harvesting), laborers pushed up against the border. On July 15, 1949, the *Monitor* reported that, in the previous thirty days, "80,000 braceros had massed on the border in order to pick a reported 900,000 acres of cotton fields in the

Valley."[31] The border remained closed to them, however. Bandits victimized the unemployed workers sleeping on the streets of the border towns, and a body a day was found in the river at Reynosa, Mexico, and downstream in Brownsville, Texas. Eventually Mexican officials backed down and cut a deal to allow the braceros to work in Texas legally, but even then Valley farmers were not interested in hiring them.[32] The Mexican government wanted them to be paid forty cents an hour, and farmers such as Burroughs believed they would be unable to make a profit paying the higher wage, as Burroughs told Ginsberg in a letter dated May 1, 1950.

Although the rest of the United States had little idea what was going on down on the Texas border, this series of events strongly shaped Burroughs's views on capitalism, labor unions, and government bureaucracies. He was acutely aware of his complicity in an exploitative system, but at the same time he reserved his fundamental right to deal with the situation on his own terms without being dictated to by government bureaucrats and wealthy landowners. He did so, he says, by treating the workers fairly and by providing for them in a way their own government would not. His labor troubles were thus an object lesson tailor made for analysis by his emerging philosophy of factualism (so prevalent in the straight-talk style of *Junky*), a philosophy of seeing things as they were, not as those in control wanted people to see them.

Applying this philosophy, Burroughs crafted a detailed indictment not only of the border's agricultural economy but of the United States in general. In a remarkable letter to Allen Ginsberg, dated May 1, 1950, he put all of the pieces of his three years of farming experience together and revealed what was (to him) a swindle of huge proportions. Says Burroughs, "[T]he present U.S. policy is the result of lobbying by a few big rich in Texas and Mexico. They are the only ones to benefit." When you go into farming in the Valley, Burroughs tells Ginsberg, you take out a loan with a local bank for your land and machinery and other costs. The banker in the Valley loans you this money, knowing full well that in order to make a profit you have to use illegal labor — "hooking" the farmer on illegal labor, so to speak. Then, in collusion with Border Patrol agents, says Burroughs, the Big Holders could (as he told John Tytell in 1974) "very selectively" bust the laborers you hired and send them back to Mexico. The cutting off of the supply of laborers in the summer of 1949 created the equivalent of what junkies call a "panic." The net result was that small farmers would go belly-up because of increased labor costs or an inability to find laborers, and the big players — the bankers — cleaned up by foreclosing on farm loans.[33] In *Junky,* Burroughs compares farming to shooting craps: "The Big Holders are the house, and the small farmers are the players. The player goes broke if he keeps on playing, and the farmer has to pay or lose to the Government by default. The Big Holders own all the Valley banks, and when the farmer goes broke the bank takes over. Soon the Big Holders will own the Valley."[34]

Locally, he says in his letter to Ginsberg, the Big Holders are a family named "Benson." "In the Valley," he says, "the bank is the Benson Brothers. The Benson Brothers represent a new type of tycoon. They have neither energy nor intelligence. They just sit, and slowly the Valley falls into their hands. In a few years they will own the whole Valley. They are the final beneficiaries of the U.S. wetback policy." Calling this the "wetback deal," Burroughs is furious with "liberals" such as Ginsberg who "are appallingly naïve when you accept a routine like this wetback deal at face value. Liberals have always been suckers for Communist or Fascist undercover moves." They are "suckers" because "Fascists" know they can count on "Liberals" sympathetic to "oppressed workers," who, like Ginsberg, believe that workers are entitled to form unions and be paid a minimum wage — a wage much higher than what Burroughs and other farmers believed they could afford to pay. Government or union regulation of labor markets would thus bankrupt small farmers, Burroughs argued, and lead to foreclosures collected on by the Big Holders. Then, with all of the farms under their control, the Big Holders could replace troublesome workers altogether with expensive but efficient harvesting machines. The result would be no more small farmers and no more labor problems — only Big Holders harvesting crops with machines. The Big Holders in Mexico would benefit, too: Their workers would have to stay at home working for pay that was a fraction of the already low wages the Texas farmers paid. That, Burroughs says, was the truth behind the wetback deal.[35]

The May Day letter is an example of Burroughs's emerging philosophy of factualism: "All I am concerned with is *facts*" was his refrain in letters written during these years. Yet, how factual is his analysis of the wetback deal? For example, did Burroughs and his fellow farmers actually have to pay their laborers substandard wages in order to make a profit, as he claims they did? In *The Development of the Migratory Farm Labor System in Texas: 1900–1954,* George Coalson examines this question. Valley farmers, he says, justified their use of low-wage, illegal field hands by citing freight charges and water rates that were higher than those charged in other parts of the country. However, Coalson counters this argument with statistics showing that such low wages merely padded the already full pockets of farmers. Moreover, he says, the low overhead enjoyed by South Texas farmers created an imbalance in the commodities markets. Farmers in California and elsewhere complained that they could not compete with Valley farmers because the low wages Texans paid allowed them an unfair advantage in the marketplace.

The most dramatic issue related to illegal labor was the purported mistreatment of the laborers by Texas farmers. Burroughs sometimes claimed that they were treated well, but at other times he told stories he had heard of ranch foremen killing Mexicans when they refused to work. However, it is a fact beyond debate that there were abuses, and I refer the reader to general histories of Mexican Americans such as Rodolfo Acuña's powerful *Occupied America: A History of Chicanos* or to regional literature of the Valley such as Tomás Rivera's seminal Chicano novel *Y no se lo tragó la tierra* [And the Earth Did Not Devour Him] (1971). Rivera, a native of the "winter garden" area of Crystal City, Texas, and later chancellor of the University of California–Riverside, recounts stories of his childhood days as a migrant farmworker that closely resemble the previously quoted newspaper accounts of laborers being transported in crowded, unsanitary cattle trucks and being forced to work until they collapsed.

Back in the 1940s, though, Valley farmers such as Burroughs adamantly denied that such abuses occurred. In the 1950 report of the President's Commission on Migratory Labor, Valley farmers ascribed to themselves humanitarian motives in hiring Mexican aliens and denounced those people who were "selfish enough to be jealous of a dollar that they resent those poor people coming over here to make a living and send something back to people who have never had a full day's meal in their lives. . . . One woman from Raymondville testified that the ladies in her community had organized a Junior Service League which operated a child welfare clinic, provided a library for Mexican families, and distributed food to the needy. . . . In addition, one employer stated that the farmers provided medical care, housing, firewood, lights, and water for workers."[36]

Burroughs's letter to Allen Ginsberg in which he says he fed, housed, and provided medical care for the workers he hired is remarkably similar to this testimony, and the truth is that many Anglo farmers practiced this sort of benevolent paternalism. Some went further: Carrol Norquest,

Burroughs's Edinburg neighbor, helped his workers gain citizenship. His son, Kelly, remembers the fun and warmth of his family's relationship with the Mexican laborers. Still, in the eyes of some Mexican Americans who were not lucky enough to work with farmers like Norquest, such stories amount to a South Texas version of "plantation literature."

I raised these and other issues — in particular, the larger question of how involved the Big Holders actually were in the creation of the wetback deal — with both Ted Marak and John Snider, whose family had farmed the Valley since the teens and who was a cash buyer for the produce shed in Pharr where Kells, Burroughs, and Marak sold their crops.

Ted Marak farmed with Kells at the same time Burroughs did and thus is an excellent judge of Burroughs's description of Valley agriculture in the 1940s. He had never read any of Burroughs's works or letters, and I made copies of this material for him and asked him to give me his opinion of what Burroughs had to say. In many respects, he thought Burroughs was very accurate and was delighted to see that someone had captured the life they led back then: "Terrific! Terrific! He had it nailed," Ted told me when I read him a description of all the things that could go wrong in the Valley for farmers ("I should have hung on to that hundred acres on the lower lift; I should have took up them oil leases; I should have planted cotton instead of tomatoes"). For him, Burroughs had truly captured the cracker-barrel conversations small farmers had in the 1940s. He also confirmed what Burroughs said (in *Junky*) about South Texas farmers making a lot of money during the War — "people thought they were sharp operators when in fact they were just riding a lucky streak."[37] "Man, they did," said Marak. "Sure, it was patriotic to take those inflated prices, too."

Burroughs and Marak thus shared many similar experiences in the Valley; however, since Marak had grown up as a poor farm boy in Oklahoma during the Depression — as opposed to Burroughs, who had spent the Depression in private boarding schools, Harvard, and abroad in Europe — he did not always see things the way Burroughs did. For example, Burroughs, in his May Day letter, reverses what he had told Allen Ginsberg earlier about the mistreatment of Mexican farmhands and says they were treated well, with few exceptions. When I asked Ted about this, he replied,

TM: Mexican Americans were just a bunch of goddamn wetback pigs, and they treated them like dogs. Well, I mean they were treated like chattel.

RJ: Did you have to pay them that little in order to make a profit?

TM: Hell no, you exploited these poor fuckers. . . . [T]hey were getting 30 cents, and a tractor driver was getting 40 cents. You got a seven-thousand-dollar tractor and a guy making 40 cents an hour playing ring around the rosies — this is idiotic. I said to Kells, you're paying them, but we're going to have the best. Give those tractor drivers at least 50 cents. And any kid that they've got that can lift up a hoe, give him 10 or 15 cents an hour. He can go out there and make food for the day anyway. And bring these wages up, 35, 40 cents. And Kells said, "All right." And I raised wages, and I thought I was going to get lynched by all the other farmers. This is sacrilege, they thought. Paying these goddamn wetbacks, blah blah blah. Certainly they could have, but everybody was greedy, redneck assholes in my book — maybe I shouldn't call them that. They were just greedy, and they had no compassion for these people, none at all. And I'll tell you what these Jackson guys [Kells's neighbors] did. They would say, "Well, we need some pants for the little boy," and these jerks would go to town and say it cost one price and then sell it to them at another price and gouge them. For clothes, for food, for medication, for everything. And that just irked the shit out of me.

I also asked Marak about Burroughs's complaints that the illegals were constantly under threat of being returned to Mexico and that this in turn threatened Burroughs's livelihood as a farmer.

RJ: Did you ever have any trouble getting laborers?

TM: Never.

RJ: Burroughs says the Border Patrol was a constant threat, busting his workers and sending them back across the border.

TM: Yeah, well, you know Burroughs was a square-head. I used to make a deal with the Border Patrol. Finally they'd say, "You know we got problems in California, and Washington's bitching about this," and I'd say, "How many do you need?" And they'd say, "Ted, we need about sixty from you." And I'd say, "How about twenty five?" And they'd say, "All right." They didn't have buses, they had trucks. And I'd always send Eusebio. And I asked him what time will they be back [across the border], and he'd say, "In time for work." They'd run them through. We were only nine miles from the river.

This may be the only time anyone has ever called William S. Burroughs a "square," and Marak's point is a good one: Burroughs thought he understood the system down here, but he didn't. There were evidently easy ways to ensure a steady supply of workers. Compared to Ted, who had learned how to figure all the angles and cons while working as a floor boss in a major Las Vegas casino, Burroughs must truly have seemed a "square-head."

Like Ted Marak, John Snider agreed with Burroughs's version of reality, but only up to a point. I read to him from Burroughs's letters about how poorly Mexicans were paid in their own country compared to what they could make in the States ($3–$7 per day) and how Burroughs said he had heard of only one farmer who ever cheated the illegals out of their money. He confirmed the salary numbers but added that he had never heard of *any* employer cheating the field hands: "I don't know who that would be," he said. He also agreed with Burroughs that, had Valley farmers paid the higher, minimum wage sought by government bureaucrats, they wouldn't have been able to make a profit at all. And he agreed with Burroughs's statement that the laborers were "generally well treated."

However, Snider had serious disagreements with Burroughs's statements about the "Benson Brothers" being behind a wetback deal that was meant to bankrupt small farmers. To any South Texan, it is apparent (as it was to Snider) that the "Benson Brothers" that Burroughs calls the "Big Holders" in the Valley were undoubtedly the *Bentsens* of South Texas, as in the family of Sen. Lloyd Bentsen Jr.[38] Burroughs's May Day letter refers to the senator's father, Lloyd Bentsen Sr., and his brother, Elmer Bentsen. Their father, Peter Bentsen, moved the family to the Valley in 1918 and worked as a land agent for John Shary, the "father of the Texas citrus industry." Over the next two generations, Peter Bentsen and his sons created a South Texas dynasty in oil, real estate, and banking.[39]

By the time Burroughs came to the Valley in the late 1940s, the family was branching out into politics. Lloyd Bentsen Jr. was elected to his first term as a U.S. Representative in 1948; he would go on to become one of the most influential and powerful Democratic leaders of the postwar period, garnering the vice presidential nomination (under Michael Dukakis) in 1988 and serving as Bill Clinton's first secretary of the treasury. I quote some facts from *The Handbook of Texas Online* that confirm Burroughs's assessment of the Bentsens' power in the region in the late 1940s: "Lloyd and Elmer Bentsen became the premier colonizers and developers of Hidalgo County. . . . Elmer and Lloyd were principals in the Elsa State Bank,

Elmer a president and director and Lloyd on the board of directors. Lloyd was also a principal in the First National banks of McAllen, Mission, Edinburg, Raymondville, and Brownsville."[40]

Nonetheless, were the Bentsens really behind the wetback deal Burroughs describes in both *Junky* and his letters? The farmer I interviewed laughed at Burroughs's claim that the Bentsens were "the bank," saying that there were many bankers in the Valley at the time. Therefore, the Bentsens were not trying to "swallow up" the Valley by bankrupting farmers, he told me, and they were not dishonest. In response, I read a passage from *The Handbook of Texas Online* that reflects Burroughs's view of the Bentsens as unscrupulous businessmen: "[Lloyd] Bentsen [Sr.] did not accumulate land and monetary fortunes without problems. In 1952–1955 he had courtroom difficulties in Texas and Washington D.C., over land sales. He was accused by five plaintiffs of conspiracy and fraud in the sale of Ramsmeyer Gardens, supposedly irrigated land fit for citrus. . . . In another land dispute, buyers of Valley lands from the Bentsen Group claimed that the sellers had failed to maintain and tend citrus plantings. . . . No fraud was ever found, although damages of $5000 to one plaintiff were later mandated by the court."[41]

It is possible that the land Kells was dry-farming might have been just such unfit land, and we know that Burroughs bought his land from one of the Bentsens' real estate agents, Roy Hines ("Roy the real estate man" in *Junky*). Burroughs also tells a story in *Junky* — reminiscent of the Ramsmeyer Gardens story — in which an unscrupulous land developer sells irrigated land and then pulls the plug on the water supply, leaving the "suckers" high and dry on worthless land. Although Burroughs does not implicate the Bentsens in that particular deal, that is the side of the Bentsens that Burroughs and Ted Marak saw: He heard "all dark stories" about the Bentsens, Ted told me, and thought "there was something to" Burroughs's view that the Bentsens were behind the wetback deal.

However, in a telephone interview with me in December 2001, John Snider emphatically denied the Bentsens were the kind of people who would calculate such a deal, and he had special knowledge to back up his argument: He knew Lloyd Bentsen Sr. ("the Old Man") very well and accompanied him on business trips to Rio Grande City. On these trips, the Old Man often talked about the land fraud charges his enemies made against him, and he told John his side of the story. Taking Bentsen's point of view, John explained that during World War II, Valley farmers needed to grow all the food and cotton they possibly could in order to support the war effort: "Food and fiber" was a rallying cry. Therefore, in South Texas, with a year-round growing season, the government practically forced farmers to expand their operations.

Eventually they had to develop land that had previously been dry brush country, and some of this land, sight unseen, was sold to Midwesterners seeking to get in on the wartime farming boom. Much of this land, it turned out, was unirrigated, but the idea was that irrigation lines would follow. However, when the war ended and the demand for "food and fiber" plummeted, the irrigation lines were never built — leaving the buyers with unirrigated land. Thus, according to Lloyd Bentsen Sr., he and his brother were simply victims of bad luck and their own desire to serve their government during the war. "Now, they [the Bentsens] weren't saints," Snider added, "but they weren't the bandits that a lot of people say they were. Now, that's all there is to it. They couldn't have been. We weren't the Wild West down here. Mr. Lloyd and I talked about this. I used to ride with him out to the ranch, and he would talk about this. He said he got a lot of bum rap. The Bentsens were people, just plain ordinary people."

Still, unflattering stories about Lloyd Sr. show up in various histories of Texas politics. The following tale is worth repeating because it took place in 1946, the year Burroughs first came to the Valley. It is from *The Establishment in Texas Politics: The Primitive Years, 1938–1957*, a book by George Norris Green:

> The governor [Allen Shivers, son-in-law of John Shary] was also embarrassed by some of his business deals, especially by one of his real estate transactions. In 1946, when he was running for lieutenant governor, Shivers had bought an option on 13,500 acres in the Rio Grande Valley from millionaire citrus grower Lloyd Bentsen, Sr., for $25,000. (Bentsen had earlier made a fortune in the "immigrant land business," selling valley land without the vital water rights.) Six and a half months later Shivers sold his option — one day after it had expired — back to a Bentsen-owned company for $450,000. Three months after Shivers became governor, the State Board of Water Engineers granted precious, but restricted, water rights on the Bentsen land. Because of the lack of water in the Rio Grande River, this was the first time in more than twenty years that the board had granted a new permit. . . . According to Shivers, who was never able to think of any reason for the 1700 percent

> increase in the value of the option, Yarborough's criticism of the deal only showed that Yarborough did not believe in "our American system of free enterprise."[42]

Interestingly, Shivers's defense of his huge profits was to accuse anyone who objected to them of being a communist — rhetoric used by Burroughs himself when anyone tried to meddle with his business interests. But the Shivers-Bentsen story also suggests that Burroughs had a point when he says farming was controlled by the Big Holders, who had access to the inner corridors of power and could use it — quite profitably — to their own advantage. Off the record, longtime Valley residents will tell you that this was the reason behind Lloyd Jr.'s run for the House of Representatives in 1948: The family wanted the influence public office would give them.

Overall, though, if you put Burroughs's version of reality in a larger perspective, it is unlikely that his, Kells's, and Ted's small farming ventures failed because of the wetback deal supposedly rigged by the Bentsens and other Big Holders. Certainly, Burroughs's *perception* that the farm game was rigged against him was a psychological factor in his decision to call it quits in late 1949. For once, however, his timing was good: Back-to-back hard freezes hit the Valley in 1950 and 1951. Ted Marak told me how his and Kells's operations were destroyed by the 1950 freeze: "I had every penny I had in a tomato crop. When that freeze was coming, they warned us, but Eusebio said, 'No, it's not going to freeze.' And I said, 'How do you know?' and he says, 'The snails.' He says, 'If the snails are going up the trees, it's going to freeze. If they're staying on the ground, it's not going to freeze.' Sure enough, they stayed on the ground, but it froze anyway, and it took us out." You can't blame snails for being inaccurate meteorologists, and you also can't blame the Big Holders for two hard winters.

However, many longtime residents of the Valley will tell you a story that confirms some of Burroughs's gloomy predictions about the future of South Texas farming. Facing increased labor costs, farmers stopped planting crops that needed to be harvested by hand ("stoop labor") and started planting crops that could be harvested by machines instead. In this sense, when Burroughs says a minimum wage will mean no one makes any money, he is correct: Today, the handpicking of crops is almost a thing of the past, and the variety of crops grown in the Valley is thus greatly reduced. In one of the richest agricultural areas in the United States (and thus the world), you are hard pressed to find an independent farmer's market selling basic vegetables. In the Valley, there is one chain of grocery stores, HEB, and its produce comes from all over the United States, shipped down here in a constantly running fleet of tractor trailers. Less and less of it comes from the Valley, and a good portion of our "local" produce now comes from the "free" country of Mexico, where Burroughs wanted to move his farming operation in order to escape the wetback deal. Meanwhile, unemployment in the Valley is the highest in the United States, hovering around 15 percent.[43]

Burroughs's experiences as a Texas farmer were unique with respect to his having to break the law in order to make a legal living — that is, having to hire illegal laborers and pay them a substandard wage. In other important respects, though, his experiences were more universally those of farmers throughout the United States. Like Burroughs, these farmers were faced with growing government intrusion in their lives, to the point where it appeared that, at least in farming, the free-enterprise system no longer existed.

Even more so than the wetback deal, it was this fundamental erosion of the capitalist system that led Burroughs the farmer to leave the States for the "free" country of Mexico. After the war, Burroughs discovered, the old rules that had allowed his grandfather and uncle to make vast fortunes based on their own genius and hard work no longer applied — at least to farming, that proud bastion of independence and self-sufficiency. "The law of supply and demand no longer holds," Burroughs wrote to Jack Kerouac in May of 1949 from Pharr. "Scarcity of commodity does *not* insure a high price. In the future I will not plant anything without a government support price on it."[44]

Burroughs is here referring to the complicated system of price supports and acreage allotments created during the New Deal in order to ensure continuous food production and to protect farmers from foreclosure in tough economic times. During the war, as John Snider confirmed, farmers in the Valley were encouraged to produce as much food and raw materials (such as cotton) as they could, and as an incentive, the government guaranteed these farmers a good price on their crops. "So they threw it wide open," Snider told me.

After the war, however, when Burroughs was starting to go into farming, it was feared that farmers would continue to raise crops at the same volume they had during the high-demand days of the war and, as a result, commodity prices would fluctuate wildly — as they had done at the conclusion of World War I. The key to stabilizing commodity prices was production control. Farmers, it was believed, could not voluntarily restrain themselves, so the government created an incentive: Only farmers who agreed to reduce the acreage they planted would receive the guaranteed support price (parity) on their crops. Those who did not follow the allotments would not receive the support. The plan worked: Farmers were willing to sacrifice their individualistic character for the security of a subsidized support price on their crops. Burroughs hated such controls, railing against the "D of A Bureaucrats telling us what, where and when to plant," as he wrote to Jack Kerouac. Nonetheless, as Burroughs told Kerouac in a May 1949 letter, he planted only crops that would receive a support price.[45]

In 1949 six basic crops were supported at 90 percent of parity — corn, cotton, wheat, rice, tobacco, and peanuts.[46] Burroughs and other Valley farmers planted cotton in order to cash in on the government deal. Ted Marak recalled how the system worked in the Valley:

> TM: Say you had a hundred acres. If you could prove that you had raised cotton on that hundred acres for two years past, you'd get parity on fifty acres, or about half what your acreage was — to hold down the production of cotton. Parity was good money in those days.
>
> RJ: They'd pay you more to raise less?
>
> TM: Yeah, that's right. And that damn old Redlands [North Edinburg] stuff.

To take full advantage of this system, says Marak, he, Kells, Burroughs, and other farmers spent a lot of time studying the details of government acreage allotments on cotton. Editorials in the *McAllen Evening Monitor* frequently referred to the arcane nature of such regulations. These arcana show up in odd places in at least a couple of Burroughs's books. For example, in *Queer,* Lee tries to pay Allerton not to work on a Saturday night so that he will have dinner with him. "Like the Wallace Administration," says Lee, "I subsidize non-production. I will pay you twenty pesos not to work tonight."[47] The reference is to Henry Wallace, Roosevelt's secretary of agriculture who created the system of farm subsidies and acreage allotments Burroughs railed against as a South Texas farmer. Another reference occurs in *The Last Words of Dutch Schulz,* Burroughs's screenplay about the life and death of the famous beer-baron and mobster. In the screenplay, Schulz is busted by the Feds for tax evasion, and, knowing how much farmers hate government intrusion in their lives, he has his trial venue moved to the rural Midwest. In the courtroom scene, you hear whispered complaints by Midwestern farmers about "[e]xperts from Washington telling us what to plant." The scene then switches to the "office of the Bureau of Agriculture. Sullen farmers look at forms. A bureaucrat sits at a table behind a pile of forms." The stage directions say the bureaucrat "talks in a weary nasal tone: 'It's all explained in the forms . . . ⅔ of present crop is the quota on any crops specified in section 13D unless exempted under section C.'"[48]

Regulation of farming was, therefore, a hotly debated topic in the 1940s. In 1948 Democrats wanted a fixed price-support system to remain in place, whereas Republicans favored a more flexible price-support mechanism.[49] Burroughs was clearly on the side of the Republicans, complaining about government controls and threatening, albeit impotently, to revolt: "And if any obscenity bunch of bureaucrats think[s] we are going to sit on our ass and the Wrath of God take over, they will learn that we are not Liberals," he wrote to Jack Kerouac in reference to this system of controls.[50]

When I read the previous quotation to John Snider, he said, "We did it. We sat on our ass because we didn't have no choice." My interview with John Snider continued:

RJ: So you think they needed regulating?

JS: They had to, or we would have been asshole deep in cotton. [After the war] people kept right on planting and planting. . . . They never slowed down. So they [the Department of Agriculture] came in and said, "You people won't govern yourselves, so we're going to have to govern you. You got fifty acres, we're going to let you plant thirty-five acres tops."

RJ: How would the government stop you from planting fifty acres?

JS: You disc it up. You either disc it up or you don't harvest any.

RJ: And how would the government stop you from harvesting it?

JS: They won't gin it.

RJ: That was Burroughs's problem. He was a radical individualist. He wanted to be able to do whatever he wanted to.

JS: You could.

RJ: No, you couldn't plant fifty acres if the government said thirty-five.

JS: Yes, you could. You just couldn't sell it. [Laughs]

Burroughs found himself facing this essential contradiction in his life: He wanted to operate in a free market, but, as a farmer, he would have to capitulate to a system of controls on his behavior in order to survive. Those who know Burroughs's books will recognize here that he was coming up against a classic example of what he would later call the "control machine." Thus, his ideas on how individuals are both subtly and overtly controlled by others (especially by faceless enemies, such as bureaucrats) were crucially refined by his experiences as a farmer.

Although such views on the "control machine" would later brand him as a member of the counterculture, it is important to know that Burroughs's views on farming were mainstream Republican ones, and it would be a Republican — Dwight Eisenhower — who would win the White House a few years later. Eisenhower's secretary of agriculture, Ezra Taft Benson, articulated this conservative response of Burroughs and other farmers to twenty years of liberal farm policies in a memoir titled *Farmers at the Crossroads: (as Told to Carlisle Bergeron):* "'Then came the New Deal,' he wrote, 'and its massive intrusion into the producing, marketing and pricing of agricultural products and its vast apparent intention to remain in such activities. I do not question in the slightest that heroic measures were needed in those days for agriculture and other segments of the economy as well. But they should have remained emergency measures and should not have been permitted to accumulate tendencies toward subordinating the whole economy under the permanent control of the Federal Government.'"[51]

Control of farmers is the consistent theme of a 1951 book titled *Subsidies for Farmers,* which is a collection of essays on the topic from the late 1940s that appeared in farm journals as well as in mainstream magazines such as *Harper's* and *American Mercury.* Again, as in Ezra Taft Benson's views, you can hear clear echoes of Burroughs's antigovernment rhetoric in the views many of his contemporaries expressed. For example, in *Harper's* (November 1948), Nathan Robertson compares a "free-enterprise system" to what he calls our nation's "safe-enterprise system" and points out, as Burroughs had to Jack Kerouac, how such a system undermines the old laws of supply and demand: "Fundamentally, a free-enterprise system . . . is one in which there is a minimum of government or monopoly interference — in which the natural laws of supply and demand rule. In that kind of system an individual entrepreneur takes all the risks and, as a reward for bearing those risks, is entitled to all the law of supply and demand will permit him to win. . . . Today, instead of having a nearly free enterprise system in this country — as we used to have and as most people still seem to think we have — we are operating under something quite different. It is a drastically revised system — revised by monopoly and by government supports. . . . It might be called the 'safe-enterprise system.'" By 1948, says Robertson, one in six U.S. citizens was receiving some kind of direct support from the government, a figure probably higher than most Americans realized.[52] Some of those who received support, such as William S. Burroughs, were still among the most vocal critics of welfare.

In several of these farming articles from midcentury, there is an underlying metaphor that helps explain how Burroughs could have come to be writing about cotton in a book called *Junky*. Some farm analysts actually made a direct comparison between price controls and drug addiction, an example of how — even before Burroughs wrote *Junky* — "addiction" had become a powerful metaphor for the controlling influence of bureaucrats and law enforcement. As one agronomist wrote in a 1949 article, "But here is the really scary part: That's the controls, the regimentation. The socialization, if you want to call it that. . . . We have a taste of it now. The bigger bite we've taken, the more bitter it has been. And the bigger bite we take, the harder it is to go back. It's a habit-forming drug. And the higher the supports are set, the more rigid the controls you get."[53]

Other agricultural researchers made this same comparison between subsidies and drugs: "What is true is that where government becomes involved in price-support operations, and the greater the surpluses become, the more difficult it is to effect retreat. In this matter interference with the price mechanism is not much different from the use of drugs. It is easy to begin. It is much harder to taper off the dosage." What farmers needed was the "reduction cure," which Burroughs describes in *Junky*.[54] And that is in fact what conservative farmers were proposing — a phasing out of supports through a flexible price-support system. You can't go cold turkey from 90 percent of parity to no supports at all.

Although Burroughs may not have been as "hip" as Ted Marak, as seasoned as John Snider, or as knowledgeable as professional agronomists, apparently he was a quick study and came to understand, on a deep level, the plight of American farmers — and of the laborers they employed. Toward the end of his correspondence with Ginsberg over farm matters, he went one step further: Rather than just complain about the problems he and other farmers faced, he suggests a solution. "I am quite willing to allow anyone who works for me to share in the profits in proportion to the work he does," he says and adds that he had instituted such an arrangement with his workers in South Texas. He thus proposes as his answer to bureaucracy and fascism a "cooperative" system that he doesn't elaborate on but does define in opposition to bureaucracy, "the most inflexible and therefore the deadest of all political instruments."[55] In later years Burroughs would write extensively about cooperative societies in his novels, and it would be the "inflexible" nature of bureaucracy that the cooperative starkly opposed: In the Johnson family cooperative *(The Place of Dead Roads)*, for example, and among the "Articulated" *(Cities of the Red Night)*, everyone works toward mutually-agreed-upon goals (such as food production), and management and workers regularly trade hats, moving up and down the labor scale. Burroughs's experiences in South Texas provided him with a negative example that clearly influenced his creation of these utopian communities in his fiction: Captain Mission's articles of freedom include "[n]o white-man boss, no Pukha Sahib, no Patróns, no colonists" (*Cities*, xiv) — all roles Burroughs had played (albeit self-consciously) in South Texas in the late 1940s.

Outside of his fiction, though, Burroughs was more often a realist than an idealist, and by the 1960s and 1970s he had even reconsidered some of his views on the evils of "bureaucratic socialism." When Burroughs was a farmer in South Texas, he hated the "control" the government had over him, but he changed his mind over time, at least with regard to farming: As he told the editors of *Semiotext(e)* in 1975, "A certain amount of control is absolutely necessary. Where is all the food coming from — it is brought in, right? The whole unseen bureaucracy is bringing that food and putting it in shops, providing power, etc. If those people didn't work, millions would be starving overnight. So any system must find a way to keep those people on their jobs."[56] This is a far cry from the South Texas farmer of the 1940s who complained bitterly about being told what and where and how much to plant. John Snider seemed to have the same retrospective wisdom: "And now we look back at it and think well you stupid sons-of-bitches . . . because you can never get two farmers together to agree on the hour of the day and they both got watches on."[57]

Still, I doubt Burroughs would have changed his mind about either a minimum wage or labor unions: Late in his life (1994), these issues were indirectly raised by his starring role in a television spot for Nike shoes. Not surprisingly, the intelligentsia and hipsters lambasted Burroughs for selling out. In particular, a younger generation of activists who came of age in the early 1990s saw in Burroughs's Nike ad an implicit endorsement of the company's exploitation of overseas workers: Just as Burroughs employed field hands in the 1940s and paid them substandard wages, Nike now employed Third World laborers at wages far below the minimum they would be paid if they were American workers. In fact, the twenty-five cents an hour Nike was paying Indonesian teenagers in the 1990s was roughly the wage Burroughs was paying illegals in the late 1940s. When Doug Grant, an admirer and friend of Burroughs, asked Burroughs why he agreed to do the advertisement, Burroughs laughed and said, "Don't you know? The money!" Critics of globalization, however, find little humor in the fact that an Indonesian boy was paid slave wages for sewing up Nike's professionally endorsed soccer balls while Nike's CEO paid himself a yearly salary of two million dollars.[58]

If Burroughs was aware of such criticism before he died in 1997, he did not respond to it. If he had, it is likely he would have told these idealistic protesters the same thing he told Allen Ginsberg in 1949, when Ginsberg accused Burroughs of paying slave wages: If you can't make a profit, you can't pay anybody anything.

WILLY EL PUTO

When I tell people who know something (but not a lot) about William S. Burroughs, that he was a cotton farmer in South Texas in the 1940s, the first questions they ask aren't about what kind of crops he raised or how much land he owned. They want to know, "So where did he score junk?" and "What about the boys?" Anyone who has read *Queer,* however, knows that the first question answers the second, according to a formula that Burroughs himself gives us: When he's on the junk, he has no interest in sex; when he's off, his sex drive comes back with a vengeance, and he goes cruising for young men. In the Valley he was off junk; therefore, the logical conclusion is . . . And so I went in search of gay McAllen and gay Reynosa of the 1940s to see whether Burroughs was a character in it. If so, what people could tell me would help me reread *Queer,* his classic novel of "outing" himself in Mexico in light of the experiences he had in Texas and Reynosa just before he "jumped" and went to live in Mexico City.

The Valley, as far as I can tell, was no more homophobic than the rest of the United States in the immediate postwar period. It was certainly not acceptable in most situations to be openly gay; in fact, the relatively benign term *gay* did not even exist. But from what people in their seventies and eighties have told me, there was a recognized "crowd" of homosexuals (men, not women) who more or less let their lifestyle be known without suffering any serious harm for doing so. Would Burroughs have found this group while living in the Valley? It seems likely, but it's also clear from reading *Queer* and *Junky* that Burroughs despised the kind of effeminate homosexual he thought gave being queer a bad name and was more interested in seducing straight young men who were, so to speak, seducible.

I do not have any definite proof to connect Burroughs to gay McAllen, only circumstantial evidence. One of my contacts is a woman in her midsixties named Betty Jo Noser, whose father, John Noser, was the "Carrot King" of McAllen in the 1940s. During my first interview with Betty Jo, I showed her a picture of Burroughs. She peered at it through her glasses and said, "He was gay, wasn't he? You didn't tell me that, right?" I hadn't, and I asked her how she knew. She told me her father was active in the little theater in Pharr in the 1940s and that two of his friends who were part of the troupe were a well-known gay couple from McAllen. Burroughs knew these men, too, she says, because she remembers seeing him with them. I subsequently interviewed one of these men, a seventy-five-year-old, well-respected businessman in McAllen. He either didn't remember Burroughs or didn't want to talk about him with me: "He looks like a lot of men," he told me when I showed him Burroughs's 1950 Mexico City College ID photo. Still, I don't doubt Betty Jo's unsolicited testimony that she knew at the time — through Burroughs's association with recognized gay men — that Burroughs was gay.

If Betty Jo Noser did in fact see Burroughs and identify him as gay, she is the only person I interviewed on this side of the border who made that connection. Kells Elvins, on the other hand, was suspected of being queer by Valley-born farmers who knew him in the 1940s. When I asked John Snider whether he knew Kells Elvins, the first comment he came out with was, "He was as queer as a three-dollar bill." Really? I asked him. I told him no one had ever said that about Kells, certainly not Burroughs himself, who was gay as well as his best friend. How did he know Kells was gay? "His mannerisms," he told me, without elaborating. "That sonofabitch was as queer as a three-dollar bill." According to John, he was not the only person who felt that way about Kells. He told me a story of a carhop waitress at the Hub in Pharr who was fed up with Kells's drunken behavior late one night after Kells had been to Reynosa: "He [Kells] was drunk, because Nevada — I'll never forget that redheaded cross-eyed gal — she was, I think, the ugliest woman I ever knew in my whole life, but she was the sweetest thing that ever was. She said, 'That drunk queer son of a bitch stumbles over that table one more time, I'm gonna hit him with a chair!'"

Like Betty Jo Noser, Snider remembered Kells in the company of the same well-known McAllen gay couple. In fact, when I asked him to elaborate, he listed a number of men who were recognized as homosexuals and said Kells was in "that crowd" — a case of "guilt" by association, which evidently often happened to Kells. Some of the men he named were bisexual, not homosexual, he told me. In the lingo of 1940s' McAllen, they were "double-clutchers" — a reference to the two clutches used in driving heavy trucks. As a vegetable broker, John would keep late hours and sometimes saw one of these double-clutchers cruising for boys on Highway 83 after midnight, wearing a pith helmet and driving a convertible. This eccentric character was later the publisher of a politically conservative national magazine. I don't know whether Burroughs knew him, but he certainly would have agreed with his conservative views, and he would no doubt have admired his style and his "I don't care who sees me attitude" — the pith helmet, after all.

As for Kells Elvins, I asked Pat Paris, who dated Kells and knew him for years, whether she ever believed Kells were gay or bisexual:

PP: Oh, my God, *nooo waay.* No, no, no.

RJ: Well, why, for example, did John Snider think this? Was it his mannerisms, the way he dressed? How did he dress?

PP: Very plain, very conservative. Preppy.

RJ: How did preppy go over in the Valley back then?

PP: As an oddity.

I sent this interview to Peter Elvins, Kells's son, and he had the following to say about his father's sexuality: "Kells once said to me, 'Considering the way Mama treats me, it's a miracle that I didn't become a pansy,' which brings up the question of his sexual orientation. He always seemed to be the epitome of a womanizer, but then I notice several people in your interviews expressed the opinion that he might be queer, and my sister Tao once told me she was convinced that Kells was bisexual. I presume she was basing this on his close friendship with Burroughs and a number of his lovers, like Kiki in Tangiers. Burroughs himself, however, assured Ted Morgan (and James [Grauerholz], too, I believe) that there was never anything physical between him and Kells. I get the feeling that nobody really had a handle on who or what Kells really was."[1] I also asked Peter about Kells's appearance as it related to his perceived sexuality, and he replied, "Pat Paris describes Kells's dress as 'very plain, very conservative, preppy,' but Kells undoubtedly wore that attire, considered an oddity in the Valley, just to shock people. I never saw him looking preppy in the East, where such clothes would have been considered normal."[2]

In *Junky,* Burroughs provides us this snapshot of a preppy Kells in his prime, in Mexico City around 1950 or 1951: "Rollins was in front of his apartment, walking his Norwegian elk-hound. He was a solidly built man of my age, with strong handsome features and wiry, black hair a little gray at the temples. He was wearing an expensive sports coat, whipcord slacks, and a suede leather jacket. We had known each other for thirty years."[3]

From talking with people in Mexico who knew Kells and Burroughs and with B. J. Noser and other locals, it is clear that such sophistication and fashionable attire could mean only one thing to people down here — you were queer. You could "just tell." For example, Blondie, a cabdriver in Mexico who knew Burroughs, described a man accompanying Burroughs to Joe's Place (probably Kells) as being *entacuchado,* meaning not only a well-dressed man but also a *katrin* (dandy), a type of man so familiar that he is pictured in Mexico's popular bingo-type "chalupa cards."

Anna Mae Kelly did not say this about Kells directly, but she too noted his sophisticated and European manner and appearance. In other words, you were definitely suspect if you looked the way Kells did, and that's how the locals saw him, certainly not the way Kells saw himself or thought he was seen. After all, only a few years after Kells left the Valley, Marlon Brando, who was in the Valley to film *Viva Zapata,* was supposedly arrested for wearing Bermuda shorts on Main Street in McAllen — or at least so goes a persistent local legend.

Other than Betty Jo Noser, however, none of Burroughs's South Texas friends and acquaintances I have spoken to identified him as gay. Pat Paris said, "No, no," he did not appear gay. "Very strong features," she told me, "no mannerisms." Ted Marak, who knew Burroughs at the same time as Pat and, as a Vegas casino manager, was an expert judge of personality, said, "No, I couldn't have made that kind of call on that man." Maybe not, but in a scene from the midfifties text "Word," it appears that Burroughs might have been practicing a bit of sexual colonizing with the laborers he hired to work his South Texas farm: "In the barn attic came on the wetback sleep with hard-on under thick cotton pants . . . sits up with fierce eyes, smile sweet, bright red gums, look down and stretch his body, and I reach slow and touch it. He sit me down and make the strip motion, and I undo belt silent and shaking and shove my pants down slow. Cock spring out hard, turn around, sink slow fence post in hole, quicksand, rubber boots slow in, the boy shudder and sigh. Black widow fall on the wetback's copper neck, bit him; die in quick convulsions allergic shock — come five times."[4] The scene, described by James Grauerholz as a "fantasy orgasm death trope, for which *Naked Lunch* is the best example," is apparently set in the Valley: Burroughs never refers to a "wetback" in any other setting, nor would it make sense to do so. Grauerholz believes the scene might well be true — up to the spider bite part, at least.[5]

It's more likely, though, that if Burroughs were looking for boys, he would have done so not in Pharr or McAllen but across the border in Reynosa. Reynosa's famous Zona Rosa was just the kind of place Burroughs loved. Times Square had allowed him to enter a world where dreams can become reality, and those were the kinds of places he really liked. St. Louis was hardly one of them. Huntsville, New Waverly, and Houston certainly were not. In East Texas he had a nosy neighbor looking over the fence, wondering what that interesting-looking tomato plant was. Down here in the Zona Rosa, though, he could wander around, as he did, where nothing was true and everything was permitted (to quote Hassan Sabbah, one of Burroughs's influences). There were fabulous nightclubs such as Joe's Place, which catered to the family crowd until 10 P.M., then became a fantasyland for adults, featuring topless dancers and even drag shows at 4 A.M. There, anything went. According to the cook at Joe's Place, it was possible to go into the bar at Joe's (or elsewhere in Reynosa) and end up spending the night with a boy — although it wasn't very common. Queers were easily spotted, he said: "You can tell them when you see them." As Juan Ochoa observes, however, if that's what you wanted, a cabdriver could locate it for you — be it a young man, women, a little grass, some peyote, a cockfight.

It's therefore not surprising that stories of "Willy the Queer" turned up on the other side of the border, rather than in Pharr. My source for stories of Burroughs's gay reputation in Reynosa is a former cabdriver named Ernesto Garza, also known as "El Blondie" because of the blonde hair he inherited from his German-born father. Blondie was born in 1927 and arrived in the Pink Zone in 1932. He drove a cab in Reynosa in the late 1940s, and he also chauffeured acts from Mexico City and Monterrey to perform in the clubs in Reynosa, including Joe's Place. He was friends with Carlos "El Pelacuas" (Baldy), another cabdriver. Both Blondie and Carlos (now deceased) knew Burroughs. In an interview for *Beat Scene,* a British magazine, I asked Juan Ochoa to tell me how he discovered that in Reynosa Billy Burroughs was known as "Willy El Puto" (Willy the Queer):[6]

> JO: I was interviewing Rodolfo Villarreal, who ran a cabstand in Reynosa back then . . . [and] I noticed Blondie kept fidgeting around. He'd take off his hat and scratch his head and get his face really close to the picture of Burroughs in *Texas Monthly.*[7] I had asked him, does this man look familiar, and he would say, "He looks like a lot of people," which is what I expected people to say,

you know, "They all look the same to me," just another gringo down here. And I wanted to smoke, and Blondie and some of the other old men followed us outside, and I tell them, "You might have known this man as Guillermo. His name was William," and Blondie's looking over my shoulder and says, "Could it have been Willy?" And I just figured he was showing off his English, and I said, "Sure, it could have been Willy," and he starts repeating over and over, "Hello, Willy!" and I said "You sound like you're used to saying that. Do you have a friend named Willy?" "No," he said. "That's Willy." And he tells another cabdriver, "Don't you remember him?" And he says, "What Willy?" and Blondie says, "Willy El Puto. You remember Willy El Puto! You know, the queer, the puto gringo who used to come walking down here. He didn't live in McAllen, did he?" He asked me this. People who live on the border here, America is summed up in McAllen. But Blondie was a lot more precise about it. He said, "He didn't live in McAllen. He lived in Pharr. The guy I'm talking about lived in Pharr." And then I knew that we were talking about the same guy. That it was William S. Burroughs who was "Willy El Puto" — Willy the Queer.

RJ: Well, you hadn't told them anything about him being a queer, had you?

JO: No, no, I had told them he was an American writer, probably one of the most influential writers of the second half of the twentieth century. I compared him to Hemingway. And remarkably, these men were well read, and they knew who those writers of the Lost Generation were, but they weren't Beat fans. And I start asking him, "Well, how did you know this man?" and he got a bit defensive. "Well, it wasn't me who started that puto business," he said. "That was Carlos El Pelacuas." We have discussed this several times since. Especially when we were doing the film for Matt McClung [*Border Beats*[8]], he really opened up, and he told me, "Now he walked and he talked like a man, but his stance, *sus parrados,* that kind of gave him away, but that wasn't enough for you to out someone." He said, "What I think happened, because it was Charley [Carlos] who outted him, something happened between Charley and Willy. Because Charley was that way, he loved to befriend his fares, to find out what they wanted."

RJ: So Willy told him what he wanted . . .

JO: Exactly. He probably tried to cruise Charley. Burroughs might have been one of those gringos who asked him, "Why aren't there any boys in Boys' Town?" Something like that must have happened between him and Charley or that Burroughs tried to put the make on him. That was what Blondie figured. I don't think he really got pissed, but by the wink in Blondie's eye — and I'm not saying Charley and Willy had a relationship — I think Charley kind of saw it as comical. Here's this weird eagle trying to pick me up.

RJ: Yes, but didn't Blondie say that, to be queer in Reynosa, you would be "burned" [*quemado*]? What did he mean by that?

JO: That you would be outted. And once everybody knew, it doesn't matter what level of prominence you achieve, you will always be Willy El Puto. And that's the reputation he was talking about.

RJ: So they would taunt him in the streets of Reynosa?

JO: Well, Charley would start as soon as he rounded the block: "Hello, Willy! Hello, Willy!" That would quicken Burroughs's pace — they also called him "Longlegs" [*patas largas*], and they would tell the kids, "If he takes to running, he's going to catch you." They would do a merry-go-round [around] him, with Burroughs in hot pursuit. "Cabrón, chinga tu madre," he'd be cussing them in Spanish and English.

Some of this was just a performance, Blondie believes: "I think he chased after the kids more for show than anything else. You know, to show that he was one of the guys." However, there was real anger that these street performances could not mask. Burroughs "would try his best to ignore them [the children]," says Blondie, "but you could see he would get rigid — and red as a fire truck. You would think his blood was going to pop out of his ears he got so red. You could see his jaw clenched and grinding." As Juan Ochoa has pointed out to me, in *The Place of Dead Roads,* Kim Carsons (one of Burroughs's fictional alter egos) looks exactly the same way when he is angry. Carsons, by the way, responds to being called a "fairy" by emptying his six-gun into the offending parties.

These newfound stories of Burroughs being outted in Reynosa and subsequently held up to public ridicule add yet another, rather sad, chapter to his life story. In *Junky* and in *Queer,* Burroughs wrote about similar incidents set in Mexico City, but there are key differences in the Reynosa stories. In *Queer,* Lee (Burroughs's alter ego) responds to such harassment by masking his anger in comic routines, similar to Burroughs's street performances in Reynosa; however, he also pulls a gun on his accuser, something Burroughs actually did in Mexico City, but never in Reynosa. When we read to Blondie from Burroughs's account of these incidents in Mexico City, in which Burroughs pulls a gun on his tormentors, we got the "full-bent-over-slap-his-knee laugh attack," as Juan Ochoa describes Blondie's reaction. "Oh no," Blondie said. "There's no bite in him," meaning he didn't see Burroughs drawing a gun on anyone. A comparison of Burroughs's actions in Reynosa with his later actions in Mexico City thus shows a rapid degeneration in his behavior, from childish anger to drunken pistol waving, behavior very much in line with his ultimate act of insanity in Mexico — the accidental shooting of Joan Vollmer.

Two scenes in *Queer* have obvious parallels with Burroughs's experiences in Reynosa but show him acting out with a gun in a way he did not do when he was living in the Valley. In one scene, Lee and Allerton are walking together, leaning on each other and laughing, and a Mexican calls them "cabrones." "Lee called after him, 'Chinga tu madre,' then added in English, 'Here I come to your little jerkwater country and spend my good American dollars and what happens? Insulted inna public street.'"[9] The Mexican considers attacking them, but Lee puts his hand on his gun and warns the man away.

Blondie tells a similar story about Burroughs being taunted on the streets of Reynosa, right down to Burroughs's identical curse — "Chinga tu madre." In both stories, a performance masks Burroughs's anger: In the *Queer* scene, it is relieved by a W. C. Fields routine ("Insulted inna public street"). However, unlike in Reynosa, Burroughs resolves the conflict in cool, tough-guy fashion by revealing his pistol, an action that Blondie says would have been out-of-character for Willy El Puto.

Another scene in *Queer* that has obvious antecedents in Reynosa is the story of Joe Guidry's "seduction" of a police officer (in *Queer*). In *Queer,* Lee encourages Guidry to tell Eugene Allerton the following story of how he "made the cop on the beat":

> He's the *vigilante,* the watchman out where I live. Every time he sees the light on in my room, he comes in for a shot of rum. Well, about five nights ago he caught me when I was drunk and horny, and one thing led to another and I ended up showing him how the cow ate the cab-

> bage. . . . So the night after I make him I was walking by the beer joint on the corner and he comes out *barracho* and says, 'Have a drink.' I said, 'I don't want a drink.' I proceeded to take his pistola away from him, and he goes into the beer joint to phone for reinforcements. So I had to go in and rip the phone off the wall. Now they're billing me for the phone. When I got back to my room, which is on the ground floor, he had written *'El Puto Gringo'* on the window with soap. So, instead of wiping it off, I left it there. It pays to advertise.[10]

Although Lee (Burroughs) is not the main actor here, the story is evidently a conflation of Burroughs's own experiences in Mexican bars: In *Junky,* he rips a phone out of a man's hands to prevent him from calling the cops; pulls a gun on a Mexican cop; and, later the same night, ends up sleeping with a policeman — who robs him.[11] The one element in the *Queer* story that is missing in *Junky,* however, is the moniker bestowed on Guidry — El Puto Gringo — an insulting nickname very close to the one Carlos invented for Burroughs after outing him in Reynosa ("Willy El Puto"). It is thus quite possible that Burroughs added this detail based on his Reynosa experiences. Still, in Reynosa, he wasn't pulling guns on cops and tearing phones off of the wall.

Kells Elvins (as Rollins in *Queer*) evidently confronted Burroughs about this dangerous behavior the day after Burroughs pointed a gun at one policeman and slept with another one later that night:

> "You're going to get your head blown off carrying that gun," he [Rollins] said. "What do you carry it for? It's passive and feminine."
>
> "How do you mean?"
>
> "A provocation. Look what happens last night. You end up getting pogged by a middle-aged Mexican cop . . . or maybe he was just probing you for money. *'Thees gringo, he got it somewhere.'*"[12]

This exchange, omitted from the published version of *Queer,* reveals Elvins as an adept psychologist. Elvins points out to the disheveled and desperate Burroughs that waving a pistol is simply a "passive" substitute for dealing with his very serious problems. Moreover, it's a "provocation" in a sexual sense and thus "feminine": All of his outlaw posturing is really just a mask for his desire to be violated by authority, in this case getting "pogged" by a Mexican cop. Lacking Elvins's letters to Burroughs, there is no definitive statement on Elvins's view of Burroughs's homosexuality, but we do have the following passage, also omitted from *Queer,* in which Rollins expresses his disapproval: "And if you want to go to bed with a member of your own sex, of which I certainly disapprove, I should think you would want to dress well and come on a little. At least take a bath. You won't get anywhere waving a rusty pistola."[13] This is vintage Elvins: Bad behavior is bad but is even worse when you perform it improperly dressed.

Both stories — Blondie's eyewitness account and Burroughs's literary version — are revealing. Of the first-person narrative *Junky,* Burroughs says that it is a book he "wrote" but that, in *Queer* (which is told in the third person), he was "written."[14] Burroughs thus wanted us to see Lee in ways that Lee does not see himself. James Grauerholz has pointed out to me that the testimony of Blondie and others lets us see Burroughs from the deeper perspective of "witnesses who will bring the real Burroughs in those years back to life: persons of no latter-day importance, but who saw our subject from 'outside' viewpoints."[15] In spite of Burroughs's ruthless self-examination and willingness to expose himself by being "written" in *Queer,* the novel, finally, cannot show us what these outsiders observed when Willy El Puto crossed the border and walked the streets of Reynosa.

Moreover, *Junky* and *Queer* do not directly address the reasons Burroughs's behavior deteriorated in the year after he left Texas. Certainly the switch from heroin to alcohol contributed to his belligerence, for by all accounts he was a better junky than a drunk. Something more was at work, though. Approaching middle age, having failed as a farmer in Texas, and seeing his plans to own land or open a bar in Mexico frustrated by Mexican laws, Burroughs had started to despair about his future. Moreover, his relationship with Joan was on the rocks, and she had even filed for divorce in Cuernevaca in 1950 (they later reconciled).[16] Although he had never hidden his sexuality from Joan, his affair with Lewis Marker and other "boys" (available for three pesos, or forty cents) was probably wearing on her.[17] In *Junky* and in *Queer,* then, we see Burroughs falling apart in Mexico. In Texas, at least, he had the routine of being a farmer. In Mexico he was facing the void.

Today, when I walk down Miguel Alemán street in Reynosa past the faded glory of bars such as Trevino's (now the Eurodisco) and Joe's Place (now the garish "1040" disco), past the Dragon Roja and the gay nightclub El Gato Negro, and beyond the few remaining trios hoping to play for the handful of tourists patronizing restaurants such as Sam's, I cannot help but think back to Reynosa's glory days, when the streets would have been full of wealthy gringos, musicians, cabdrivers, and street vendors. There is Billy Burroughs, long legged and red faced behind his glasses, striding past Rodolfo Villarreal's cabstand. The chant starts up — "Hello, Willy!" — initiated first by Carlos and then taken up by children on the street lining Burroughs's path to the bar at Joe's Place, where he will drink until 4 A.M. To this day, when Blondie and his friends see a gringo in Reynosa they suspect of being queer, they joke with one another, "Look! There goes Willy."

After leaving the Rio Grande Valley in late 1949, Burroughs moved to Mexico City, where he studied Mayan archeology at Mexico City College. This is his 1949 college ID photo. Courtesy James Grauerholz.

Kells Elvins (seated) and Ted Marak, South Jackson Road farm, 1947. Courtesy Ted Marak.

Ted Marak and Pat Paris, Boca Chica beach, 1947. Courtesy Ted Marak.

Obie Dobbs and Pat Paris, Boca Chica beach, 1947. Kells Elvins (background), throwing a ball to his dog, "Bopper." Courtesy Ted Marak.

Eugene "Tiger Terry" as a member of the Skulls Club. High school yearbook photo, 1943. Courtesy Corsicana High School.

Luis Alejos with his brother Jaime and other musicians, Joe's Place bar, 1949. Courtesy Luis Alejos.

Feeding the lions at Joe's Place, Reynosa, Mexico, 1952. Wearing glasses and seated, José Ortega. Far left, Roberto Pérez (the lion tamer). Courtesy Luis Alejos.

Postcards featuring Joe's Place, exterior and interior, circa 1940s.

Blondie and interviewer, Juan Ochoa, Summer 2002. From Matt McClung's documentary, Border Beats. *Courtesy Matt McClung.*

Texas lawmen, including "Whispering Tom" Mayfield (wearing a white hat) circa 1912. Courtesy Museum of South Texas History.

Vail Ennis, sheriff of Bee County. Courtesy Bee County Sheriff's Department.

THE TEXAS OILMAN ROUTINE

William S. Burroughs was a prototypical American in his desire to be left alone to do whatever he wanted with no outside interference. He certainly did not want anyone telling him what to do in his private life, as occurred in Reynosa. That was his basic problem as a farmer, too: The government told him what and when and where to plant his crops, and he couldn't stand it. Texas was full of ornery characters like Burroughs but none more so than the self-made millionaires called "wildcatters," a breed of fiercely independent oilmen who, in Burroughs's words, "were an uninhibited bunch, they just did what the fuck they wanted — totally unlike the conservative prissy Presbyterian East-coast stuff these guys came up from."[1] By the 1940s, the image of the Texas wildcatter who struck it rich overnight had replaced the cowboy as the dominant image of a Texan in the national consciousness. Burroughs admired these self-made men such as Clint Murchison Sr. and David Harold "Dry Hole" Byrd, and he shared their conservative political views, especially their rabid hatred of communists. Still, he was also aware what slick con artists the wildcatters could be.

Burroughs probably first met these colorful Texas oilmen not in South Texas but in East Texas, where the real oil finds in the Lone Star State began back in the 1920s. Subsistence farmers living in broken-down houses could find themselves suddenly sitting on top of a fortune. Burroughs no doubt had similar ambitions for his ninety-nine-acre "ranch" in New Waverly. Just as likely as hitting it big, though, you would either hit a dry hole or the oilmen would con you into a lease that kept you out of the money. Burroughs was a close student of every kind of rip-off, and he observed the slick oilmen at work in East Texas, as he told Ted Morgan in 1984:

> I'd seen how they operate way up in East Texas. . . . See, they'd talk it up, and they'd talk it down, then they'd come in, they don't buy anything, then they talk it down, they get the leases finally for very little. "Well, we don't think we're going to drill

> this. The reports are very bad. I know you're probably disappointed, but so are we. That's the way it is, heh, heh!" They give them a boost first, and on the strength of that, a lot of these guys had spread themselves, gone out and bought stuff on time, so then they were really strapped. Then the other guy came through. Then they had the oil leased up at the lowest possible prices. They had to be careful because other oil people could move in. They had to do it fast and know what they were doing. They had to be damn sure the oil was there.[2]

The South Texas oil fields were developed much later in Texas, and natural gas was not even considered worth drilling for when Burroughs lived in the Valley. By the late 1940s, however, oil drilling had long been under way in Hidalgo County. A November 9, 1948, letter from Burroughs to Allen Ginsberg shows that Burroughs was in fact trying to find oil on his property in Edinburg, which would, he hoped, produce some "quick $."[3] Ted Marak remembers the oil fever from those days and his and Kells's attempts to get rich quick by drilling on their land in "Tex-Mex": "They made a find over there on Tex-Mex (yeah, there was a fault). I'm out busting brush getting a-dollar-an-acre leases. Kells and I must have put together umpteen-hundred acres of ground, and I had enough money to get on a few, and they kept blowing gas, and you couldn't give it away in those days, and the last one that I didn't get in on and I didn't have the money and I was going to Vegas, sonofabitch if it didn't come in." [Laughs][4]

Both Burroughs and Elvins had land in Tex-Mex, which refers to land on the Texas-Mexican railroad survey on the northeast side of Edinburg. In *Queer,* Lee (Burroughs's alter ego) begins the "Texas Oilman" routine by saying, "'You know, it looks like we might bring in an oil well. They're drilling now over in quadrangle four, and from that rig you could almost spit over into Tex-Mex where I got my hundred-acre cotton farm.'"[5]

Of course, Burroughs, like Ted Marak, never did strike it rich; however, from his own experiences and from listening to Kells's stories about South Texas oilmen, he did hit on some profitable material for his novel *Queer.* I doubt there is a better or more accurate portrait of a Texas oilman than this one in *Queer,* the title of which has probably led to its neglect by oil-field historians: "First thing, you must look like an oilman. There are no young oilmen. An oilman should be about fifty. His skin is cracked and wrinkled like mud that has dried in the sun, and especially the back of his neck is wrinkled, and the wrinkles are generally full of dust from looking over blocks and quadrangles. He wears gabardine slacks and a white short-sleeved sport shirt. His shoes are covered with fine dust, and a faint haze of dust follows him everywhere like a personal dust storm."[6]

The routine continues with a detailed description of how the oilman cons landowners in the Valley into leasing their land to him, using tactics similar to those Burroughs observed in East Texas. (In fact, some of the names of the landowners used in the text — Scranton and Bane — were the names of Burroughs's East Texas neighbors, transplanted to the Valley).[7]

Once the drilling rights have been secured, the oilman approaches a banker (such as Kells Elvins's friend Clint Murchison Sr.) to finance the drilling, convincing him that these local "good old boys" are also involved: "You go to the bank and talk to the president: 'Now Clem Farris, as fine a man as there is in this Valley and smart, too, he's in this thing up to his balls, and Old Man Scranton and Fred Crockly and Roy Spigot and Ted Bane, all of them good old boys.'" The site for drilling is the fault line Ted Marak described: "'You see this quadrangle here? That's Tex-Mex. Now there's a fault runs right along here through Jed Marvin's place. I saw old Jed too, the other day when I was out there, a good old boy. There isn't a finer man in this Valley than Jed Marvin.'"[8] The Texas oilman is able to lull the bank president into acquiescence with his good-old-boy patter and convinces him to finance the drilling operation.

Next, you need a driller, says Lee. Living on the McAllen-Reynosa border, Burroughs knew the likely place to find an available one: "He has to be a real rip-snorting character. They look for him in Boy's Town — the whore district in border towns — and they find him in a room full of empty bottles with three whores. So they bust a bottle over his head and drag him out to sober him up, and he looks at the drilling site and spits and says, 'Well, it's your hole.'" The routine ends with the inevitable dry hole being drilled, which reminds the Texas oilman of his friend "Dry Hole" Dutton, who "brought in twenty dry holes before he got cured. That means 'get rich' in the salty lingo of the oil fraternity."[9]

The oilman routine is of course pretty over the top and set the tone for Burroughs's even more outrageous routines in *Naked Lunch;* however, quite a lot of the routine has a clear basis in fact. Dry Hole Dutton, as Burroughs told Ted Morgan, was based on an actual Texas oilman: "He brought in — God knows — twenty dry holes before he 'got cured.' There's a picture of

'Dry Hole' with a false beard and a luscious blond on each arm, taken in Mexico City."[10] In his wonderfully titled 1951 book, *The Lusty Texans of Dallas,* John William Rogers provides this portrait of Dry Hole, whose real name was David Harold Byrd: "For the sheer exuberance, friendliness and energy which characterize oil men as a race, it would be hard to find a more astonishing example than David Harold Byrd. Byrd is a slightly stout gentleman with a round, friendly, faintly comic face and a smile that is engagingly youthful in spite of his fifty years. Somewhere in his background there must have been clown blood, for in social contacts he talks a stream of antic stories which he acts out with engaging gusto."[11]

Apparently, like Burroughs, Byrd enjoyed performing routines. But here's the "Dry Hole" part: "[B]efore he finally struck success he had drilled fifty-six wildcat wells throughout Central West Texas which were all dry holes. His first producer came in along the Balcones Fault zone. But as a result of his prodigious string of failures he is still sometimes referred to as 'Dry Hole Byrd' in a play on his initials." Rogers also describes elaborate parties Dry Hole threw in Dallas, at which around fifty cases of hard liquor were consumed.[12] *The Handbook of Texas Online* adds to this account the interesting detail that Byrd owned the Texas School Book Depository building at the time of the Kennedy assassination. Byrd, evidently no fan of JFK, had the window from which Oswald shot Kennedy removed and mounted on a wall in his home.[13]

Burroughs probably knew about Byrd through Kells Elvins and his association with legendary oilman Clint Murchison Sr. As Burroughs told Ted Morgan,

> [Kells] made some oil investments that gave him about $600 a month. [Clint] Murchison gave him some tips. He was doing all right. I remember Kells was telling me about Murchison. He'd be sitting around with his entourage, and he'd say, "Hey, Clem, when are you gonna get yourself cured?" That means get real rich. You know, 20–30 million. Clem's only got a couple of million. Then he would give out occasional tips. So he gave Kells — he liked Kells — he gave Kells tips that yielded him this income. And [Kells] said once, "Tell me about the man, Burroughs, tell me about his hands." And I could see his hands were twisted, he had terrible arthritis. And I could see, with second sight I saw — I said, "His hands are twisted. Being down there with all that shale." And Kells says, "Yes, the man's got arthritis, that's right, Burroughs." So

> I told him, "If the man is your friend, he'll give you some good tips." And he did. And Kells got this $600 a month. I think it was a little more than that.[14]

Dallas-based oilman Clint Murchison Sr. (1895–1969) was as flamboyant a character as Burroughs and Elvins and was known for coming up with crazy business deals. Burroughs stole the phrase "getting cured" from Murchison and used it and other details in the Texas oilman routine in *Queer*. The shale on Murchison's hands could well refer to the fact that his company, Tecon, performed the dangerous work of removing shale from the Panama Canal. During the time that Burroughs lived in South Texas, Murchison was a co-owner (with V. F. Neuhaus) of the McAllen State Bank and a garrulous fixture on Tenth Street, always ready to shoot the bull or listen to a financial pitch.[15]

Burroughs must also have learned oil-field lore on the weekend trips he took to Corpus Christi with Tiger Terry and Kells. By 1951, according to *The Centennial History of Corpus Christi*, oil reserves within 150 miles of Corpus amounted to 8 percent of the nation's total. It was a real boom time: "Development of the Mustang Island Field in Corpus Christi bay brought the greatest oil boom in the city's history. The discovery well came in on April 1, 1949. Some 18 months later, it had more than 100 wells, with some 200 more scheduled."[16] Corpus, therefore, must have been full of wildcatters just around the time Burroughs returned to Texas in April of 1949, or Burroughs might have visited there when he returned to Texas in 1950 to renew his travel visa to Mexico.

In his interviews with Ted Morgan, Burroughs records some of the outlandish behavior of these Corpus Christi oilmen: "The oil men were a really riotous, far-out bunch of people. There was one of them, for example, he had a yacht, and he would sail around Corpus Christi, places like that, then he would get drunk, blasted out of his mind, and go into town and pick up masses of people from bars and take 'em out to his yacht, and in the morning he would throw 'em all off: 'Who the hell are you? What are doing on my yacht?' He would have his security men take them off or throw them off. There were always scandals going on, people falling into the water and drowning, all that kind of thing."[17]

Evidently the waterfront bars in Corpus Christi were quite a scene during this period. However, when I contacted the man who was writing the history of oil exploration in the area (a former reporter for the *Corpus*

Christi Caller-Times), he knew little about such outrageous stories or the characters involved. As far as I have been able to ascertain, then, Burroughs's is the only account of that colorful community at midcentury, but it sounds as if his stories are the tip of the iceberg.

Burroughs was obviously a fringe dweller in this kind of society, but he felt a natural affinity for these self-made men with tremendous wealth who could act as they pleased. Such a life was what being an American was about, after all. It is not surprising to find out, then, that the Texas oilmen were — as was Burroughs — vociferous anticommunists. In fact, Burroughs was such a rabid anticommunist that even his close friends, such as Allen Ginsberg, thought he was being facetious when he ranted against "the commies." But he was serious.

So was Clint Murchison Sr., a major contributor to Sen. Joseph McCarthy's campaigns. The Texas oilmen had made their first millions in the forties and were not about to let a bunch of commies take it away from them. As one oilman told *Fortune* magazine in 1954, "We all made money fast. We were interested in nothing else. Then this Communist business suddenly burst upon us. Were we going to lose what we had gained?" McCarthy was the hero of Texas oilmen and bankers, and he enjoyed more support in Texas than in any other region of the country. Thus, Texas Democrats (so-called Texas Regulars) voted for Eisenhower, a Republican. McCarthy, observed the *Fortune* magazine reporter, was admired by Texans "not just for attacking Communism but for linking it with the New and Fair Deals."[18] Again, this is a sentiment Burroughs openly shares in his letters as well as in published routines such as "Roosevelt after Inauguration."[19] Dick Russell, whose book *The Man Who Knew Too Much: Hired to Kill Oswald and Prevent the Assassination of JFK* links Murchison to not only McCarthy but also Jimmy Hoffa, Richard Nixon, Jay Edgar Hoover, and the Kennedy assassination, tells the following anecdote about Murchison's vituperative anticommunism: "Back in 1951, after General Douglas MacArthur was relieved of his Korean command by President Truman, H. L. Hunt accompanied MacArthur on a flight to Texas for a speaking tour. Hunt and Murchison were the chief organizers of the pro-MacArthur forces in Texas. They would always remember the general standing bareheaded in front of the Alamo, urging removal of the 'burden of taxation' from enterprising men like themselves, charging that such restraints were imposed by 'those who seek to convert us to a form of socialistic endeavor, leading directly to the path of Communist slavery.'"[20]

Compared to the views of these rich, influential Texas power brokers who supported McCarthy, Burroughs's rhetoric against communism ("I tell you we are bogged down in this octopus of bureaucratic socialism," he told Jack Kerouac[21]) and against Roosevelt's New Deal sound pretty mainstream Republican. And that's the point: Burroughs was not some crank in terms of his political views at the time. He was actually reflecting the position of the rich and powerful Texans he sometimes ridiculed but also admired — such as the Texas oilmen and other maverick millionaires.

That was in the 1940s, though, when Burroughs was still trying to follow in the footsteps of his grandfather and his Uncle Ivy, both highly successful capitalists. As he came to change his beliefs about the necessity to control farming, so, too, in later life did he come to see the consequences of the world's "addiction" to oil. Consequently, in his novels of the late seventies and early eighties, Burroughs cast the Texas oilmen not as people who are admirable for their "I don't give a fuck" attitude but as villains. In *The Place of Dead Roads,* for example, the Texas oil millionaire Old Man Bickford is part of the opposition to the space program of the Johnson family (the heroes of Burroughs's final trilogy of novels). Similarly, in one of his most popular set pieces performed for college audiences in the 1980s, "Pay Color," Burroughs, in ominous tones, demanded of the industrial powers that had destroyed the planet for profit, "Pay back the green you stole for your money. . . . Pay back that green to flowers and jungle river and sky."[22]

Back in the 1940s, though, Burroughs would have liked nothing better than to strike oil and be "cured" of having to find a respectable way to make a living. He was not a lucky man, though. As he writes (autobiographically) in *Interzone,* "When Willy Lee shows, the desert wind is blowing dust into empty bars and hotels, jungle vines are covering the oil derricks." However, his experiences among the wildcatters were not dry holes. They would take their place in the slowly emerging worldview of his yet unwritten works.[23]

THE WRATH OF GOD AND THE LIBERAL IMAGINATION

As is true for the intellectuals of every generation, William S. Burroughs felt the need to define his own philosophy in relation to existing political labels and schools of thought. By the late 1940s, when he was farming in South Texas, Burroughs had already rejected the Marxist philosophy urged on him by his Harvard professors in the mid-1930s; witnessed firsthand the horrors of communism's opposite, fascism, in Vienna in the late 1930s; and concluded that Roosevelt New Dealers were merely communists in disguise.

In this respect, *Junky* (first published in 1953) can be seen as a book in which Burroughs staked himself out in the political landscape of the postwar period. A novel by Allen Ginsberg's Columbia professor Lionel Trilling is typical in this respect. Characters in *The Middle of the Journey* (1947) must sort through various possibilities for political and cultural engagement — "communist, anti-communist, anti-anti-communist, liberal."[1] Burroughs had to sort through the same labels, and at midcentury, the publication of *Junky,* as well as his letters to friends, made it clear that Burroughs was neither a "liberal" nor a "communist," the two nastiest words in his vocabulary at this time. A true radical individualist, he invented his own political label for himself: He was a "factualist." "All arguments, all nonsensical considerations as to what people 'should do,' are irrelevant. Ultimately, there is only fact on all levels," Burroughs wrote to Allen Ginsberg back in 1948 in a letter about his South Texas farm.[2]

In *Junky,* Burroughs the factualist makes a clear, unemotional case that drugs are not the real problem — it is the police state arising from the illegality of drugs that is the threat. As Allen Ginsberg says in his 1977 "Introduction" to *Junky,* only the "cognoscenti" at the time could "appreciate the intelligent fact, the clear perception, precise bare language, direct syntax and mind pictures — as well as the enormous sociological grasp, culture-revolutionary attitude toward bureaucracy and law, and the stoic cold-humor'd eye on crime."[3] No one had ever read a book about drugs that took on anything less than a hysterical tone. "[T]he more one argues, verbalizes, moralizes the less he will see and feel of fact," Burroughs told Ginsberg with regard to factualism.[4] The flat, hardboiled tone of *Junky,* devoid of any message about the morality of doing drugs, reflects this philosophy, as does Burroughs's separation of the myths surrounding drugs from the straight facts about their use and effects. One hundred thousand hip readers snatched up copies of the first editions of *Junky* in the mid-1950s.[5] In *Naked Lunch,* published six years after *Junky,* the members of the Factualist party are the heroes.

You have probably noticed that Burroughs's original discussions of "factualism" had a particular audience — Allen Ginsberg — and that it was Ginsberg who in later years was Burroughs's first knowledgeable critic about books such as *Junky.* In a previous chapter ("The Wetback Deal"), I discuss the way in which Burroughs's South Texas experiences contributed to this factualist philosophy as it was expressed in his growing hatred of liberals, communists, government bureaucrats, and cops. Left out of this discussion of the development of Burroughs's philosophy, though, was this personal level involving Ginsberg. Burroughs was refining his worldview — what we would today call a "conservative" or "libertarian" view or what Ginsberg styled "libertarian conservatism" — in letters he wrote from Texas and Louisiana to Ginsberg and (to a lesser extent) to Jack Kerouac.[6] Kerouac, as time proved, was just as conservative as Burroughs and was a receptive audience for Burroughs's rants against communists and labor unions, social forces that threatened Burroughs's livelihood as a self-righteous son-of-the-soil farmer. His letters to Kerouac are full of colorful indictments of "Liberals," "Revenooers," "New Deal Freudians," "cancerous bureaucracies," and other rhetoric that would make contemporary, right-wing talk-radio hosts jealous of its creative abuse of the Left. Ginsberg, on the other hand, played the part of the rebellious child, and evidently he argued with Burroughs, in particular, about the minimum wage and workers' rights as they related to Burroughs's South Texas farm. Burroughs therefore wrote his most detailed discussions of his farming operations to Ginsberg in an attempt to show him how the world really worked. And he probably had other motives related to Ginsberg, as these letters reveal.

Beneath their debate over workers' rights was the real drama: Burroughs thought Ginsberg was aligning himself with a group of liberal thinkers, which included Ginsberg's father, Louis, his professors Lionel Trilling and Mark Van Doren, and Ginsberg's neo-Freudian psychiatrists. Burroughs feared these liberals would eventually force Ginsberg into conforming to the will of the larger society, and, in particular, he foresaw that they would try to "cure" Ginsberg of his homosexuality. No longer queer, no longer an individual, Ginsberg would settle down into an acceptable nine-to-five job and become a card-carrying liberal or, worst of all, fulfill his ambition of becoming a labor lawyer. Farming, the topic of many of their letters from this period, allowed Burroughs to carry on a real-world, economic discussion with Ginsberg that would, Burroughs hoped, persuade Ginsberg to see the world in the same factualist, antiliberal terms Burroughs did. Moreover, as Ginsberg later suspected, Burroughs might also have written these provocative letters — ostensibly about farming — for purposes of seduction, much as Lee in *Queer* keeps Allerton entertained with his outrageous routines, such as the Texas oilman.

To understand these surface and underlying messages of Burroughs's and Ginsberg's "farm" letters, it is helpful to know a little about each man's class background and the intellectual atmosphere in which they were raised.

Allen Ginsberg's father and mother were both children of Russian émigrés. He was a socialist, she a communist. In New York in the 1920s, they were Greenwich Village intellectual communists and free love experimenters who vacationed at a communist nudist camp. Louis's poetry was published in the *New Masses* on the basis of both his prosody and his politics. They named their first son Eugene after Eugene Debs; their second son, Allen, recalled going to communist cell meetings with his mother where "the speeches were free everybody was angelic and sentimental about the workers it was all so sincere you have no idea what a good thing the party was," as he writes in his poem "America." The members of the Ginsberg family thus shared a vision of defending the rights of downtrodden workers, and, as a young man, Allen vowed that if he were admitted to Columbia University, he would become a labor lawyer.[7] As he writes in his tribute to his mother, "Kaddish," "Prayed on ferry to help mankind if admitted . . . by being revolutionary labor lawyer. . . . I wanted to be President, or Senator." It was an ambition he held for many years, even after his intellectual friends at Columbia, including Jack Kerouac and Lucien Carr, ridiculed his idealism. Carr asked him, "You want to be a labor lawyer? You've never worked a single day in your life!"[8] Still, in spite of Carr's (and later Burroughs's) derision, Ginsberg held on to this noble ambition, and at one point in early 1950, he was working as a reporter for a union newspaper called the *Labor Herald*.[9]

William S. Burroughs's upbringing was hardly conducive to producing a communist sympathizer or union supporter. His grandfather was a capitalist in the grand tradition: He had invented an improvement to the adding machine and, on the basis of his own talent and hard work, made a fortune. Ivy Lee, Burroughs's uncle, was one of the original public relations men in New York, and his most famous client was John D. Rockefeller. To Burroughs, such wealthy industrialists represented the natural winners in a system of laissez-faire capitalism. As he told Conrad Knickerbocker in a 1965 interview, "The whole world of high finance interests me, the men such as Rockefeller, who were specialized types of organisms that could exist in a certain environment. He was really a money-making machine, but I doubt he could have made a dime today because he required the old laissez-faire capitalism. He was a specialized monopolistic organism. My Uncle Ivy created images for him."[10]

Burroughs does not judge these men; in fact, part of his nostalgia for the old America where you could still buy morphine over the counter and there was no income tax was the free playing field of laissez-faire capitalism. Men such as Rockefeller were "specialized organisms" that naturally thrived in such an environment. In South Texas in the 1940s, Burroughs himself hoped to find such an environment.

However, as a proponent of old-style capitalism, Burroughs was out of step with the intellectuals of his time. At Harvard in the mid-1930s, many of his professors were card-carrying communists intent on radicalizing Burroughs and his generation of students. At the urging of a philosophy professor, Burroughs read the *Communist Manifesto* but did not buy Marx's argument: "Everyone's gonna work, but who's gonna make them work?" he asked the professor. In *Queer,* Lee tells Allerton, "You know, when I was at Princeton, Communism was the thing. To come out flat for private property and a class society, you marked yourself a stupid lout or suspect to be a high Episcopalian pederast. But I held out against the infection — of Communism I mean, of course." These impractical professors at Harvard thus failed to convince him that a communist was anything other than a leech trying to suck the lifeblood of the rich.[11]

Unions, similarly, were simply another form of communism (i.e., fascism) to Burroughs, as was Franklin D. Roosevelt's web of bureaucratic agencies created during the New Deal. Burroughs's attitude toward unions was not different (as he admits in a December 1949 letter to Ginsberg) from that "so ably and vigorously expressed by Westbrook Pegler," a conservative news columnist who called organized labor leaders thugs and who stopped just short of saying FDR was as big a fascist as Mussolini or Hitler.[12] As Jack Kerouac writes about Old Bull Lee in *On the Road,* "His chief hate was Washington bureaucracy; second to that, liberals, then cops. . . . We'd all learned from him."[13]

Ginsberg is Carlo Marx in *On the Road,* and, as Kerouac says, Marx was Burroughs's student: "[He] sat at [Burroughs's] feet."[14] As a pupil, though, Ginsberg was rebellious — thus Kerouac's naming of Ginsberg after Burroughs's nemesis, Karl Marx. This rebellion might even have had an Oedipal aspect to it. Kerouac, playing amateur psychoanalyst, told John Clellon Holmes in 1948 that Burroughs was a father figure to Ginsberg.[15] Louis Ginsberg, Ginsberg's real father, recognized this and repeatedly warned his son about Burroughs's pernicious influence. However, it wasn't just Ginsberg's father Burroughs was replacing. In trying to get Ginsberg to reject the socialistic policies of the government and the labor unions, he was also forcing Ginsberg to reject his mother and his memory of her youthful, activist days.

During the years Burroughs was writing to Ginsberg about his South Texas farm (1946–1950), Ginsberg would vacillate between these two worlds — that of his parents and Columbia professors and that of Burroughs.[16] Burroughs, on the other hand, was squarely in the camp of old-style capitalists that the United States had produced and rewarded. When Ginsberg showed signs of becoming a liberal, Burroughs became furious, because a liberal — hardly better than a communist — was the enemy of that old freewheeling American entrepreneurial spirit. These letters are, therefore, at one level a portrait of Burroughs as a laissez-faire capitalist written to and received by Allen Ginsberg, a Columbia student, ambivalent homosexual, would-be poet, would-be labor lawyer, and champion of the poor.

Burroughs's experiment in becoming a classic American capitalist began in April of 1946, when the courts in New York ordered him to go back home and live with his parents in St. Louis. There he was supposed to straighten himself out and search for a way of life that was more legitimate than being a drug user and drug dealer. Luckily, his boyhood friend and early literary collaborator, Kells Elvins, was back in town. Kells always had a get-rich-quick scheme going, although his ideas (and Burroughs's) read like parodies of their grandfathers' industriousness. Years later, Burroughs recognized this in his portrait of *Naked Lunch*'s "K.E.," the "hottest idea man in the gadget industry":

> "Think of it!" he snaps. "A cream separator in your own kitchen!"
> "K.E., my brain reels at the thought."[17]

That summer in St. Louis, Kells and Billy spent time "inventing" a new system of dry-cleaning clothes. It was no adding machine, but at least they were showing some signs of the industry practiced by Burroughs's grandfather and Kells's father. At that time, Burroughs writes (facetiously) to Ginsberg that he was "giving my attention to money making enterprises variously engaged in patent medicines and household appliances." One such medicine was a fluoride tablet to prevent tooth decay; however, he says, the FDA was shutting him down — a complaint that apparently became real a few years later when his South Texas business partner Kells Elvins was shut down by the FDA for manufacturing chicken feed from cockroaches.[18]

Burroughs's first letters from Texas to Ginsberg in late 1946 show that he is once again excited about a new scheme for making money. Kells has convinced him to move to the Rio Grande Valley with him, where they will make a fortune growing grapefruits and oranges. Of course that scheme, too, would eventually be ruined for him by Border Patrol agents and interfering bureaucrats as part of what he called the "wetback deal." His letters to Ginsberg from 1947 are mostly from his other farm in East Texas, where he was raising a very different crop — marijuana, identified as "hay" in their correspondence. Once again, he claimed the government was interfering in his business plans. In a letter from East Texas, he tells Ginsberg he needs more seeds for planting because the government has found a means of sterilizing hemp seeds — "a dirty, underhanded, bureaucratic trick."[19] He is having better luck with his poppies, which he plans to harvest for opium production. Here he was one step ahead of the Feds, who hadn't yet thought to sterilize poppy seeds.

That was the problem with the United States in the postwar period, according to Burroughs: The "revenooers" kept interfering with the natural, competitive order. A November 9, 1948, letter to Ginsberg stresses the breakdown of laissez-faire capitalism as a system in which, formerly, the best and the brightest would be the winners. Case in point: Ginsberg had just graduated from Columbia but could find work only as a dishwasher. Burroughs tells him that his "intelligence" will be a "highly undesirable" commodity in the job market because all employers are looking for is "technicians." As an independent farmer, he himself is not looking for a job. "Financially things look very good," he reports to the dishwasher poet back in New York. He thinks he will gross five thousand dollars on peas, and he also has an oil deal going. The cotton will bring in even more money in the summer. "Make everything pay is my motto," he tells Ginsberg. Along these lines, he suggests that Ginsberg tell the naïve Jack Kerouac to get a professional editor to help him prune down the sprawling manuscript of *The Town and the City* (1950) to "marketable proportions." Again, "make everything pay" is his motto.[20]

In this letter and others, we see the beginnings of a crucial ideological debate between Ginsberg and Burroughs, one that is played out over the next two years in their letters about farming. At this point, their lives are starting to take on the characteristic poles of political ideology in the United States: Burroughs was a conservative (or "anticommunist," to use the lingo of the day) who believed you ought to pull your own weight and stay independent, whereas Ginsberg was a liberal who believed people need the active help of the government and unions in solving social and economic problems. The youthful Ginsberg still believed in the ideal of a "progressive" communal society his parents taught him, while Burroughs believed society needed to leave him alone and let him do whatever he wanted to do. To him, liberalism was simply a plot to create conformity — politically, economically, and, as his letters to Ginsberg consistently argue, sexually.

A major subtext of Burroughs's farm letters and rants against liberals, therefore, is a discussion of the young Ginsberg's confusion over his sexual identity and what liberals had to say about it. Burroughs knew that the progressive society proposed by midcentury liberals would have no room for sexual deviants, and, as it turned out, he was correct. In late 1948 Burroughs thus worried that the "New Deal Freudians" — a phrase Burroughs used in a letter to Jack Kerouac and one that neatly conflates both his political and sexual agendas with Ginsberg — had taken hold of Allen.[21] Accordingly, in the November 9, 1948, letter in which he talks about carrots and oil deals, he also connects liberalism with homophobia. He was surprised, he tells Ginsberg, about his enthusiasm for a brand of psychoanalysis that has "cured" their friend William Scott Gilmore — perhaps even cured him of his homosexual tendencies. Regarding Gilmore's analysis, he says that "anyone who is 'fully analyzed' will turn out to be a nice liberal."[22] In an earlier letter (from February 1947), he elaborates on the psychiatrist's role in creating a society of conformists: "What [psychiatrists] want is some beat clerk . . . someone so scared and whipped down he would never venture to do anything that might disturb the analyst."[23]

This idea of a conformist as a liberal and a radical individualist as a conservative needs explaining to anyone raised in more recent times, when the meanings of these labels have practically been reversed in the popular consciousness. In a review of Rick Perlstein's biography of Burroughs's contemporary Barry Goldwater, Louis Menand makes what appears to be the counterintuitive point that the real radicals in U.S. society had always been the "conservatives" and that the kind of freedom conservatives were fighting for was similar to the call for freedom made by the "counterculture" in the sixties. Writing in the *New Yorker,* Menand says of Perlstein's *Before the Storm* that it is a "history of the early nineteen sixties in which John Wayne, William F. Buckley and Young Americans for Freedom take roles usually assigned to Allen Ginsberg, Herbert Marcuse, and Students for a Democratic Society. . . . Goldwater's hatred of the establishment and its writings was, at its very deepest level, not very different from the New Left's and the Counterculture's: he believed that top-down managerial liberalism was a threat to individual autonomy. . . . Goldwater just didn't like being told what to do."[24] To many of us who were not children of the sixties but were children *in* the sixties (or later), it may seem inconsistent — if not downright paradoxical — that conservatives are their own brand of radical individualists. However, this was the kind of radical individualist Burroughs was in the 1940s: He, too, just didn't like being told what to do.

This view of conservatives and liberals was well documented in the 1930s and 1940s by conservative newspaper columnists such as Westbrook Pegler, whom Ginsberg made fun of, but who was read seriously by Jack Kerouac; his father, Leo; and William S. Burroughs.[25] In an essay from the early 1940s titled "The Evolution of the Liberal," Pegler describes how originally, in the 1920s, a liberal was someone who was "first of all opposed to discipline or regimentation" — a reaction to their having had to become soldiers and fight in World War I. After the war, Prohibition gave the nascent liberals yet another reason to rebel against conformity. The "kernel" of 1920s' liberalism, says Pegler, was "individual rights and rebellion against compulsion beyond the minimum restraints necessary for the regulation of traffic."[26] However, writing in the 1940s, twenty years later, Pegler has to wonder when the liberals of the 1920s became the "goose-steppers" they hated in their youth. His answer is a gradual influx of communistic ideals

(New Deal policies, unions) that became associated with "liberalism." In defense of the common man, he says, liberals support militaristic unions run by fascists who tell a man he "has no right as an individual to conduct himself as an individual" — the very line Burroughs used to warn Ginsberg against "the New Deal Freudians."[27] Burroughs's views in his letters to Ginsberg from 1948 and 1949, in which he rails against liberals and their suppression of individual rights, are right in line with Pegler's.

That's what Burroughs meant by a liberal — and he certainly was not one. In the November 9, 1948, letter, in which Burroughs argues that psychiatrists are out to make everyone "straight" and "liberal," Burroughs declares that he has come up with his own philosophy, quite distinct from liberalism: "Myself, I am about to annunciate a philosophy called 'factualism.'" Factualism, he says, will distinguish itself from liberal (and Freudian) thinking by creating a distrust of language and undermining the conventional moral (and liberal) response of doing what one "should do." Alfred Korzybski's work in linguistics influenced Burroughs, and factualism seems to be based in part on Korzybski's idea that a word is not the thing it represents and that words therefore get in the way of real facts. Says Burroughs, "[T]he more one argues, verbalizes, moralizes the less he will see and feel of fact. Needless to say, I will not write any formal statement on the subject. Talk is incompatible with factualism."[28]

Burroughs might not have written a formal statement on factualism, but you can see this worldview applied in his letters to Ginsberg about his "labor troubles" in South Texas. Ginsberg as audience is key here. Writing these letters, Burroughs knew that his description of the wetback deal would incense Ginsberg, who, at the time, was very much the Carlo Marx of Kerouac's novel and was holding fast to his youthful ideal of being a labor lawyer and defender of the working poor.[29]

Their opposing views on labor are the subject of letters from the spring and winter of 1948. In one of them, Ginsberg, anguishing over his complicity in Herbert Huncke's theft of some books from an apartment Ginsberg was subletting, wrote to Burroughs about the connection between crime and ethics, and Burroughs responded in factualist fashion: Many legitimate enterprises were actually criminal in nature, he said, including his own cotton farm in South Texas, which was a viable operation only because Burroughs hired, at slave wages, illegal laborers. Controversy over the mistreatment of these workers in South Texas had made the national news, and Burroughs used these events to give Ginsberg a lesson in realpolitik.

In the Rio Grande Valley, he says, small farmers cannot afford expensive harvesting equipment, so they are forced to use cheap labor (two dollars for a twelve-hour workday): "If Valley farmers had to pay a living wage for farm labor they would be ruined. A farm worker's union is the farmer's nightmare. If anyone wants to live dangerously in a noble cause, let him organize farm labor in Texas. Maybe Jerry Rauch [Ginsberg's roommate] would like to take on the cause."[30]

Ginsberg had apparently been on the Democratic side of the hotly debated Taft-Hartley Bill, passed by Republicans in 1947, which legalized nonunion, right-to-work laws throughout the United States and required union leaders to take an oath that they were not members of the Communist Party. The bill passed over the objections of President Truman, who called it a "slave labor" bill and who ran for reelection in 1948 in part on a platform to raise the minimum wage from 40 cents an hour to 70 cents.[31] Ginsberg and his roommate Jerry Rauch were no doubt in favor of such a minimum wage law, whereas for Burroughs it was a "nightmare" that would put him out of business. In his factualist tone of the day, he tells Ginsberg to send Jerry right down to Texas, where, he implied, Rauch could be shot alongside striking workers. As described in an earlier chapter, Burroughs had in fact heard stories (which I cannot confirm) of striking workers being machine-gunned in the fields.[32]

Burroughs's "nightmare" was the institution of a minimum wage for farmworkers, but that was hardly comparable to the nightmare that many illegal laborers in South Texas were experiencing. In the most unsentimental (and seemingly unsympathetic) terms, Burroughs goes on to tell Ginsberg of the mistreatment of these workers: "I do not mean to convey the impression that Kells and I sit under a palm leaf sun shelter, rifle in hand 'suppressing' the workers. The whole deal is handled by labor and vegetable brokers. . . . Some brokers go into for rough stuff, some don't. I recall one broker mentioning casually that 'his foreman had to shoot 2 wetbacks last night.' But like I say, I don't have anything to do with it personally."[33]

This horrible story is told for effect and certainly reflects the thoughtless colonial side of Burroughs's personality that Herbert Huncke found suspect. Nevertheless, his story is probably at least in part meant to bait Ginsberg, who was himself baiting Burroughs with his liberal mindset and intention of becoming a labor lawyer. In *Queer,* written just a few years later, such outrageous stories, fascinating and repellent at the same time, are told by Lee as a means of seducing Eugene Allerton — and Burroughs, similarly, may well have been trying to keep Ginsberg interested in him by shocking and provoking him into response. Ginsberg, in his "Recollections of Burroughs Letters," does not say this directly about the letters from the late 1940s but does say of Burroughs's much more openly sexual letters from the early and mid-1950s that, in them, Burroughs "wooed with extravagant self-deprecatory suggestiveness" and that they were "a parody of his feelings, lest his desire be considered offensive."[34] The letters from the 1940s, such as this one, have a teasing quality to them ("I don't have anything to do with it personally," he says, hardly hiding his hypocrisy) that also reveals affection masked in "routine." (Ginsberg, too, eventually read between the lines and accused Burroughs of hiding a "sex interest" in him.)

These letters about farming and farm labor led up to an event that exacerbated this ideological and personal rift between Burroughs and Ginsberg: They were both about to go to jail. A March 18, 1949, letter informed Ginsberg that Burroughs had lost quite a lot of money when the "[b]ottom fell out of carrots."[35] On April 5, 1949, Burroughs's bad luck in farming preceded even worse luck, and on April 16 he wrote to Ginsberg regarding his New Orleans bust: "Just took a fall. Possession. The bastards are trying to send me to the State joint at Angola which is one of the worst in the South."[36]

This wasn't just a fall for Burroughs, however, because it ended up involving Ginsberg: The feds had found copies of their correspondence, which referred to East Texas "tea" (marijuana) that Burroughs had shipped to Ginsberg. Burroughs told Ginsberg to be careful; instead, his warnings put Ginsberg in a panic. In New York, Ginsberg gathered his incriminating notebooks and letters — filled with his most personal confessions — and piled them into the car of Little Jack Melody, one of the many Times Square hoodlums Burroughs had introduced to Ginsberg. Predictably, Little Jack had stolen the car they were riding in, and the police spotted them and gave chase. Melody wrecked the car, and out spilled Ginsberg, his letters, and his journals. Ginsberg, Melody, and Melody's moll, Vicki Russell, were all arrested, and subsequently so was their roommate, Herbert Huncke.[37] The cops evidently read through Ginsberg's stuff because they began taunting him: "So you're a big fag, eh? So you like little boys, eh?" John Clellon Holmes has the police ask "Stoffsky" in his fictionalized but factual account of the arrest in *Go: A Novel* (first published in 1952).[38]

Ginsberg's father and his liberal Columbia professors Lionel Trilling and Mark Van Doren had long warned him of Burroughs's nefarious influence, and now their dire predictions had come true: He had been arrested and thrown in jail, and his picture had been splashed across the pages of the New York papers. Out on bail, Ginsberg was lectured by Van Doren, who told him that hearing the "clank of iron" might do him some good. However, with the cooperation of a Columbia alumnus who was a district attorney, Ginsberg escaped incarceration by pleading insanity. He was subsequently admitted to Columbia Presbyterian Psychiatry Institute, where he remained for eight months.[39]

In South Texas, where he had retreated after his fall, Burroughs had been hearing from Ginsberg about these troubles. The "wrath of God" had descended on him, Ginsberg told Burroughs. Always the factualist, Burroughs thought this reference to Blake's idea that suffering caused transcendence was all dramatic nonsense. He wrote to Jack Kerouac that the *real* wrath of God was being visited on *him* at his farm in South Texas, where bureaucrats were telling him what to plant and deporting the laborers he needed to pick his crops. By comparison, Ginsberg's arrest was nothing. In fact, Ginsberg's problem, Burroughs wrote Jack Kerouac, was not the crime he committed but the fact that he let Louis Ginsberg, Mark Van Doren, and Lionel Trilling talk him into seeking psychiatric help instead of trying to beat the charges against him: "If I was in Al's place I would say 'Go ahead and place your charges, if any.' His present position is insufferable. . . . I don't see anything to gain from the Medical Center deal, a lot of New Deal Freudians. I wouldn't let them croakers up there treat my corn let alone my psyche."[40]

During his eight-month stay in the psychiatric institute, however, Ginsberg rejected Burroughs's advice and his analysis of him, siding instead with his father and Trilling. Louis called Burroughs an "immoralist" (early twentieth-century code for "queer") and told Allen that Burroughs was "dangerous not because he rationalizes but because his end product of thought and attitude results, eventually, if carried out in action, in danger and disharmony and chaos." He worried that his son had abandoned the family's "zeal for a progressive, democratic society."[41]

Burroughs knew, however, that his greatest nemesis was Ginsberg's mentor and Columbia's preeminent scholar and critic, Lionel Trilling. In 1960 Burroughs expressed his disgust with Trilling's influence on Ginsberg by claiming that if he cut Ginsberg up he would "find Lionel Trilling inside." Although today Trilling is sometimes seen as a forerunner of neoconservatism, Burroughs, at the time, viewed Trilling as the type of liberal that Westbrook Pegler described — one whose moral intentions masked an agenda that would suppress individuality and freedom.[42] Burroughs had a point. Particularly during the early years of the Cold War, it became the duty of intellectuals in the United States to transform themselves into pro-U.S. propagandists and support a kind of homogeneity in culture and thought.[43] As Trilling wrote in a 1952 issue of the *Partisan Review* dedicated to "our country and our culture," even "the most disaffected intellectuals" needed to come together at this time of cold-war crisis. Oddly, Burroughs and Trilling actually shared similar views about communism and the threat that big government posed to individual freedoms, but Trilling would never have been able to see Burroughs's drug use and homosexuality as an expression of those freedoms, and he deplored the underworld of the United States that men such as Burroughs populated.

Perhaps it was simply Burroughs's homosexuality that threatened Trilling. Like Louis Ginsberg, Trilling could not envision homosexuals as participants in a "progressive society." For example, in his influential collection of essays from 1950, *The Liberal Imagination,* Trilling argues that, while the individual homosexual should not be persecuted, homosexuality, if openly condoned in society, would produce "a society different from our own" — certainly not a better one.[44] Burroughs knew that there was no room for him in this "progressive, democratic" society of Louis Ginsberg and Lionel Trilling, nor would there be for Allen Ginsberg, the future writer of poems titled "America" and "Howl." Ginsberg himself later wrote that taking the advice of the "crew cut psychologists" out to "cure" him would have forced him "to reject everything I held dear, to reject Burroughs, reject Huncke, reject — you know, reject my own homosexual feelings, reject any compassion I might have felt towards my friends."[45]

Back in 1949, however, Allen Ginsberg was initially swayed by Louis Ginsberg's and Lionel Trilling's views about society and his place in it, and in a letter to Jack Kerouac he concluded that "reality, as [Bill] well knows, is that familial and social community which we, as madmen, have discontinued."[46] Once again, renewing his "zeal" for a "progressive society" (as his father had put it), he baited Burroughs by writing to him of his ambition to become a labor lawyer, and he taunted Burroughs with the very words Lucien Carr had once said to him (Ginsberg): "Trouble with you is you never had to work for a living. . . . As for me, I have nothing better to do than to help those less fortunate than myself."[47] Burroughs, who did work for a living (as a farmer), responded in kind: "I hope you are not serious in this labor leader idea. My opinion of labor leaders and unions is very close to the views so ably expressed by Westbrook Pegler, the only columnist, in my opinion, who possesses a grain of integrity."[48] Ginsberg, in similar disbelief, drafted a response to this letter, saying that Burroughs's "b.s. about Stalinism and cops and the welfare state is just a W. C. Fields act," that is, one of Burroughs's well-known, semiserious routines of the Texas oilman type.[49]

Ginsberg underestimated Burroughs's seriousness. In a letter written on the first day of midcentury, January 1, 1950, Burroughs complained to Jack Kerouac that Allen was being brainwashed: "Allen, by the way, has been utterly corrupted by those Liberal psychiatrists. He talks of becoming a labor leader! I wrote him what I think of labor leaders, Unions, and Liberals. . . . Allen is aligning himself with a cancerous element that will stifle every vestige of free life in the U.S. . . . The word Liberal has come to stand for the most damnable tyranny, a sniveling, mealy-mouthed tyranny of bureaucrats, social workers, psychiatrists, and Union officials."[50]

Ginsberg, to use the parlance of *Naked Lunch,* had entered the "reconditioning center," and Burroughs was horrified at the thought of Ginsberg becoming an "IND" (from *Naked Lunch*): a case of Irreversible Neural Damage. Even worse, Ginsberg had apparently gone straight: "A turning point has been reached in that I am no longer going to have homosexual affairs," Ginsberg wrote to Kerouac on February 27, 1950. Perhaps not coincidentally, the woman he dated reminded him strongly of Joan Burroughs, almost as if Ginsberg were finding his heterosexuality through Burroughs's own taste in women — independent, intellectual women.[51]

On May Day (May 1, 1950), Burroughs wrote Allen a long letter that conflates his many concerns about Ginsberg's apparent conversion to liberalism. Once again, the overt subject is the labor trouble on Burroughs's farm. For this reason, the May 1 date of this letter was probably no accident. In Mexico, where Burroughs was living, May 1 is el Día del Trabajador, or Worker's Day, a holiday celebrated in more than seventy countries (but not in the United States, where, in 1894, Congress designated Labor Day as the first Monday in September to distinguish it from the socialist's May 1 celebrations).[52] Ginsberg, as an employee of a union newspaper and the son of communists, could not have failed to see the significance of the May 1 date on Burroughs's letter.

To begin with, Burroughs, forgetting the previous letters he had written about workers being shot on the job, now maintains, like a benevolent patriarch of the antebellum South, that the workers were "generally well treated" by him and other individual farmers. The government, on the other hand, deported these workers — and worse: "I have observed that the Welfare Gov. makes liberal use of guns and blackjacks in their dealings with the underprivileged." Moreover, he says, the big Mexican landowners hardly treated their native workers any better, forcing them to stay at home in Mexico, "where they can work for two pesos a day or starve." Burroughs, as an individual, thus treats the workers better than either government does; however, he says, *"You can only pay a certain wage and make money. If you don't make money you can't hire anybody at any wage."*[53] Burroughs italicizes this for emphasis. He is exasperated that he has to explain the obvious to Ginsberg and other supporters of a minimum farm wage. Quite paternalistically, he seems to be telling Ginsberg, "Let me tell you what that means when you are the one doing the paying for the labor."

What, then, was the ethical basis for economic exchange in society? Glossing Aristotle's *Politics,* Burroughs explains to Ginsberg: "There are two bases for any ethical system. (1) *Aristocratic code* (2) *Religion.* Liberals reject both which leaves them with exactly nothing."[54] In Aristotle, aristocrats are defined not by material wealth but by their wealth of virtue. Poor or middle-class citizens, therefore, could technically be aristocrats if they were virtuous, in a secular sense. Religion, on the other hand, sets up a prescribed moral order, or "some Cosmic order," as Burroughs says. A citizen who lacks either set of values, he says, is free to act without consideration for "any interests other than his own." In the context of this letter, such people acting without consideration would be the land-rich Mexicans who were starving their people and U.S. government bureaucrats who "make liberal use of guns and blackjacks in their dealing with the underprivileged" — an opinion that echoes Westbrook Pegler's argument that, in defense of common people, liberals turn into fascists.

This is not his position, he tells Ginsberg. Apparently adopting the aristocratic code, he thus proposes his "cooperative" model of farming and points out that he had already instituted profit sharing with his hired laborers in South Texas.

But he doesn't stop there: Farming and labor may be the ostensible subjects in the letter, but once again Burroughs switches from those topics to his other major battle against the forces of liberalism, Ginsberg's plan to "overcome queerness": "I think you will find it is not as simple as that. The fact is that no one at present understands this condition, though, of course, psychiatrists will claim to understand anything." The May Day 1950 letter concludes on this serious note: "I am concerned with *facts* on all levels of experience," he writes, adding, "I hope you will realize that this letter is not a joke, and that I mean what I have said. You are too intelligent to talk in this way."[55] Evidently Ginsberg, who was still a young man and somewhat bewildered by Burroughs's intentions, thought Burroughs was joking around in letters like this one.

"What was Burroughs's game?" Ginsberg must have wondered. Certainly he could understand their political differences, for those fell into fairly well-defined categories: Ginsberg and Burroughs were not the only Americans fighting over labor issues. Finally, at some point in 1950, however, Ginsberg seems to have understood the other fairly obvious intentions of Burroughs's letters as they related to Ginsberg's sexuality, and he wrote to Burroughs that his skepticism about Ginsberg's going straight was simply because he wanted to have a sexual relationship with Ginsberg. Stung, Burroughs replied to him almost a year later, saying, "You said in one of those square letters you wrote to me: 'You don't really want me to get over being queer. You should know enough psychology to realize that.' Even if I had a sex interest in someone I would still be glad to see him switch to women if he could make it and wasn't just putting down a con on himself."[56] Ginsberg was right, though: Burroughs did have a sexual interest in him, even though he does not admit it here. Finally, in 1953, when Burroughs was back in New York City, this five-year conversation about sex and politics was consummated not intellectually but physically, and the two had a brief sexual relationship that lasted for perhaps two or three weeks. This physical aspect of their association was dissatisfying for Ginsberg, who preferred younger men, but not for Burroughs, who pined for Ginsberg for several years after Ginsberg rejected him sexually. Still, Ginsberg remained Burroughs's lifelong friend and student, and, in large part because of Burroughs's influence, he became America's most "out" homosexual writer.

Burroughs was also successful with Ginsberg on the other front of their farm-related debates of the 1940s — the issue of the American liberal. By the late 1960s Ginsberg, the one-time budding labor lawyer, finally understood the failure of the American liberal. "It seemed to me," he said of Lionel Trilling's generation of "poet critics," that, "in so disowning the new open poetics and freedom of mind, desire, imagination, [they] were setting the mental stage for repression of political liberty in the long run." The *Partisan Review* crowd, he said, would not be willing to go to jail in opposition to the emerging police state.[57] Eventually Ginsberg was in fact willing to do just that and was won over to what his father and Trilling had foreseen: "philosophical anarchism," that is, a disbelief in any rigid system of social governance.

Ginsberg's real education on the subject, however, would have to wait until the late '50s and early '60s, when he visited the "communist paradises" of Cuba, Russia, and Poland, where he was harassed and threatened with imprisonment for being an intellectual and a homosexual.[58] The son of a communist and a socialist, Ginsberg finally had to admit, as he did to Tom Clark in 1965, "Yeah, I no longer feel — I didn't ever feel that there was any answer in dogmatic Leninism-Marxism — but I feel very definitely now that there's no answer to my desires there." His about-face on the issues he had debated with Burroughs in the late 1940s is evident, but even more interesting is his suggestion to Clark regarding whose philosophy had replaced Marxism for him. *Someone,* he says, needs to do what Marx did and go into the British Museum and sit there and read and come up with a new plan to save the world because communism and capitalism did not work out the way they should have. Who alone could come up with such a plan? Who has the intelligence and experience? "William Burroughs is almost working on it," he told Clark.[59]

This is a fascinating development in their intellectual relationship, which lasted until both men died in 1997. In 1948 the young and bewildered Ginsberg could not separate the "Red-baiting" that was making the newspaper headlines from Burroughs's anti-union, anticommunist rhetoric in letters about labor trouble in South Texas. Of course, in the forties, it was not just intellectual; as much as Burroughs was trying to win an argument with Ginsberg, he was also trying to keep him free from liberal conditioning that would rob him of his individuality, including his homosexuality. That was the "real Wrath of God."

It must be said, however, that Burroughs also developed beyond the views he expressed to Ginsberg in his letters from the late 1940s. Whereas in those years Burroughs's motto was "make everything pay" and he struggled to convert Allen Ginsberg from a liberal into a laissez-faire capitalist, in his later years Burroughs recognized the dark forces underlying this aspect not only of his personality but also of Americans in general. In 1992, near his home in Lawrence, Kansas, Burroughs, with Ginsberg sitting beside him in a shaman's sweat lodge, underwent a cleansing ritual to rid himself of what his close friend Brion Gyson had called "the ugly spirit." It was this spirit that Burroughs blamed for many of the tragedies in his life, including the death of Joan Burroughs. The ritual cleansing was reportedly a success. However, the shaman told Burroughs he was very nearly defeated by this spirit, which he said was the most malevolent he had ever encountered.

The next day Burroughs was interviewed by Ginsberg, who asked him to describe this powerful spirit's identity. "Well, . . . it's very much related to the American tycoon," Burroughs said. "To William Randolph Hearst, Vanderbilt, Rockefeller, that whole stratum of American acquisitive evil — monopolistic evil. Ugly evil. The Ugly American. The Ugly American at his ugly worst."[60] Although he denied that the spirit was part of the lineage he had inherited from the wealthy, successful Burroughs and Lee families, he must have recognized within himself this basic American dilemma — that of attempting to achieve wealth and total personal freedom without robbing others of their rights and freedom.

Many years before, in South Texas, Burroughs had faced these contradictions in real terms and tried to explain them to the young Allen Ginsberg. At the end of his life, he was still wrestling with his inner demons, and Allen Ginsberg, his old comrade, was there to see it, no longer sitting at Burroughs's feet, as Carlo Marx had in *On the Road,* but sitting beside him.

THE WILD WEST

So far I have characterized William S. Burroughs as a radical individualist, and that's true; however, he was more than just someone who bucked the system. In this respect, when Ted Morgan calls Burroughs a "literary outlaw," he does not mean Burroughs simply broke literary laws; he means Burroughs also broke drug laws, sex laws, gun laws, and censorship laws. In other words, he was a *real* outlaw. And where do American outlaws run to when they are in a fix? They make for Texas and the border, of course, which is what Burroughs did twice in his lifetime after being busted for drugs. The second time was in 1949 in New Orleans. Awaiting trial and possible imprisonment in one of the grimmest prisons in the United States, Angola, Burroughs lay low and impersonated a farmer in Pharr, Texas, just five miles from the border. At any time, he could *brincar el charco,* as locals in South Texas say: He could "jump the puddle."

Therefore, it's probably no accident that in South Texas he was known as Billy, as in Billy the Kid, a morphine-using, pistol-flashing outlaw whom Burroughs admired and, during this period of his life, may well have been imitating. One of his South Texas pastimes, for instance, was to practice shooting a pistol from the hip on the quick draw, "disintegrating" grapefruit, as Ted Marak told me, thrown by him or Kells Elvins. A year after Burroughs left the Valley, Hal Chase has described him in Mexico City as still being "in this Western-gunman phase, impossible to be around. [He came on to me] in all sorts of different ways, like a real rough, ironic guy, a cracker."[1] The South Texas border would have been the perfect place to play out this role.

As an outlaw, though, he couldn't really exist without some tough, Wild West–style lawmen of the type he had read about as a boy in the pages of Zane Grey, J. Frank Dobie, and Jack Black. Black's true crime memoir, *You Can't Win,* served as a model for Burroughs's own true crime memoir, *Junky,* and in it Black and his partner, the Sanctimonious Kid, cross paths with one of the most feared of Western lawmen — Bat Masterson. "He has a reputation as a killer and he earned it," the Sanctimonious Kid tells the young Jack Black. "When he was a marshal of Dodge City bad men rode from the Texas Panhandle and from Deadwood, Dakota, to shoot it out with him, and he dropped them all. Nobody knows how many; he probably don't know himself."[2] Burroughs must have felt that same sense of awe when he too encountered a couple of famous South Texas lawmen — Sheriff Robert Vail Ennis of Beeville, Texas, and "Whispering" Tom Mayfield, constable of Pharr. With their steely eyes, tall white hats, and horn-handled six-shooters slung low on their hips, these South Texas lawmen could well have stepped right out of a Western dime novel.

Burroughs had the pleasure of meeting Sheriff Ennis — the "Texas Hell-bent Sheriff," as a 1947 *Time* magazine called him — in April of 1948: Traveling down to the Valley to buy some land and passing through Beeville, he was arrested by Ennis for drunken driving. The April 29, 1948, issue of the *Beeville Bee-Picayune* reported the following facts of the arrest: "State vs. William Burroughs; driving while intoxicated; guilty; fined $250 and costs, and drivers license suspended six months." Burroughs's version of these facts is, of course, far more colorful, and he obviously relished telling the full story to Ted Morgan in a 1984 interview:

> I was arrested for drunken driving by one of the meanest cops in South Texas, Vail Ennis. He was famous, boy, what a nasty piece of work he was. Shortly before, Ennis had arrested two people for forgery. They were handcuffed together, and he went into a phone booth to make a phone call, and one of them had a concealed .38 revolver. He whipped it out and shot Ennis four times in the gut, but they were not in vital places. Ennis hauls out his .44, puts six bullets in one, calmly reloaded and put six bullets in the other. Two for one. He recovered.
>
> I was driving and I was really drunk and I got out and started fucking Joan by the side of the road. But somebody came by in a car and saw this, and the next thing I knew here is Ennis, Vail Ennis and his deputy, and he looked around, saw the scene. Billy was in the car, he was only two years old then. So [Ennis] said, "Alright, get in the car." He took us back to town. . . . I was only in there overnight and was charged with drunken driving and had to pay a fine of $173. "This here feller was disturbin' the peace while tryin' to get a piece," [Ennis told the Bee County justice of the peace].
>
> While I was in the jail that night some kid came in with blood all over

> his face, scared shitless, and I heard the story from Ennis. He said, "If I hadn't a knowed his papa, I'd have killed this little fuck." He had beaten someone, had taken their money. He said, "I didn't do nothing." So Ennis rolled him around the block three times and by the time he came back he was willing to reach out and point out the money he had stolen. Ennis had beat the living shit out of him, just beat the shit out of him. He was ready to crawl under the bunk when Ennis came in. He was a mean son of a bitch, but there was a certain integrity and fairness about the man. . . . So I had to send a telegram to my family, "For Godsakes send the money or I will be here in Beeville jail." This was on the way down to Pharr, Texas, where I had my cotton.
>
> He was a little tin God. Mean son of a bitch. I got along well with this horrible piece of work. He wasn't the sort of person who would stop someone for long hair. He was a killer, there's no doubt about that. He'd killed about nine people. He was a killer, he didn't fuck around. But he made a clear distinction between criminals and people who were not criminals. He saw right away that I was not of the torturable [*sic*] classes and nobody should hit me over the head with a gun or anything like that.
>
> He was very puritanical, he didn't drink, and he didn't smoke, he didn't approve of drinking and smoking. Just shooting people. As Joan said, "You could see him with a look of faint disapproval on his face as he drills someone through the guts." That's a mean old man. He looked old. He was tall, very tall and thin with narrow shoulders and large arms that tapered down and big forearms, that kind of a build, with very pale gray-blue eyes. He wore a Stetson, and he carried a .44 double-action Colt with a horn handle. . . . Kells was so glad to see me, he said, "My God, I thought that Ennis would have beat you to death."[3]

And he might have done just that: Although Burroughs's Wild West rhetoric occasionally echoes that of the fabulist Jack Black (e.g., "He was a killer, there's no doubt about that" matches Black's description of Bat Masterson — "He has a reputation as a killer and he earned it"), his description of Ennis and his stories about him are dead-on accurate in most respects, from what I have learned. For example, Burroughs was not exaggerating Ennis's brutality: A 2002 history of Bee County recounts stories about several Mexican Americans who were unnecessarily beaten and pistol-whipped by Ennis.[4] In *Last Words,* Burroughs recalls Ennis quipping, "They'll talk, or they won't be in a condition to talk, one way or the other."[5] Nor was Burroughs exaggerating Ennis's fearsome appearance. John Snider, who had a run-in with Ennis in the mid-1940s, told me, "Son-of-a-bitch's got arms on him like a gorilla. They hung way down, and he was built like a gorilla. I don't believe you could hurt the son-of-a-bitch with an axe."

Burroughs's story about Ennis being shot four times by a handcuffed prisoner who pulled a concealed weapon while Ennis was making a phone call is also accurate. In fact, it appears that Burroughs, whose memory was prodigious, had read a 1947 *Time* magazine article describing the incident: "Bleeding but upright, Vail turned from the phone, pulling his Colt from his hip holster; he pumped six shots at the manacled prisoners," *Time* reported. "Deliberately, he reloaded and pumped six more. When the smoke cleared away, both men were dead." The article goes on to quote a Beeville resident saying, "They might as well have gone out and hanged themselves as to pull a gun on Vail."[6] Ennis was sheriff, judge, jury, and executioner, all in one.

Other aspects of Burroughs's story, however, tell us as much about Burroughs as they do about Ennis. It is revealing that, while Burroughs was appalled by this "horrible piece of work," on another level he had a grudging respect for him. Apparently he had a genuine sense of identification with redneck Southern sheriffs. In 1944 Burroughs, Jack Kerouac, Allen Ginsberg, and Lucien Carr had regularly performed charades for each other, and one of Burroughs's favorite alter egos was "Old Luke, the Tobacco Farmer." Ginsberg recalled that Old Luke's personality was that of a "psychotic Southern Sheriff."[7] Therefore, in Burroughs's description of Ennis there is both condemnation and a degree of understanding. Ennis was a cold-blooded killer, but there was a "certain fairness," Burroughs says, in his ability to distinguish between real criminals and minor offenders. In reality, Ennis was every bit as discriminating as Burroughs says, but not in a good way: In his eight-year career (1944–1952) as sheriff of Beeville, Ennis killed eight people, almost all of whom were Mexican American or African American, which explains why Burroughs, in his encounter with Ennis, felt safe: Burroughs was "not a member of the torturable [*sic*] classes."[8]

While Burroughs was certainly aware that it was his lily-white skin and daddy's money that saved him in his encounter with Ennis, his interview with Ted Morgan only touches on this social reality of the "frontier," much as his description of the Valley as a whole ignores the Jim Crow type of segregation and discrimination that Anglos practiced against Mexican Americans during this period.[9] South Texas in the 1940s could be a virulently racist place, and, depending largely on whether you were white or non-white (Mexican American, African American), you saw Vail Ennis in very different lights. As Richard Rudeloff, Ennis's biographer says, "Ennis was either a ruthless killer who totally disregarded the civil rights of the citizens of Bee County, or, on the other hand, he was a vigorous and dedicated peace officer who need be feared only by those who violated the law."[10] In support of the former view, Carlos C. Guerrero Jr., who grew up in Beeville and worked as a Beeville Police Department communications officer for thirty-four years, says that Ennis singled out Mexican Americans for abuse. "When Ennis came upon some 'Pachucos' standing on the corner of town or in a beer joint," Guerrero says, "he would tell them, 'You better leave and go on,' or, 'If I see you again, I'll shoot you or kill you 'Meskins.' It was like the old West. They were afraid of getting shot."

One incident known to Burroughs involved Ennis and the family of Carlos Guerrero's wife, Angelita (Rodriquez); it is still talked about today.[11] The Rodriguez family lived on the Wilson Farm, seven miles west of Beeville. On July 7, 1945, Ennis drove there to serve a child custody order to Geronimo Rodriguez, who had failed to return his children to their mother after a weekend visit. According to Ennis's court testimony, the family refused to turn over the children and told him to leave the property. According to surviving family members, however, when Ennis asked to speak to Rodriguez, he was told that Geronimo was out working the ranch and that the children could not be turned over without his consent. They asked Ennis to wait for Rodriguez, but Ennis became angry and drove back to town.

When he returned to the Wilson farm, he was backed up by Texas Ranger Frank Probst and Joe Walton, a civilian Ennis had deputized on the spot. He also returned armed with a Thompson .45 machine gun, a weapon he sometimes bolted onto the hood of his Hudson Hornet and operated from inside the car using a chain mechanism. Ennis set this heavy gun up on a tripod outside the farmhouse and called out to the family. Twelve members of the Rodriguez family, including women and children, were inside. Felix Rodriguez, the grandfather, heard Ennis's calls and went to the screen door. Ennis, for no reason, opened up on him with the Thompson, spraying the front of the house and killing Felix, whose body fell back inside the dwelling. Hearing the gunfire, Felix's brothers, Domingo and Antonio, ran around the side of the house. Ennis cut them down without warning, their bodies falling atop each other in the shape of a cross. One of Felix's granddaughters, only twelve years old, ran from the house in terror, and Ennis tried to cut her down, too, but the bullets hit a water cistern. Ranger Probst then threw a tear-gas grenade into the farmhouse. When the smoke cleared, Ennis entered, finding only unarmed men, women, and children huddled around the body of Felix Rodriguez. Ennis kicked and beat the adults, fracturing one man's head with a rifle butt.

Later, in court, Ennis claimed self-defense, saying Domingo leveled a 30–30 rifle at him and that Antonio was carrying a shotgun. Family members maintain, however, that the men were unarmed. To this day, the surviving members of the Rodriguez family bear the trauma of what can only be called a massacre.[12]

It is no wonder, then, that Kells Elvins was petrified when Burroughs told him who had arrested him. They both knew about the machine-gun slaughter, either from the *Time* magazine article or from accounts in the McAllen *Monitor.* Burroughs did not recount this story for Ted Morgan, but it is likely that he conflated the story with one he heard about another legendary South Texas lawman, Tom Mayfield.

Much worse than Burroughs's story of Ennis pistol-whipping prisoners is his account of Tom Mayfield machine-gunning recalcitrant Mexican workers in the South Texas fields. "Whispering Tom Mayfield was down in Pharr," he told Ted Morgan:

> He was a really mean son-of-a-bitch, he had lost his voice, years ago. He'd shout, "Stop!" and they wouldn't hear him and he'd pull out his gun and shoot them. He was a strikebreaker for the big landowners down there. Once in cotton-picking season the wetbacks went on strike. And they called Mayfield in. He opened the door with a submachine gun, "Right, you fucking Mexicans, get out there and work!" And they didn't pay any attention and then he opens up with the submachine gun, kills three of them. . . . See, there was no law except that kind of law in South Texas.
>
> There's many relatives of people that he killed have tried to get Whispering Tom Mayfield, but they never succeeded. He was another absolute mean awful son of a bitch. He was at that time a man of 60 years old but of great physical strength. Nobody would fool around with that mean son of a bitch. Our tractor driver killed our best worker in a fight. Hit him over the head with a tire iron. And before we could get to the scene, Whispering Tom Mayfield had beat a confession out of him. So he went away for five years, so we lost two of our best men just like that.[13]

I have heard the "Stop or I'll shoot" story about Mayfield from many people, including John Snider, who was in the Hidalgo County Courthouse around 1946 on the day Mayfield made this defense for shooting a Mexican he caught robbing a drugstore. Today the story is told like a joke: "I shouted 'Halt!' and he kept on running, so I had to cut him down," Whispering Tom testified in a voice so low and rasping that court observers had to lean forward in their seats to hear him. The capper is the machine-gun story, which, as far as I can tell, never occurred and is probably a conflation of the Vail Ennis machine-gun tale. On the other hand, Burroughs's firsthand account of Mayfield's rough interrogation of his tractor driver is undoubtedly true.

Separating facts from fiction about Mayfield is difficult at this late date, but doing so reveals the discrepancy between Burroughs's view of South Texas as the Wild West and the views of South Texans themselves. It also uncovers a deeper history of South Texas that was unfamiliar to Burroughs and other transplanted Midwesterners. The actual facts about Mayfield's career and character (as well as I can reconstruct them from books and personal interviews with people who knew him) are as follows. Mayfield, by anyone's standards, lived an adventurous life in South Texas. He was born in Gonzales County in 1880 and first made a name for himself in 1898, when he traveled to San Antonio and sold some horses to Teddy Roosevelt's Rough Riders. He worked the railroads in South Texas, drove a stagecoach for a while, and ended up as an assistant manager on San Juan Plantation, owned by John Closner, sheriff of Hidalgo County.

Known for his brutal methods of interrogating suspected cattle rustlers, Closner may well have taught Tom Mayfield a few techniques he later used: "I went a little too far to make the suspects confess," Closner once confided to county "boss" Jim Wells.[14] On his plantation, Closner needed someone who could supervise the workers, speak fluent Spanish, and use a gun. Mayfield qualified and was evidently a firm but fair supervisor. This reputation landed him a job as a deputy sheriff under Closner's successor as sheriff, A. Y. Baker.[15]

Like Closner, Baker was a South Texas political boss well into the 1920s; also like Closner, he was a controversial lawman whose actions came under investigation. In 1902 Baker shot a rancher named Ramón de la Cerda, who was purportedly caught in the act rustling cattle from the King Ranch. When Baker heard that de la Cerda's brother Alfredo was out to avenge Ramón's death, Baker took the law into his own hands. He found Alfredo inside a Brownsville store trying on some gloves. Alfredo was unarmed, and Baker shot him in the back. Baker was arrested, released on a bond posted by the King Ranch family, and later, in a decision that enraged the Tejano community, acquitted of the murder charges.[16]

According to border historian Benjamin Heber Johnson, this case became "a microcosm of the confusion and death" seen during the later "border wars" in South Texas (1914–1918), in which both Sheriff Baker and his deputy, Tom Mayfield, played important roles. Although this war is often overlooked in U.S. history books, it was a real and bloody conflict with high stakes for both Mexico and the United States. From Mexico, revolutionaries were making raids into South Texas and New Mexico; in Texas, Mexican Texans were rebelling against decades of Anglo discrimination and calling for the return of their land, which, through legal as well as illegal means, was now mostly in the hands of Anglo ranchers and farmers. At one point, in July of 1916, thirty thousand U.S. troops as well as a large contingent of Texas Rangers were stationed on the border to quell violence in South Texas and prevent the spread of the Mexican revolution north of the border.[17] Walter Prescott Webb calculates that as many as 5,000 Mexicans and Tejanos were killed by soldiers and Rangers between 1914 and 1918. Other authorities estimate the number of dead Mexicans and Texas Mexicans at between 200 and 1,500.[18] Even apologists for the Rangers, such as Webb, refer to the "orgy of bloodshed" conducted in this period.[19]

Sheriff Baker was involved in numerous battles and skirmishes with Tejanos and Mexicans and earned a reputation (as did many Rangers) for "killing Mexicans on sight." Tom Mayfield was privately hired as a "Special Ranger" during this period of violence and is locally famous for his part in the foiling of a revolutionary plot known as the Plan de San Diego.[20] In a more controversial incident, Mayfield and his men "discovered" the bodies of a dozen dead Mexican *sediciosos* [insurgents] in Alamo, Texas, all shot in the back. Mayfield later testified that he and his men had nothing to do with the killings.[21] On the border, finding Mexicans shot in the back became so commonplace that the San Antonio newspapers admitted they were getting bored publishing such accounts.[22] The "Stop or I'll shoot" story in which Mayfield shoots an unarmed man in the back thus has a special significance to Texas Mexicans, who to this day have not forgotten the violence of the border wars period. Understandably, they do not find stories about a Mexican being shot in the back all that funny. By the end of this period

(1918), almost half of the Mexicans living in Hidalgo and Cameron counties had fled northward or gone back to Mexico. Some never returned, and the invading Anglos consolidated their power in the region once and for all.[23]

Following the border wars, Mayfield took a job in Mexico as a security officer in the U.S. oil fields. It was probably there that he earned his nickname, "Whispering Tom": Tom, so the story goes, had his throat cut by a Mexican during a brawl. He survived, but thereafter his voice rose barely above a whisper. In his later, less spectacular, career, Mayfield served (from 1938 to 1963) as a deputy constable in the Pharr-San Juan-Alamo area. Burroughs, living in Pharr in the late 1940s, knew the aging lawman during this later phase of his career, and he no doubt heard "Ranger stories" about Mayfield — tales told by South Texans recounting the violent days of the border wars. Some of these accounts were undoubtedly true, but others were probably fabrications that transplanted Yankees, who had no understanding of the historical context of these stories (particularly those related to the border wars), were all too ready to believe: Men such as Kells and Burroughs wanted to feel as if they were living in the remnants of the Wild West they had read about as kids.

To try to get past the tales men such as Burroughs, Kells Elvins, and other Anglo immigrants heard on the border during the 1940s, I talked with Antonio Villegas Jr., who was eighty-four years old at the time and has lived in Pharr his entire life. Although Antonio knew Mayfield only in his later years, his father had been best friends with Mayfield at the turn of the century, and he told his son all about Tom. In contrast to Burroughs's stories, those Villegas related to me are decidedly "mild" West ones. He told me frankly that stories about Mayfield killing unarmed Mexicans were invented by Anglos who arrived in the Valley well after the border wars. "The Anglos liked the idea of the Valley as the Wild West, Billy-the-Kid stuff," he said. "The Mexican men who knew Mayfield back then liked and respected him," he told me. "He wouldn't go after anyone unless there was just cause." Newcomers like Burroughs, he said, knew Mayfield only when he was much older, as did younger Mexican Americans, and they feared him because of the Ranger stories about him and because of his rasping voice, which added to his fearsome image. Local historian Robert Norton agreed and was audibly upset when I told him the machine-gun account in a phone interview. "I wouldn't give that story any credence," he said. Other South Texans go even further than this in their retelling of history: They outright mock the legend of lawmen such as Mayfield.

I read Burroughs's Tom Mayfield and Vail Ennis stories to John Snider, who knew Kells Elvins and both Mayfield and Ennis. He hooted at Burroughs's tales about Tom Mayfield machine-gunning Mexicans: "I can't get over that," he said after he finally stopped laughing. His view of Mayfield, whom he knew from the 1930s until Mayfield's death in 1963, was that he was "a joke." As for the machine-gun story, he said the following:

JS: Mayfield! He wouldn't know how to operate a machine gun.

RJ: Why do you say that?

JS: He was dumb. That guy was dumb, all he was was a night watchman with a big gun, and he never was a Ranger.

RJ: I heard he had nineteen notches on the gun.

JS: Ah, shit, he probably had somebody carve them on there for him. He was a joke. A goddamn joke.

RJ: I understand he was pretty brutal when he interrogated people. He beat up Burroughs's tractor driver to get a confession out of him. Did you ever hear anything like that about him?

JS: See, Burroughs puts on that "we didn't have no law down here." We had a sheriff that was sheriff in this county for about twenty-four years straight. Nobody would run against him. You knew you was spinning your wheels. His name was E. E. Vickers [Hidalgo County sheriff, 1955–1969]. Sheriff Vickers lived in Donna, never owned a gun. Vickers could make more arrests over the telephone than any of his deputies could in the field. If he wanted this guy arrested he'd just call him up . . .

RJ: Mayfield was just a Barney Fife?

JS: He was worse than Barney Fife. I don't think they even give him one bullet. Old Bill [mayor of San Juan] bought him, found, a Black Oldsmobile, a Super 88, abandoned somewhere, and he gave it to Tom, and Tom drove that damn Oldsmobile from the Junction over to the Hub and into San Juan over to the pharmacy. And somewhere he found in a junkyard one of those silver sirens that goes on top of it and put it up on top. It wasn't connected to nothing. And he wore a big hat. Now, he would go to a funeral and go into the church, and the sonofabitch wouldn't even take the damn hat off! Big damn hat with a point on it. Oh God, it's the most ridiculous thing you ever saw. Makes him look like he's nine foot ten inches tall, and he wasn't. Tom was about five foot seven. He is short. And he wore these cowboy boots with little bitty heels on them. He couldn't hardly hide the date on a nickel with those heels.

To this man, Burroughs and Kells were just a couple of dandified gentlemen farmers from the East who were of course terrified by an old man such as Tom Mayfield impersonating a Texas Ranger with his six-shooter, pointy boots, and ten-gallon hat. Still, if Mayfield was a "joke," why is there a state highway marker dedicated to him in front of the San Juan Hotel? I asked.

JS: He was dead twenty years before they did it, because they wanted all the old folks to be dead. If you notice, these counterfeit bastards that get these memorial signs put up, they don't put 'em up until all their generation is gone. See, there's not many of even my generation still alive, and as soon as they're all gone . . . I laughed, I thought it was the funniest damn thing there ever was.[24]

Some South Texans mythologize men such as Ennis and Mayfield, while others try to humanize or even knock them down several notches. Others say Mayfield was just as mean as Burroughs says he was: One of my students from San Juan recently interviewed his grandfather about his memories of Mayfield, and his grandfather recalled that, as a child, he saw Mayfield gun a man down in front of his house, which was Mayfield's way of settling an argument. We also know that Mayfield liked to show off the notches on his gun to children in the 1940s and 1950s, obviously contributing to his formidable image.

Still, most South Texans do not like to hear outsiders such as Burroughs playing up the Valley as the lawless frontier: "See, Burroughs makes out like we were the Wild West down here," John Snider told me. At the same time, though, Valley residents cannot help themselves and love to tell stories about the days when the Valley was a frontier region with its own brand of justice. The murder of Burroughs's friend Walter Benson is a good example of — to adapt a phrase from Judge Roy Bean — the law south of the Nueces.

In an interview with James Grauerholz in 1974, Burroughs listed Benson as a South Texas friend of his who was shot to death by his father-in-law — a story Burroughs probably heard from Kells Elvins since Burroughs had left the Valley several years before Walter's murder. Burroughs had known Walter quite well. At some point during his trips down to the Valley between 1946 and 1949, Burroughs stayed at Walter Benson's apartment in a large house that is still standing at 321 Kelly Street in Pharr. Burroughs likely first met Benson either on the golf course (Walter's favorite pastime, along with drinking) or at the San Pat Vegetable Shed, where Walter worked, in Pharr. As a produce dealer, Walter Benson was famous for his ability to write down complicated produce orders he received simultaneously from two phones, one on each ear. "Walter was a brain," one of his relatives told me.

He was also a famous drinker. John Snider remembers seeing Walter drag himself up the stairs to his office after a hard night of drinking in Reynosa. By all accounts, drinking made Walter mean: His first wife left him (in the early 1940s) after he broke her nose in a fight. Walter's second wife, Helen, was the daughter of a justice of the peace, J. Loy Ramsour, and when Walter started abusing her, too, Ramsour took matters into his own hands. "I have thought it over," he told a friend over dinner in early 1956, "and I have decided the best thing to do is kill the S.O.B."[25]

"The Judge" (as he was called) did just that on April 29, 1956. With a .380-caliber pistol concealed under a long coat, he went to his son-in-law's house to confront him. He and Walter argued in Walter's study. According to Ramsour, Walter made a move to go for a gun in the pocket of his Bermuda shorts (no gun was ever found), and in "self-defense" Ramsour whipped out his gun and shot Walter three times; a fourth bullet ricocheted and wounded a family friend named Maria Kenworthy in the leg. Kenworthy's account of these events was quite different from Ramsour's. Walter made no move to go for a gun, she said. The Judge, calmly smoking his trademark pipe, simply told Walter, "I'm going to settle this once and for all now." He then removed a concealed pistol from his waistband, Kenworthy testified, and put three bullets in Walter, one in his back. Helen Benson, seeing both Walter and Kenworthy lying bleeding on the floor of the study, screamed at the Judge, "Now you've killed them both. Who do you think you are, Daddy, God?"[26]

Maybe so. After shooting Walter in cold blood in his own home while his four children were playing in the backyard, Ramsour called the Pharr police from Walter's phone and turned himself in. He was released on a bond of five thousand dollars that night, and, amazingly, he presided as justice of the peace the next day — and continued to do so until the July elections, when he was defeated.

The case came to trial in early March of 1957, a full year after Walter's death. By then, however, most people in Pharr had already pardoned the Judge for shooting Walter, whose alcohol-fueled beatings of his wife were well known. As Jim Bates, the exasperated prosecuting attorney pointed out at the trial, the defense's main argument was that the Judge had actually done the community a favor by killing Walter — an excellent example of the Texas-style "he needed killing" defense. That was certainly the substance of Judge Ramsour's testimony. According to the Judge, Walter was a recognized sexual pervert and homosexual who gave his wife Helen "love potions" in order to control her in bed. Walter was also, according to Ramsour, mixed up in a drug-smuggling plan. Jim Bates countered that, after killing Walter, Ramsour was now assassinating Walter's character.[27]

Still, with no evidence that the Judge's shooting of Benson was anything less than premeditated murder, the verdict of the Brownsville jury came back "guilty." Ramsour was sentenced to ten years in prison.[28]

However, some people I have talked with maintain that, in spite of the verdict, the Judge never spent a day in jail. According to newspaper accounts, he actually served eighteen months of his ten-year sentence before being paroled in May 1959. The case was not over, though: In 1962, as payback for services rendered by J. C. Looney (Ramsour's defense attorney) in the recent gubernatorial election, Texas governor Price Daniel issued Ramsour a full pardon. South Texas justice was finally done. To this day, Ramsour is remembered as a gentle man with no previous history of violence. Walter, on the other hand, is remembered as a bad apple who simply needed killing. "Everybody knew Walter needed shooting" is a line I have heard from more than one person who remembers the murder. Their message is that, during the first half of the twentieth century down in the Valley, cases were tried by the court of public opinion and common sense rather than by the court of law. In this respect, frontier justice truly prevailed in South Texas.[29]

In South Texas we have *corridos,* border songs about outlaw-heroes and the *rinches* [Texas Rangers] they battle. In these songs, the Mexican heroes are exaggeratedly macho and nearly indestructible; the Rangers, on the other hand, are always referred to by the epithet *rinches cobardes* [cowardly Rangers]. One of the most famous of these corridos celebrates Jacinto Treviño from Matamoros, who avenged the bullwhipping of his cousin by killing an Anglo construction foreman in San Benito. In the corrido, Treviño taunts the rinches who are pursuing and firing at him by saying that their bullets are good only for making buttonholes in his shirt. In the middle of a fierce battle, he pauses dramatically to tie his shoelaces while bullets whistle around him.[30]

Such songs were people's history, sung in response to the even more exaggerated (and racist) accounts of Ranger heroism printed in newspapers and history books and dramatized in B-movie Westerns. Obviously Burroughs did not have the same stake as the singers of the corridos. As an outlaw he needed rinches, too, but as an Anglo, he did not want them to be cowards. Burroughs's personal mythology required those lawmen to be as tough as Vail Ennis, who took four bullets and kept coming — the same way Jacinto Treviño, the outlaw, laughs off the hail of bullets "making buttonholes" in his shirt. He certainly was not interested in telling stories about lawmen such as E. E. Vickers, who didn't even carry a gun. Nor, apparently, did he know the story of real South Texas "outlaws" such as Jacinto Treviño and Gregorio Cortez, men who were hunted like animals by the law and whose families were persecuted.[31]

Ultimately, to find his own real Wild West, Burroughs would have to travel to a terrain familiar to him: his imagination. In his three final novels, *The Cities of the Red Night, The Place of Dead Roads,* and *The Western Lands,* Burroughs often borrowed from the traditions of the pulp Western that had inspired Jack Black and also influenced the young Burroughs. You would expect, however, that his own brush with the Wild West in South and East Texas would show up in these "Westerns," and, in fact, it does — not only in the general atmosphere of the settings and characters but also in specific details.

In an early scene in *The Place of Dead Roads,* Kim Carsons (Burroughs's alter ego, who is both gunfighter and writer) rides out west and takes possession of a river-front farm he has inherited from his deceased father. The next day, a neighbor sells Kim homegrown marijuana as well as several rifles and pistols. On the farm, Kim brushes up on his skills as a gunfighter. The training pays off when two men at the local saloon complain loudly within Kim's earshot about having to drink in the company of a "fairy." Kim drops them both.[32]

If you look at this setup in light of Burroughs's South Texas days, it is in some respects an idealized version of Kells's Jackson Road farm and his and Burroughs's life down there. Kells, too, inherited his farmhouse near the river, grew his own marijuana, and allowed Billy to practice his "quick draw" skills in his orchards. Billy, as is Kim, was also insulted as a queer, but unlike in the Western fantasy, he didn't have Kim's satisfaction of gunning down his enemies.

Another scene in *The Place of Dead Roads* also has echoes of the South Texas setup. Kim and the boys are hiding out in Mexico at the Fuentes hacienda, where they eat hallucinogenic mushrooms and perform mysterious rites. The local chief of police, or jefe, gets wind of these activities and complains about the *maricons* [queers] and the *brujería* [black magic] going on at the hacienda. Kim and three comrades raid the saloon where the chief is getting drunk with his "asshole cronies" and kill the whole bunch: "Twelve of those lousy macho shits died in the shootout," Kim reports.[33] Although mostly a fantasy, some of this has a basis in South Texas reality. Billy and Tiger Terry were known to use mushrooms, and Billy and Kells were suspected of performing brujería in Burroughs's homemade Reichian orgone accumulator. A further clue in an earlier novel, *Port of Saints,* connects this part of Mexico with South Texas: Down on the hacienda, they drink "Old Pharr" whisky, a play on the name of Pharr, Texas, and Old Parr, a commonly consumed whisky in Mexico.[34]

In Burroughs's reinvention of the Western, there is also a racial context only briefly mentioned in his letters and interviews. His outlaw hero, Kim Carsons, shoots homophobes and "nigger-killing sheriffs" with their "frog-faced deputies," and, as part of Kim's "shit eradication program," one sheriff is infected with botulism (used as a biological weapon) while eating in a segregated restaurant.[35] In B'dan, one of the seven "Cities of the Red Night," the Texas Rangers are lumped in with murderers such as "nigger-killing Southern lawmen" and army pilots flying "Operation Intercept" helicopters — a Nixon-era drug interdiction action on the border — while being shot at by Pancho Villa.[36]

Kim has some respect for certain lawmen, however. In a scene right out of Jack Black, Kim meets Bat Masterson, whose advice to Kim is interesting: He tells Kim to give up on being a quick-draw specialist and go to work for a rancher as a deputy sheriff.[37] In South Texas, this is very close to the career path followed by Tom Mayfield, who worked on John Closner's plantation and was A. Y. Baker's deputy sheriff. Like the stories Burroughs heard in South Texas, there is both truth and fantasy in his dramatization of the Old West. Once upon a time, he too had lived there en la frontera, on the border between fact and fiction.

As for the real Wild West lawmen he knew — Vail Ennis and Tom Mayfield — both show up either directly or indirectly in his Westerns. Ennis appears to be the prototype of several old sheriffs in his works, identifiable by his "very pale gray-blue eyes" and his horn-handled Colt pistol (as Burroughs described Ennis to Ted Morgan). For example, in "Word" in *Interzone,* a cattle rustler is hanged by an "old sheriff, eyes pale and empty as blue sky."[38] Mayfield shows up briefly as an actual character in *Port of Saints.* One of the crew members of the *Mary Celeste,* "Pecos Bridge Juanito the knife thrower" flashes back to the following scene from his past:

> Moonlight on a dusty street little Texas town. Whispering Tom Mayfield with twenty greaser notches in his gun steps from a doorway . . .
>
> "All right you fucking Mexican stop right there."
>
> Juanito clasps his hands behind his head and pivots slowly at first then suddenly speeds up throwing a knife from a holster behind his neck. It catches the sheriff in the Adam's apple and he flops like a stricken buzzard.[39]

The story, which incorporates the "Stop or I'll shoot" routine Burroughs heard in South Texas, does not have the dark humor of Burroughs's oral version because Mayfield's rasping voice does not come into play. Instead, the story appears to tell the origin of Whispering Tom's nickname. I heard from several people (and perhaps Burroughs did, too) that Mayfield had his throat "operated on by a Mexican with a machete," and this was how he lost his voice. Here, though, the story also has a revenge element — Juanito's knife avenging every "fucking Mexican" notched on Tom's gun.

Like Jack Black spinning tales from his youth about run-ins with Bat Masterson and other remnants of the Old West, Burroughs recalled all of these stories of his "frontier" days for friends and eventually for his reading public. By then, they were stories about his past, too, and he had grown out of the Billy-the-Kid phase he exhibited in Mexico and South Texas. This development can also be seen in the evolution of his books. *Junky,* like Jack Black's *You Can't Win,* was a true-crime memoir, but his later books show Burroughs was after higher game. In *The Western Lands,* he makes a distinction between the common outlaw and his outlaw character, Joe the Dead, and the distinction no doubt applied to Burroughs himself: "Joe the Dead belongs to a select breed of outlaws known as the NO's, natural outlaws dedicated to breaking the so-called natural laws of the universe. . . . Ordinary outlaws break man-made laws. Laws against theft and murder are broken every second. . . . To the ordinary criminal, breaking a law is a means to an end: obtaining money, removing a source of danger or annoyance. To the NO, breaking a natural law is an end in itself: the end of that law."[40] In

South Texas, he saw man-made laws broken every day as he put his illegals to work in the fields, and he saw laws against assault and murder broken by the very authorities who were supposed to uphold them. He came to South Texas stuck in the dime-novel universe of lawman and outlaw, but he would leave it aiming for a target more difficult to hit than the grapefruit Kells and Ted threw in the air for him — the end of law itself.

ON THE ROAD IN SOUTH TEXAS

In June of 1949 Jack Kerouac planned to visit William S. Burroughs on his farm in South Texas, but he never made it; a year later he came close to the Valley when he crossed the border at Laredo in June, a trip recorded in the famous Mexico section of *On the Road.* Kerouac's only visit to the Valley proper was in July of 1952, when he crossed the border at Brownsville, Texas, en route to his sister's home in North Carolina from Burroughs's apartment in Mexico City. In Brownsville, just across the bridge from Matamoros, he hitched a ride with a man named Hotrod Johnny Bowen, who insisted that Kerouac accompany him on an all-night drinking binge at local roadhouses. He then hitched to Harlingen, where a young Mexican medical student picked him up and drove him up Highway 77 all the way to Rosenberg, near Houston.[1]

Even before Kerouac first visited the Texas border and Mexico, though, he had, in a sense, already been there — through Burroughs's letters to him. In fact, most likely Kerouac would never have traveled to Mexico had Burroughs not paved the way for him, and *On the Road* would be missing its climactic chapters set south of the border as well as other essential elements. During the years (1948–1950) Burroughs was corresponding with Kerouac from Pharr; New Waverly, Louisiana; and Mexico, Kerouac, who was living and writing *On the Road,* was also absorbing much of what Burroughs had to say in his letters about the allure of Mexico and his bitter experiences as a farmer in South Texas. It is well known that Kerouac included whole chunks of letters from Neal Cassady in *On the Road,* but I do not think anyone has fully considered how Burroughs's Texas letters also make their way into *On the Road.*[2] Moreover, Kerouac read two novels in manuscript just before he started writing the famous "scroll" version of *Road* in April 1951: John Clellon Holmes's *Go: A Novel* and "Junk" by Burroughs, which contained the South Texas scenes later cut out of the novel when it was published as *Junky* in 1953.

It should therefore not be surprising that in *On the Road* and *Junky* (and in Burroughs's letters from the forties), Kerouac and

Burroughs express remarkably similar views on a number of topics. No doubt Kerouac's opinions were influenced by those of the older, more experienced Burroughs, but it is also true that both men were constitutionally libertarian, even conservative, in their political and social beliefs. Their shared philosophy can be boiled down to the fact that both of them, as Kerouac says of Old Bull Lee in *Road,* were nostalgic for an America that stood for freedom and rugged individualism. "What ever happened to our glorious Frontier heritage of minding one's own business?" Burroughs asked Kerouac in a January 1, 1950, letter, sent from Mexico City. "The Frontiersman has shrunk to a wretched, interfering, Liberal bureaucrat."[3] Such words found a ready audience in Kerouac, who, like Burroughs, genuinely loved the idea of frontier America.

One of these shared American ideals was of "living off the land." Kerouac had toyed with the idea — but quickly rejected it — in a 1943 letter to his most important boyhood friend, Sebastian Sampas: "However," he wrote Sammy in one of their philosophical and poetic exchanges, "a Promethean Farm would be good for vacations . . . but one can't really work there, live there, study there. If we had money, it might work, but even then, the ennui would be awful — an artist needs *life.*"[4] This letter would prefigure one from Burroughs to Kerouac five years later, when Burroughs, writing from his farm, described South Texas as "this Valley of heat and boredom," the very "ennui" Kerouac predicted would take hold on the Promethean Farm.

We know further that in the 1945 book Kerouac and Burroughs wrote together, *And the Hippos Were Boiled in Their Tanks,* Burroughs was already idealizing life on a farm or ranch as a way to live and do what you wanted to do without outside interference.[5] Soon after *Hippos,* in late 1946, Burroughs had actually established himself as a farmer in both South Texas and later, in December of that year, in East Texas. At that point, Kerouac was less interested in becoming a farmer than in becoming a writer, but in 1947 he expressed his ambition to be an American writer who celebrated "a culture of livelihood, purpose, land and natural struggle" — Kerouac's version of Frederick Jackson Turner's frontier thesis.[6]

Understandably, Kerouac wanted to know about Burroughs's real-life farm, and a few months after writing this letter to Neal Cassady's pal Hal Chase, he was writing the following to Burroughs in East Texas: "I wish you would write me once in a while and tell me about your life on the ranch. When are you going to grow grapefruits or something?"[7] Obviously Kerouac had not visited Burroughs's East Texas farm, where it was not possible to grow grapefruit, but Allen Ginsberg, Neal Cassady, and Herbert Huncke were all at Burroughs's East Texas "ranch" in the summer of 1947. Kerouac loved the idea of these hipsters pitching in and doing farmwork: "I think it is amazing how Bill put you to work on his ranch," he wrote to Cassady. "What the place probably needs is an old hand like yourself, 'Horseskinner' Cassady from Arkansas. I wish I were there, I'd really go to work too — just for the hell of it."[8] Of course, Kerouac's idea of Burroughs's ninety-nine acres of East Texas swamp as being a "ranch" shows how little he understood about ranching or farming, but he is certainly enthusiastic about the *idea* of a ranch on which they could all live and work.

In the summer of 1947 Kerouac went west (as described in *On the Road,* chapters 3 and 4) to visit Cassady in Denver, with stops along the way in Iowa, Nebraska, and Wyoming. In Cheyenne, he partied during "Wild West Week." His idea of owning a ranch must have been influenced by that trip because, when he finished the manuscript of *The Town and the City* a year later, he wrote to Cassady of his next ambition: "I've made up my mind to become a rancher, I've learned all about it in books, and [am] going to learn the rest this summer working on ranches in Colo., Ariz., or Wyo."[9] He envisions the ranch as a kind of commune. In a June 27, 1948, letter to Neal, he wrote, "I need a life situation like a ranch. . . . Neal, what I want is a big home with about twenty people in it, whole families at the same time, something going on all the time, someone leaving, someone coming, someone building a shelf, someone mending a fence, someone sewing, someone cooking, someone reading, someone eating, so on, and on on on. . . . I want the Shakespearian gamut of things in one big tumultuous house."[10] The idea, as he puts it in a subsequent letter, was "something really cooperative, and free. . . . *Partnership* in such endeavors means protracted vacations for all, rotation of responsibility and duties, opportunity for travel, a real workable routine."[11] Neal Cassady quickly warmed to the idea and began discussing plans for a cooperative ranch with his wife, Carolyn.

Thirty years later, in his fictional works Burroughs defined a "cooperative" in terms similar to Kerouac's, particularly with regard to the "rotation of responsibilities and duties." In *The Place of Dead Roads* (1981) he writes, "The Johnson Family is a cooperative structure. There isn't any boss man. People know what they are supposed to do and they do it. We're all actors and we change roles. Today's millionaire may be tomorrow's busboy. There's none of that ruling-class old-school tie. . . . 'Hey boy, manicure my toenails and look sharp about it . . . and you, boy, don't slack at the ceiling fan, I'm sweating my bloody balls off . . . saddle my horse nigger.' We are showing that an organization and a very effective organization can run without boss-man dog-eat-dog fear."[12]

I do not know for sure whether it was Burroughs or Kerouac who first defined a cooperative in this fashion, but I suspect it was Burroughs. After all, he had shared his profits with the hired workers on his South Texas farm. Unfortunately, Burroughs was never to realize this ideal of cooperative living: He ultimately had no profits, so he had no profits to share, he told Allen Ginsberg.

In May of 1949, however, when Neal and Jack were both still high on the idea of farming and ranching, Burroughs's advice from Pharr, Texas, was practical rather than theoretical. As a "professional farmer," he advised them not to buy good farmland if they were simply looking for a place to live. If they wanted to farm, though, they needed to keep in mind what he had learned through bitter experience in South Texas: Commodity prices were going down, but the expenses of farming were going up — the price-cost squeeze that caught Burroughs. Cattle, he says, are "strictly a rich man's deal," and people who think they can make money by raising them would do just as well making bets at a horse track.[13]

There was criticism from another quarter as well: Carolyn Cassady. In an interview with me, she expressed what had been her major concern over the ranch idea: "I don't recall any mention of Burroughs when we planned the ranch. That idea just grew little by little as big-hearted Jack wanted to include everyone, even if only as guests. We didn't even think of it as a 'commune,' a concept not yet evolved. I was just concerned my privacy with my two men might be jeopardized and that a lot of confusion, personality conflicts, mechanics could arise with their friends. Like, 'Who's the boss around here?' I like order, and I'm pretty set in my ways."[14]

She had personal reasons for not wanting to do this — privacy — but she also had philosophical motives that were strongly at odds with the cooperative idea that Jack and Burroughs shared: They didn't want a "boss-man," while Carolyn wanted to know "Who's the boss around here?" She likes order, which the cooperative structure lacked in the sense that everyone would periodically change hats. Neal's vision of the ranch was similarly disordered: "No hard and fast, naturally, rules or obligations or expectancies or any such bourgeois strains in our veins toward them."

And Carolyn Cassady was right that Burroughs was not included in the plan. In fact, Neal specifically excluded him: "I don't really mean to include

Burroughs (a probable impossibility anyhow) but I do love him and Joan so much you know."[15] You have to wonder why Burroughs — of all their friends (most of whom were welcome at the ranch) — was left out. Perhaps Neal knew by this point that Burroughs was not someone he could easily con, and that was not the cooperative spirit Neal was looking for in his ranch guests.

Still, Carolyn indulged Neal in "games of penny pinching" in order to finance the ranch idea. For once, as Carolyn says in her memoir, *Off the Road,* Neal did not go out and buy a new car but saved money instead — at least for the moment. Ironically, he would use the ranch money to buy a 1949 Hudson: the *On the Road* car. From wanting to be rooted sons of the soil, Kerouac and Cassady became the opposite: mobile and rootless, criss-crossing the country on mad dashes to some party or woman, on what farmer Burroughs saw as a trip "carefully selected to symbolize the basic fact of purposelessness."[16] This is a far cry from the sentiment Kerouac expressed to Hal Chase just two years earlier in 1947, when he was first discovering the United States as his real subject, calling it "a culture of livelihood, purpose, land and natural struggle." By making that choice of purposelessness over purpose, Kerouac forever abandoned the golden ideal of agrarian America he longed for and instead threw himself into, even helped create, a decidedly rootless America.

In spite of Burroughs's criticism of the "on the road" trip as symbolizing purposelessness, the book that came out of the trip actually dramatizes many of Burroughs's own views, a testament to how much attention Kerouac was paying to what Burroughs had to say against FDR, cops, liberals, and unions. As he describes Burroughs in *Road* (as "Bull"), "Bull had a sentimental streak about the old days in America . . . [when] the country was wild and brawling and free. . . . His chief hate was Washington bureaucracy; second to that liberals; then cops. He spent all his time talking and teaching others."[17] Certainly Kerouac had his own conservative worldview, but it is likely that Burroughs's influence (particularly his hatred of cops) can be felt in particular *Road* scenes such as those set in Oakland, where Sal Paradise (Kerouac) and Remi Boncoeur are hired as security guards to keep order in a sailors' barracks. In a letter Kerouac wrote to Neal Cassady about the irony of this situation, he says, "Yes, Neal, I am a cop — it is one of the funniest things ever to happen to me." But it is not Neal whom Kerouac really wants to know about his new job: It is William S. Burroughs.

"I can hardly wait to tell Burroughs about it," he adds.[18] Later, when Kerouac wrote up these scenes in fictional form in *On the Road,* that original audience of Burroughs is still there.

Perhaps Burroughs's presence is there in other ways, too, in the Oakland section of *Road* because, while Kerouac was playing cop in Oakland, Burroughs was playing outlaw in Texas, and Kerouac's buddies Allen Ginsberg and Neal "Horseskinner" Cassady were visiting Billy on the "ranch" in New Waverly. Interestingly, Kerouac transforms the Oakland barracks into a frontier town in Texas. The guards all want to be Texas Rangers, and a Wild West atmosphere prevails in the quarters. The chief guard is a man named Sledge, who "rigged himself out like a Texas Ranger of old. He wore a revolver down low, with ammunition belt, and carried a small quirt of some kind, and pieces of leather hanging everywhere, like a walking torture chamber: shiny shoes, low-hanging jacket, cocky hat, everything but boots."

Sal Paradise wants to play at being a Wild West character, too, and when Remi gives him a .32 automatic, he "used to take out my gun and play cowboys in the dark." Burroughs went so far as to brandish guns in Mexican saloons (as recounted in *Junky*), an act that, considering Burroughs's outlaw image, is not all that unexpected. However, it is surprising to see Sal doing almost the same thing in *Road* in a scene in which he goes into a bar and threatens a queer with his pistol. "I never understood why I did that; I knew queers all over the country," he says. Kerouac actually did this, if we can believe his letters to Neal Cassady — letters that recount many of these incidents but have none of this atmosphere of the Wild West, as does *Road.* That atmosphere, I contend, comes from the influence of the cowboy junky, Burroughs, who knew real Wild West lawmen firsthand.[19]

Maybe all boys from the Midwest and back East longed to be cowboys, and some of these similarities may be coincidental.[20] However, in the case of Burroughs and Kerouac, you can sometimes see Burroughs's letters from Texas and Mexico — as well as the South Texas section of *Junky* — moving straight into *Road.* In this respect, Burroughs's direct influence on *Road* is most apparent in the Mexico section of the book. Burroughs had been trying to tempt Kerouac and Ginsberg down to Mexico ever since he left South Texas and moved there in late 1949, telling Jack in one letter, for example, that "Mexico is undoubtedly the place for you. . . . [I]t is possible to enjoy oneself without interference."[21] In the fall of 1950, Kerouac and Neal Cassady could no longer resist such advertisements and crossed over the Texas border at Laredo, headed for Burroughs's Mexico City apartment.

Readers of Kerouac's youthfully exuberant second novel will certainly recall Kerouac's dramatization of this trip in the concluding section of *Road.* Dean Moriarty (Neal Cassady) and Sal Paradise finally stop crisscrossing the country from east to west and go south into Mexico, which fully lives up to Burroughs's description of a land where anything goes: The cops are harmless, the marijuana plentiful and potent, the whorehouses extremely friendly, and the Mexican people are all Indian versions of the ultrahip Dean Moriarty. Everything the United States lacks, Mexico offers.

Kerouac had been receiving Burroughs's letters about Mexico for a year before he wrote *Road,* and he had also read the unedited manuscript of *Junky,* which concludes in South Texas. Compare Burroughs's letters and scenes in *Junky* with *Road* on the following points:

Kerouac's description of the border town of Laredo, Texas: "Laredo was a sinister town that morning. . . . It was the bottom and dregs of America where all the heavy villains sink, where disoriented people have to go to be near a specific elsewhere they can slip into unnoticed."[22]

Burroughs's description of the Valley in *Junky:* "All the worst features of America have drained down to the Valley and concentrated there."[23]

Kerouac's description of Mexican cops: "The Mexicans looked at our baggage in a desultory way. They weren't like officials at all. They were lazy and tender. Dean couldn't stop staring at them. He turned to me. 'See how the cops are in this country. I can't believe it!' He rubbed his eyes. 'I'm dreaming.'" And later, too, in the Mexico section of *Road:* "Such lovely policemen God hath never wrought in America. No suspicions, no fuss, no bother."[24]

Burroughs's description of Mexican cops: "[A] man can walk the streets without being molested by some insolent cop. . . . Here a cop is on the level of a street-car conductor. He knows his place and stays there."[25] "A Jean de Brasse here ranks with a streetcar conductor. . . . Drunks sleep right on the sidewalk of the main drag. No cops bother them."[26]

Kerouac's description of a whorehouse: "We came to the whorehouse. It was a magnificent establishment of stucco in the golden sun."[27]

Burroughs's description after returning from a trip to Mexico City: "Fabulous whorehouses and restaurants."[28]

Kerouac's description in *Road* of the "oriental" character of Mexicans: "thousands of shifty hipsters hanging around doorways and whores looking out windows and strange shops that might have sold anything and narrow sidewalks crowded with Hong-Kong-like humanity." "Old men sat on chairs in the night and looked like Oriental junkies and oracles."[29]

Burroughs's description (in far less romantic terms than Kerouac) of the oriental character of Mexico: "These areas compare favorably with anything in Asia for sheer filth and poverty."[30] A letter to Ginsberg echoes this: "[Mexico] is basically an oriental culture (80% Indian) where everyone has mastered the art of minding his own business."[31] In a letter Burroughs wrote to Kerouac just about the time he was writing (or had just completed) the scroll version of *Road* [May 1951], he says, "Mexico is not simple or gay or idyllic. It is nothing like a French Canadian neighborhood. It is an Oriental country that reflects 2000 years of disease and poverty and degradation."[32]

Some points of comparison might not be so obvious as these. Kerouac's description of border towns being "dregs" that "sink" is clearly similar to Burroughs's "worst features . . . drained down . . . concentrated there," but there may be a veiled reference to Burroughs himself: It is a place that "disoriented people . . . can slip into unnoticed," an excellent description of El Hombre Invisible and also of Burroughs's position on the Texas border ("disoriented") preparatory to making the jump when his drug charges came up in New Orleans.

There is a particular context for their parallel comments about Mexican policemen. The key point is they don't "bother" people, a word repeated in both Burroughs's and Kerouac's descriptions. The point is an important one because Neal Cassady had recently been harassed and beaten up by cops in Brooklyn. Burroughs, in a letter to Allen Ginsberg, also contrasts how a Mexican cop coolly disarms him — even after Burroughs has threatened him with a gun — compared to the cop in the States who dislocated Lucien Carr's shoulder over simple drunken behavior. Burroughs knew Kerouac and Cassady would be attracted to a land where bar fights did not end in arrests and where cops and police minded their own business.[33] "I'm dreaming," says Dean Moriarty in *On the Road,* no doubt in this context.

Kerouac's emphasis on the oriental character of Mexicans brings to mind the Mexico section of *Junky,* but this section was not added until the summer of 1952, after the composition of *Road.*[34] It is thus difficult to date Burroughs's letter to Kerouac about the oriental character of Mexicans as having been written before Kerouac finished the scroll in late April 1951; however, we know from the May 1951 letter that Burroughs is responding to one Kerouac had sent him earlier, in which he painted a highly romanticized picture of Mexico. It was evidently much the same picture Kerouac later presented in *Road*. Therefore, Burroughs's reaction to this letter would presumably have been his reaction to the Mexico section of *Road,* too — and that is of great interest. A longer excerpt from this letter follows: "Your letter reflects some staggering misconceptions on the subject of Mexico. . . . Mexico is not simple or gay or idyllic. It is nothing like a French Canadian naborhood [*sic*]. . . . Above all don't expect settled secure naborhoods [*sic*] like extended 19th century families where everybody knows everybody and no one has to take any shit off anybody."[35]

Burroughs is thus the first reader to criticize Kerouac's romanticizing of Mexico, and he zeroes in on what later (postcolonial) critics would expose in *Road:* Kerouac's false identification with the Mexican people. In his books, Kerouac often used his French Canadian Canuck status to identify himself with the people he calls, after Oswald Spengler, the "fellaheen," a salt-of-the-earth, generic race that has survived throughout history. Burroughs is having none of this from Kerouac: "Mexico is not . . . like a French Canadian naborhood [*sic*]." Kerouac has made the mistake of projecting his own identity onto the foreigners rather than seeing them as the jaded factualists Burroughs does — as a people characterized by "poverty," "slavery," and "stupidity." Coincidentally, Burroughs himself was at this very moment writing a Mexico section of *Junky* (either the end of the book, or the beginning of *Queer*), so his own work can be seen as written not necessarily in reaction to Kerouac's idealization of Mexico but certainly with an awareness of what he calls Kerouac's "staggering misconceptions."[36]

The question arises, though, as to why Burroughs revised his picture of Mexico as a gay land where everything goes, as he had originally written to Kerouac. Perhaps he no longer needed to pen such advertisements for Mexico, having successfully lured Kerouac and Cassady there for a visit. The visa problems Burroughs was having with corrupt Mexican bureaucrats might also have had something to do with his change of heart. However, his restatement of his outlook on Mexico may have occurred after reading Kerouac's version of what Burroughs had been saying to him for more than a year about Mexico: It's a place of total freedom, where everyone leaves you alone. That's the *Road* version of Mexico. Reading Kerouac's version of that myth, Burroughs offers a strong corrective, which sometimes occurs only when we see someone else saying what we have previously said or written.

There is another way, though, in which Kerouac's identification with Mexico and Mexicans places Burroughs in a different light, one that reveals his more patrician upbringing. In a section of *Road,* Kerouac falls for a Mexican girl named Terry, whom he meets in a bus station. He joins her on the migrant farmworker trail in California's Central Valley and learns to pick cotton and grapes. The romantic life of living off the land that Kerouac once had briefly becomes real for him: "I thought I had found my life work," he says about his job picking cotton for a $1.50 a day. "I was a man of the earth, precisely as I had dreamed I would be, in Paterson." Later he claims he actually is a Mexican laborer: "They thought I was a Mexican, of course, and in a way I am."[37]

While Kerouac is working as a laborer for $1.50 a day, Burroughs is *hiring* laborers for about the same pay or even less. The point of contrast with Burroughs is this: Burroughs never saw himself as being anything like the illegal laborers he employed. As John Houghton Allen points out in his Valley memoir, such a separation between *patrones* [bosses] and *peones* [workers] was both inevitable and one of the least pleasant aspects of being an Anglo farmer or rancher in South Texas: "I was only the figurehead, understand, the Mexicans would never allow me to be anything but their *patrón*. And that can be a lonely blessing."[38] Burroughs is more matter-of-fact about the patrón/peón relationship, simply pointing out that he was not the one who did the "actual work." Kerouac, however, as a French Canadian–Indian born into the working class, is able to feel solidarity with these laborers in a way that Burroughs (or John Allen) never could. The farthest Burroughs goes is to say (as does Allen) that he hopes to be reborn a Mexican — a sentiment almost as Romantic as Kerouac's identification with the fellaheen.[39] Overall, though, the distance he creates between himself and his laborers (in his letters at least) reflects Herbert Huncke's assessment of Burroughs as a farmer: "His [Kells's] father had sent him down to Texas, and of course he had nothing more to do than just sit back and collect."[40] Burroughs was a gentleman farmer; Kerouac a gentleman laborer.

Kerouac's *On the Road,* written "spontaneously" in twenty-one days and based closely on Kerouac's own real-life adventures, is a book of such openness and a near telepathic ability to communicate (as Ginsberg said) that readers often confuse its content with the truth or facts. One of the book's discrepancies, as Burroughs rather testily points out in *The Adding Machine,* has to do with South Texas and Old Bull Lee's Reichian orgone accumulator in Algiers, Louisiana. The disputed scene in Kerouac's novel begins with Old Bull Lee asking Kerouac and Cassady (who are visiting Bull

Lee in Louisiana), "Say, why don't you fellows try my orgone accumulator? Put some juice in your bones. I always rush up and take off ninety miles an hour for the nearest whorehouse, hor-hor-hor!" A description of the accumulator follows: "The orgone accumulator is an ordinary box big enough for a man to sit inside on a chair: a layer of wood, a layer of metal, and another layer of wood gather in orgones from the atmosphere and hold them captive long enough for the human body to absorb more than a usual share. According to Reich, orgones are vibratory atmospheric atoms of the life-principle. People get cancer because they run out of orgones. Old Bull thought his orgone accumulator would be improved if the wood he used was as organic as possible, so he tied bushy bayou leaves and twigs to his mystical outhouse."[41] Burroughs hated this scene in *Road* and explained why in an essay in *The Adding Machine:* "Kerouac described my orgone box in *On the Road* — a pretty good trick as he never set foot on the South Texas farm. He had me taking morphine. . . . The fact is that I was not using junk at that time, and even if I had been I certainly would not have done so in an orgone accumulator. . . . In Algiers . . . I was far too busy with a habit to build an accumulator. Neal Cassady did visit me at the South Texas farm, but never used the orgone accumulator. Since Kerouac presumably got the story of my first accumulator from Cassady, whose tendency to exaggerate rivaled Jack's, it's a wonder they didn't have me throwing orgies in the accumulator for the amusement of the wetbacks."[42]

It is thus no accident that Burroughs built his first accumulator in South Texas rather than Louisiana: He was off the junk and looking for a new fix. Moreover, in the Valley he was living in a place that he felt was deadly. In response to this pestilential atmosphere, he says, he "built an orgone accumulator, and the gimmick really works. The man [Wilhelm Reich] is not crazy, he's a fucking genius," he told Jack Kerouac in a letter.[43]

One of the best descriptions of this first orgone accumulator — and similar to that in *Road* — appears in an unpublished interview James Grauerholz conducted with Burroughs in 1974: "[The orgone box] was in South Texas; Kells and I made it, and it was a sloppy job, too. . . . We had some kind of jerry-built hut to start with and sloppily nailed sheet iron inside that. Then inside that we had another orgone box made out of an old icebox which you lowered down over yourself, and then we had a little accumulator made out of one of those jerry cans, we just covered that over in burlap and various stuff — we were getting three levels. I think that's much more potent than all the levels together."[44]

Kells Elvins was also interested in immortality schemes, and he no doubt spent time lowered into the fridge, too. It must have been an odd sight. In *The Adding Machine* (1985), Burroughs says, "Kells' wetbacks watched dubiously from a distance, muttering something in Spanish about *Brujerías* — witchcraft."[45]

This gets a bit into the line of shoptalk among Beat scholars, but it is worth asking how Kerouac knew to describe Burroughs's own version of an orgone accumulator if he had not actually seen it in South Texas and it didn't exist in Louisiana. Kerouac scholar Dave Moore and I recently hashed out the details on this.[46] In *The Adding Machine,* Burroughs says that Neal Cassady visited him in South Texas, and if that is the case, perhaps Kerouac heard the description from Neal firsthand (as Burroughs believed). However, Carolyn Cassady and Dave Moore, in their editing of Cassady's letters, have created a thorough chronology of Neal's life during those years and can account for no South Texas visit. Still, it is odd that Burroughs would so definitely associate Cassady with a South Texas visit and the accumulator. If it happened, my guess is that it was during September of 1947, when Cassady spent a whole month living with Burroughs in East Texas. Billy was probably making frequent trips to check up on his South Texas farming interests, and it is not unlikely that Neal accompanied him on one of these visits. Neal never wrote about such a trip, however, and his friends do not mention it either. Moreover, even if he did make the trip, Burroughs did not build the accumulator until at least a year later.[47]

A more likely source, however, is found in several pages of *Junky* recently restored by Oliver Harris in the fiftieth-anniversary definitive edition of the book. Harris's version includes the long-missing chapter 28, which is a five-page discussion of the theories of Wilhelm Reich and of Burroughs's construction and testing of a Reichian accumulator. In the original "Junk" manuscript read by Kerouac just before he wrote *Road,* this material was embedded in Burroughs's account of the Valley, so Kerouac knew something about the contraption. Readers of the published book did not, and without this section, they must have been puzzled by Burroughs's references to "orgones." According to the restored chapter, the accumulator actually revitalized Burroughs in the Valley: "After using the accumulator for several days my energy came back to normal. I began to eat, and could not sleep more than eight hours. I was out of the post cure drag."[48] Anecdotal information confirms Burroughs's renewed vitality. Blondie, for example, recognized pictures of Burroughs taken a couple of years later in Mexico

City — when Burroughs was back on heroin and had lost weight — but said the man he knew in the Valley in 1949 was heavier.

Kerouac would have read chapter 28 before writing *On the Road* and would thus have read Burroughs's description of the accumulator and instructions for how to build one. Still, the description of the contraption in chapter 28 is fairly dry and scientific compared to Kerouac's humorous account of it in *On the Road* — one much more in line with the description Burroughs gave to James Grauerholz decades later: "[I]t was a sloppy job."

The question remains, though: Why did Kerouac transplant the orgone accumulator from South Texas to Burroughs's junky pad in Algiers, Louisiana? Obviously, for purposes of compression (too many confusing settings) and sensation: Every odd idea of William S. Burroughs is poured into the Old Bull Lee section in *Road*, regardless of whether they make sense together. Like Burroughs's construction of the accumulator, Kerouac's portrait of Burroughs in *On the Road* is "a sloppy job." A junky in an orgone accumulator? Never. Burroughs in South Texas, trying to kick, drinking Kells's homemade gin, and suffering in a land Reich would say was plagued by DOR (Deadly Orgone Radiation)? Yes. He needed all the levels he could get.

ASUSTADO

The Death of Joan Burroughs

It's the most infamous event in the controversial life of William S. Burroughs — the night he accidentally killed his wife, Joan, in a Mexico City apartment while attempting to shoot a drink glass off her head. The press styled it a "William Tell" killing. The shooting took place on September 6, 1951, at a party in the third-floor apartment of John Healy, who worked downstairs at the Bounty bar, a watering hole for Americans attending nearby Mexico City College, such as Burroughs. That evening, Burroughs had arranged to sell a .380 Czech-made Star pistol, but the buyer never showed up at the party. Several other people were in the living room of the multiroom apartment when Joan placed a glass on her head and (by most accounts) announced — as if it were a regular routine with them — that it was time for her and Bill to perform their William Tell act. Burroughs aimed the Star .380 badly, missed the glass, and put a bullet in the upper left portion of her forehead. Joan died a couple of hours later at the Cruz Roja hospital. Burroughs was thirty-seven years old. He was not yet a published writer.[1]

Initially, Burroughs confessed the truth before a group of reporters and said that he had killed her by attempting to shoot a drink glass off of her head. This started the William Tell story. However, immediately after Burroughs made this statement, his lawyer, Bernabé Jurado, swooped in and had him change his story — right there in front of the assembled members of the press. No, he told Burroughs, you were checking the gun for bullets, and it accidentally went off. Don't you remember? This doctoring of the story was of course reported by the press, who also added a jealousy angle: Burroughs had shot his wife because of a love triangle, the third "angle" of which was never determined, but it might have been the Marxist novelist (and former husband of better-known Marxist novelist Josephine Herbst) John Herrmann, who was a friend (and possibly a lover) of Joan's. The Mexican press discovered that Burroughs and Joan had recently considered getting divorced, and Burroughs's defense lawyer had to go out of his way to establish how much Burroughs loved his wife and how happily married they were. One can only speculate what the jury would have thought had they known that Burroughs, at the time of the shooting, had just returned from a South American vacation with his paid lover, Lewis Marker, and that Marker was in John Healy's apartment when Bill shot Joan.

The facts of what happened that night have always been a subject of intense interest for not only Burroughs scholars but also American literary historians in general, for there is no other literary murder in the twentieth century that is quite so fascinating — or so tragic — in all of its elements. No one has studied this case more, however, than William S. Burroughs's longtime companion, secretary, and collaborator, James Grauerholz, who has spent two decades sorting through the circumstances of Joan's death. The result of his investigations is an exhaustive paper titled "The Death of Joan Vollmer: What Really Happened?" In it, Grauerholz takes the reader through all of the existing evidence much as a juror would be taken through a trial. Of course, in the end we are left with as many questions as answers, for although it is nearly certain that Joan's death was an accident, there are still nagging questions about Burroughs's unconscious intentions, which will never be fully sorted out. It is arguable, however, that Burroughs himself spent the rest of his life sorting them out in more or less veiled ways in his writings. As he says in his "Introduction" to *Queer,* "I am forced to the appalling conclusion that I would never have become a writer but for Joan's death, and to a realization of the extent to which this event has motivated and formulated my writing."[2]

My own contribution to this aspect of Burroughs's biography has been in researching Burroughs's time in South Texas with regard to the way his experiences on the border might somehow have presaged the disastrous events of September 1951. After all, he shot Joan less than two years after they left the Valley. I also wanted to know what the local reaction was to the story. I found out a good deal more than I expected to.

Pat Paris remembers hearing the news of Joan's death, but long before it occurred, she had forebodings that something tragic was going to happen to Kells and Billy and their crowd: "He and Billy used to go across [to Mexico] and buy alcohol and make their own gin. I began to distance myself from Kells, right after he introduced Billy to that group of people. I thought they were dangerous. I lived at home with my mother and father and my sister and my nephew, and I felt like someday something tragic was going to happen. Yes, I just felt they were too far out. You see, I was fairly naïve and probably Kells was; when we met him [in 1945] he was not like that."[3]

She was therefore not at all surprised by the news in September of 1951 that Billy had shot Joan. "Do you remember the local reaction to the news?" I asked her. "If it was in the paper," Pat said, "I don't remember it. I just remember word got around, but I didn't have much contact with any of those people. It wasn't [a surprise]. Well, I said, something was going to happen." In a later interview she told me it was Kells himself, back for a visit to the Valley in 1956, who told her the news.

Pat Paris did not remember the story showing up in the local paper, but it actually did, both in Harlingen and McAllen. The Harlingen paper even ran the story on the front page. Jim McKone, who lived in McAllen and worked for the *Monitor,* remembers the local coverage and recalls hearing a very particular response to the story of the man from Pharr killing his wife in Mexico City by attempting to shoot a drink glass off her head and missing: "People in McAllen said, 'It sounds like something someone from Pharr would do,'" according to McKone. "There was this big city-little city rivalry between McAllen and Pharr — there still is," he explained. "People in McAllen saw this as a reason to make fun of Pharr."[4]

Valley newspaper coverage of the story was mostly drawn from the Associated Press wire stories, but since Burroughs had lived in Pharr and owned farmland, there was a local angle, too. *The Valley Morning Star* for September 8, 1951, featured the story of Joan's death on the front page, headlined "Wealthy Pharr Man Held in Death of Wife: William S. Burroughs Says Shot Accidental in Mexico City." The story led off as follows: "Mexico City (AP): A wealthy Texan whose wife was shot to death Thursday night was quoted by police Friday as saying he had fired at a glass of gin balanced on her head. Later he denied this. William Seward Burroughs, 37-year-old Pharr, Texas, rancher and a member of the Burroughs adding machine family, was lodged in the penitentiary." The jump to page two reads "Wealthy Pharr Man Held in Death of Wife."

A separate story just below the main story is headlined "Friend Sure Case Accident," and it is an interview with Kells Elvins. In fact, this description of Burroughs by Elvins amounts to — as far as I know — Kells's only statement about Burroughs to appear anywhere in print. (Elvins's letters to Burroughs are lost.) In the article, Elvins says that he is "certain" the shooting was an accident and that Burroughs "was very much in love with his wife. They had been married about five years. She was very attractive." Calculated or not, such talk helped establish the belief that Burroughs was married to Joan, for any other arrangement would have been suspect, and Elvins claims they had been married for five years. The truth, though, was that Burroughs and Joan had never married but considered their cohabitation to amount to a common-law marriage. The fact that they were "very much in love" was also important in that the Mexican papers had reported the "jealousy angle." If he truly loved her and yet shot her, it must have been an accident; if his love were suspect, he might have had reason to miss the glass. Even more devastating would have been the revelation that Burroughs was a homosexual.

Elvins also discusses his friend's character in this interview. What he says supports Burroughs's innocence, but it also gives a glimpse into Burroughs's personality in a way that suggests that it was not purely accidental that Burroughs found himself in the middle of such a bizarre story: "I have known him for years," Elvins says of Burroughs. "He is a very interesting person. He has a very, very fine mind, if a bit unusual. His interests are varied. He did quite a bit of work in anthropology, especially among Aztec and Mayan ruins." It sounds like a letter of recommendation more than it does a description of a man who has just shot his wife while drunk at a party.[5]

Joan, on the other hand, receives very little attention in the various local newspaper articles: The focus is on the grandson of the inventor of the adding machine, whose mind is "fine" but "a bit unusual" and whose "interests are varied." Joan is described by where she grew up (Ossining, New York), her father's profession (a chemist), and the identity of her previous husband (Paul Adams). Apparently, she had neither a mind to speak of nor any interests.

The McAllen paper, *The Valley Evening Monitor,* did not pick up the story until September 9, when it ran it on page two under the headline "Pistol Slip Killed Wife, Pharr Man Says." A subtitle reads "Wed in Pharr," but no evidence of Burroughs's marriage to Joan Vollmer is given — nor is there any record in Hidalgo County of the two marrying there. A much more interesting follow-up story appeared in the *Monitor* on September 11, 1951. It is illustrated by one of the *La Prensa* photos of Burroughs after he was arrested ("his hair disheveled and his clothes wrinkled," as the *Morning Star* article describes him) and features the imperative headline "Ask Freedom for Burroughs." This headline has special irony since Burroughs would become famous as one of the century's radical individualists, but one wonders about the apparent partisanship in the headline. Was it Kells's influence?[6]

This was the most I could find out about the reaction in the Valley — until I met Ted Marak through Pat Paris, who had recently learned that Ted was living in Boerne, Texas. She had not spoken to him in more than fifty years, but he was very cordial when she called him out of the blue, and he also agreed to help me with my research. When I conducted my initial interview with him over the phone, practically the first thing he told me was that not only did he know Billy Burroughs, but he was also in the Mexico City apartment the night Billy shot Joan. "Really?" I asked and added frankly, "None of the biographies of Burroughs makes mention of you. Or at least no one who was interviewed about that night later mentioned you being there." In fact, reference to Ted Marak occurs neither in the interviews with Burroughs nor in those with Burroughs's friends who were sources for earlier biographies of Burroughs. I told Ted as much, but he was telling the truth, so he was unimpressed. Here is Ted's account of that night:

RJ: Tell me about the trip to Mexico when you found yourself at the party where Joan was shot.

TM: They [Kells and Marianne Elvins] went down, and then I came down because there was crap to do around McAllen. But I went down, and I know that I met them. If I remember right, this hotel was by that big park that's in the center of Mexico City. I know that evening we all met at the hotel. I don't know if it was a suite or how big it was. I know I met some other people at a bar downstairs. We went up. We no more than got there — I don't know what time it was — I never said hello to Billy, I don't think I even saw Kells or whomever he was with. There was a lot of people there.

RJ: How many?

TM: It was a group of people, maybe fifteen people scattered around, and I'm in a room, from here to that washroom or better [about twenty feet away], and we were smoking a little pot, and we were drinking a little. I was drinking a little more gin, and I hear this report, a revolver report. And dead silence. And then suddenly I hear Billy say, "Quit hamming it up, Joan. Get up!" And then there was a murmur, and pretty soon, well, things started happening. He'd shot Joan right between the eyes, and then everything was just bedlam.

RJ: What do you mean, bedlam?

TM: Oh, people were screaming and hollering. Hell, they said her brains were all over the goddamn wall or something. That's what people said afterwards that were there.

RJ: You didn't actually go in and see any of this?

TM: Oh, no, I heard the report. I don't know if it was a .38.

RJ: What did you hear that night about how it happened? Anything?

TM: No, because the police started coming in there, and I got out in the hall, and they're jabbering in Spanish, and I don't know any Spanish enough to get along with, and I already had a problem in Reynosa. I'd whacked a cop — and that's a federal offense — and got put up in their hoosegow for a couple of nights. . . . They had given me a persona non grata, don't ever come back to Mexico. I wasn't even supposed to be in Mexico. But I didn't know how far that went, and all I could think about was, "Well, make yourself very small, get the shit out of there." And that's what I did. It was just bedlam, women were screaming.

RJ: Do you remember anyone else who was there? Do you think Kells was there?

TM: I hadn't been drinking with him [that night]. But I'm pretty sure Kells was there. Talking with him later, I got the picture. He said Billy said, "Joan, put that piece of fruit on your head," and Joan did it, and he fired. That's when I was coming in among these people. And he [Kells] repeated what I said ["Quit hamming it up, Joan"]. It sounded like he was an eyewitness.

Keep in mind that Ted Marak had never spoken to any researcher about this night — or about Burroughs at all — until I contacted him in the summer of 2002. Nor had he, at the time, read any of Burroughs's books or any biographical accounts of his life: Ted Marak knew that Billy had gone on to fame by writing *Naked Lunch,* but Marak has lived a long, fascinating life and has known many famous (and infamous) people, so Billy's later renown was not something that strongly defined Marak's past. Realizing that Marak's knowledge of that night's events is limited to his own memories of September 6, 1951, it is clear that several details in his story prove its reliability. James Grauerholz has pointed out these details to me: "Ted's memory of the apartment does match the oral and written eyewitness descriptions I have studied. His story is quite believable. The 'big park that's in the center of Mexico City' would be Zapultepec, which indeed is quite near Colonia Roma neighborhood, at the west end of Paseo de la Peralta. 'The hotel' where 'that evening we all met' may have been west of Col. Roma near the park. The bar 'downstairs' where Ted 'met some other people' and then 'went up' to the 'suite' was of course The Bounty Bar & Grill. What this points to is the likely existence of many more eyewitnesses — or ear witnesses — who were in the vicinity of Bill & Joan at the fatal moment."[7]

James Grauerholz's characterization of Ted as an "ear witness" is important, for it accounts for the fact that Ted heard the shot (but did not see it) and heard William's reaction ("Quit hamming it up, Joan") but was in the next room and thus gets key details wrong. Perhaps he learned about them through rumors that surfaced the next day or later. For example, there was no brain matter on the wall since the autopsy on Joan revealed no exit wound; moreover, she did not put a piece of fruit on her head. However, as Grauerholz says, Ted's statement is provocative because it confirms that there were more than just the five people in the apartment that Grauerholz previously identified (Joan, Bill, Lewis Marker, Eddie Woods, and Betty Jones). These other unidentified people were not in the actual room where the shooting occurred but were in a room next to it. Ted says there were several rooms in the apartment, and in fact there were six.

More important, Ted's story corroborates a crucial element in Burroughs's defense: "Quit hamming it up, Joan," Burroughs's immediate reaction to the shooting, is the statement of a man who is not aware of what he has done — meaning that he did not intentionally mean to shoot her. Eddie Woods, who had every reason to dislike Burroughs, told Ted Morgan essentially the same story in a 1985 interview, although he did not recall with Marak's accuracy the exact words Burroughs spoke after the shooting:

> And then *bang!* — the noise, that's the first impression I had, was the noise. Next thing I knew, the next impression I had was that glass on the floor . . . rolling around in concentric circles on the floor. Then I looked at her, and her head was over to one side. Well, I thought, "She's kidding," you know. That's the first thing you think, and then I heard Marker say, "Bill, I think you hit her." And then [Bill] said, "No!" And he started towards her, you know, and Marker got there first, and I got over there, too, and then I saw the hole in her temple, a little blue hole, and Burroughs jumped on her lap and he said, "Joan! Joan! Joan!" I mean, he was out of it, in shock that this happened. Again, to me, that's evi-

> dence it was absolutely an accident. He was shocked that he had hit her, and he was trying to wake her up.[8]

Burroughs's own initial story, told to *La Prensa,* matches Woods's (and Marak's) recollections that he thought Joan was faking an injury: "At first, I thought she was attempting a joke when she fell down, and I went to where she was." It would have been at this point that he would have said, "Quit hamming it up, Joan," the line Ted Marak recalled. When I interviewed Marak on tape, he actually changed his voice to sound like Burroughs as he said this line.

One of the most obvious discrepancies between Marak's story and other accounts is that Joan did not put a piece of fruit on her head, but a drink glass. Every eyewitness account confirms this. However, Ted never claimed to have seen a piece of fruit, only to have heard the shot. Subsequently, someone (Kells?) told him the target had been a piece of fruit, or at least that's what I thought. When Matt McClung and I were interviewing Ted for a documentary on Burroughs in South Texas *(Border Beat),* I explained to Ted that his presence as an "ear witness" rather than an eyewitness might be confusing to people watching the film since many of them would know Burroughs had been aiming at a drink glass (rather than William Tell's apple) on Joan's head. "Well," he told me, "I guess I keep saying that because Billy used to shoot pieces of fruit off Joan's head in the Valley." "In Kells's orchard?" I asked him, and he said, yes, that Billy had shot either oranges or grapefruits off of her head — he couldn't remember which. His memory jogged, he continued, with Matt's camera recording his recollections about Billy and Joan's William Tell acts: "But that was something he did quite often. Joan would be walking around, he'd pick up a piece of fruit, throw it to her, she would set it on there, and 'bam!' he would hit it off. He was a good shot. Just missed once. . . . Well, Billy was a hell of a shot. As an example, you could throw a piece of grapefruit across the lawn and he could 'bam!' hit it moving. So that night when he shot Joan . . . I knew that Billy had tried to shoot something off Joan's head. It just came to my mind. Okay, you know, Billy's drunk, and I thought, 'Well, Billy's shot again.' That's a hell of a place to shoot, crowd of people and all."[9] This eyewitness account of Billy's shooting fruit off Joan's head frankly took me aback, for no one has ever reported seeing Billy and Joan perform such an act prior to the ill-fated evening in Mexico City. In Ted's mind, though, Billy and Joanie were just up to their usual antics, but with an unexpected twist.

Although no one has ever reported seeing Billy and Joan practice the act, Burroughs's contradictory statements on this point have long led to speculation that he and Joan might well have done so. At first he denied the whole William Tell story, sticking to Jurado's invented version that the gun had gone off by accident. As Burroughs told Conrad Knickerbocker in a *Paris Review* interview in 1965, "I had a revolver that I was planning to sell to a friend. I was checking it over and it went off — killed her. A rumor started that I was trying to shoot a glass of champagne from her head, William Tell-style. Absurd and false."[10] Later Burroughs revised this account to say that he had in fact tried to shoot at a glass but had "Never. Never. Never" performed the William Tell act with Joan before that night — as he told Howard Brookner in a 1980 documentary film. "Just an absolute piece of insanity," he said.[11]

The latter is certainly true, but Lewis Marker's testimony seems to corroborate Marak's story that Burroughs had done this before. Marker, who became more and more inebriated in his 1985 interview with Ted Morgan, had the following to say on the subject: "But at the very tail end, Bill said something to the effect that he was going to do a William Tell thing, you know, with the glass on the head. . . . There was some mention of William Tell; there was no suggestion, that I recall, that it had been done in the past, you know, but clearly, the implications are obvious, you know. Probably even mentioned the glass on the head or something like that, since [they] didn't have an apple. . . . You could ascribe it to confidence in his marksmanship, or anything you want to ascribe it to, but there was no particular indication that I could see, as to why she was agreeable to the little act."[12]

Although he makes no direct assertion that Burroughs and Joan had done this before, it seems clear that Marker is implying that he could not understand why Joan would have been "agreeable" to the act unless they had practiced it before: "Clearly, the implications are obvious, you know."

If this was the case, we can extend the life-and-death drama Bill and Joan were performing well back into the mid-1940s. It is an eerie scene to imagine, Billy shooting fruit off Joan's head in a South Texas orchard, and it certainly confirms Pat Paris's feeling about these people — that they were just "too far out . . . something tragic was bound to happen." Of course, Ted's testimony also puts Burroughs's inconsistent story about the shooting in a new light. Burroughs either blanked their rehearsals out of his mind, or he was simply lying. And you can see why he might. Looking back on those William Tell routines in the Valley must have been too painful, so clearly did they presage what was to occur later. Why were he and Joan rehearsing her death? he must have asked himself, and no sane answer came back.

In the "Introduction" to *Queer,* Burroughs says — to be blunt — that shooting his wife made him become a writer. His life was a nightmare thereafter, and the only way he could find his way of it was to "write his way out," as he says — not only in the writing of *Queer* but in other stories as well, as I have argued in relation to his story "Tiger in the Valley." He never got over shooting Joan and was, as James Grauerholz points out, still writing about her in his journals just days before his own death in 1997.

Perhaps the wisdom of the Mexican people is helpful in explaining his life in this respect. In Mexico, when you witness an act of violence or a tragic event, it stays with you and in a sense haunts you. Blondie, Juan Ochoa tells me, was deeply affected by the sight of Gene Terry's lifeless body that night at Joe's Place: "[Blondie] saw the body draped in a tablecloth when they were taking it out. He noted that it was limp and still oozing blood. But my Uncle said Blondie was traumatized by it. I asked him, 'Did it scare him?' and my uncle said, 'It certainly left an impression.' That's the term in Spanish — *asustado* [frightened] — and you have to go and get a *curandero* [spiritual healer] to give you a 'sweep' so you can sleep at night."

Folk wisdom in Mexico ascribes *susto* [a fright, scare] to an outside agency. The sight of something horrifying — such as your wife with a bullet in her head — steals your soul and leaves you prey to this fear. Like a possessing entity, the fear must be removed in order for you to regain your sense of well-being and wholeness. A curandero can accomplish this through a variety of means. Most commonly, you are given a susto tea made from anis (the tea is also blessed), or you undergo a sweeping with tree branches that removes the spirit. If successful, this cure leaves the patient free of the unsettling fears brought on by the original trauma.

Late in life Burroughs did try to have "the ugly spirit" removed in a home exorcism. His own cure for possession had been to write — writing as exorcism. It did not work, though, if you read the "Foreword" to *Queer* carefully. Even thirty years after writing the book, he felt this same drag or fear as he reread the work and realized he was under the "constant threat of possession." Perhaps, however, if that fear had ended, Burroughs would have stopped writing. In Mexico, his condition would have been clear: The death of Joan left Burroughs asustado.

ATROPHIED AFTERWORD

Of course, any biography is just a rough approximation of the truth.
— William S. Burroughs

In the summer of 2001 James Grauerholz and I drove up Jackson Road toward Edinburg in my oil-burning Mazda pickup. Grauerholz was Burroughs's longtime companion and is now his literary executor. More than that, he is Burroughs's official biographer and one of the preeminent Beat scholars. He has made it a point to visit every place Burroughs lived, and he is passionately interested in all of the details of his good friend William's past, particularly the period before William S. Burroughs was William S. Burroughs. In this respect we talked about being biographers and about trying to re-create the past through interviews, research, and plain old sleuthing.

James told me about his and William's interest in time travel, and I told him that, after doing so much research on the Valley of that period, I sometimes imagined I was actually back in the 1940s. We drove past orange groves and old farmhouses off Jackson road and past the raised banks of a canal bringing water from the Rio Grande to the farm fields, and if you let your eyes look in just the right direction, you could almost feel you were back in those times. As we drove along the business highway through Edinburg, James, with an acute eye for history, pointed out old buildings — warehouses, bars, restaurants — that Billy and Kells might well have frequented.

We left Edinburg and headed east out into the country where Burroughs's land was. Since I am a professor of American literature, James picked my brain about Burroughs's place in the canon. I told him I considered Burroughs one of the great American writers of the twentieth century and would put him in a line with writers such as Twain, Melville, and Hammett, who were particularly attuned to this country's most original contribution to the English language — argot, slang, subterranean lingo. Among European writers, I said, he had to be mentioned with the great innovators in print, such as Joyce and Beckett. "I put my money on the right horse, then, you think?" he asked me. I nodded, understanding. You see, James could well have attached himself to another great writer: In fact, when James moved to New York City in 1974 (at the age of twenty-one), he first sought out Allen Ginsberg. However, Ginsberg — always prescient in such matters — pointed out to James that it was Burroughs he was really interested in. Ginsberg introduced the two.

We drove down Monte Cristo past the boys' reform school and a golf course and turned onto César Chávez, where Billy's Edinburg land is. That day, it was planted in purple cabbage. James got out of my truck, surveyed the land, and was drawn to the northwest corner of the property, where there was a berm. He stepped up onto the mound and said, "This is how I imagine William would have stood, right here." He placed his arms akimbo and surveyed the productive fields. Not much in the vista would have been out of place fifty years ago, and again it was easy to imagine time had turned back. But we were both biographers standing in a field of cabbage that, except to us, had no special significance.

James is one of the great literary men in the United States and a remarkable man in his own right. Burroughs attracted extraordinary people to him throughout his life and all across the world, including in the Valley. Through my research I have had the great pleasure of meeting Ted Marak, Pat Paris, Blondie, Luís Alejos, Anna Mae Kelly, and many others who lived in the Valley in the 1940s. Pat Paris, in her late seventies now, is a beautiful, gracious, and highly intelligent matriarch of the Valley. El Blondie, who worked as a cab driver for decades and is now a retired civil servant, has a Solomon-like wisdom about him. Luís Alejos, who dragged Terry's body out of the lion cage, has a brother who did the musical scores for Sam Peckinpah's Mexico films *The Ballad of Cable Hogue* and *The Wild Bunch,* and Luís himself continues to perform masterfully in musical trios. For Ted Marak, Billy Burroughs was among dozens of major twentieth-century figures he knew in his career as a casino operator around the world. It cannot have been an accident that these South Texans and norte mexicanos all knew Kells and Billy. Something back then worked to set these people in each others' path, something that continues to bring together brilliant, talented people who are undoubtedly finding each other right now.

Of course, it was Kells who brought them all together. For that reason, Kells is much more central to this book than he is to any other book about Burroughs. His son, Peter, encouraged my research throughout the writing of this work, and our correspondence includes the following summary of his father's fascinating life: "I knew that he was a complex individual with many sides — the straight-arrow married Harvard student and the accountant at Price Waterhouse whom I don't remember, the psychologist in Huntsville, the notorious womanizer, the brave Marine, the abusive husband in Mexico, the alcoholic playboy of the Western World, the occasional writer of short stories."[1]

As I learned more and more about Kells's adventures in South Texas, I kept thinking of Grauerholz's comparison of Kells to Neal Cassady because the association rings true. Billy hung around Kells because Kells was guaranteed to have something of interest going, no matter where he lived — and he lived all around the world. But I also began to discern something about Kells's feelings toward Billy. It was Kells who, in 1938, first encouraged Burroughs to be a writer, and it was Kells who later suggested, just after Billy left the Valley, that he write down a factual account of his life as an addict. Why would he have suggested this to Billy? I have to think he did so because, as a trained psychologist, Kells knew his friend was deeply troubled in many ways. Perhaps by putting his experiences on paper, he could begin to address those problems. Later, when he wrote the sequel to *Junky* — *Queer* — Burroughs directly subscribed to this theory of writing as a cure.

It was difficult finding people who knew Billy down here, but I had no trouble finding people who remembered Kells, either personally or professionally. My neighbor across the street remembered him as one of his father's associates in the oil business.

To do the research for this book, I have often had only to drive down the road a few miles or, in the case of my neighbor, cross the street. Behind that neighbor lived Joe Ortega's niece, whose sister provided me with the postcards of Joe's Place published in this book. Pat Paris lives a few blocks from me. Another neighbor's parents knew Kells and were present at a dinner party Pat threw for Kells on his last trip to the Valley. And so on . . .

Grauerholz has told me that for this reason — Kells's place on the social register — the type of research I have done on Burroughs in the Valley could probably not be done anywhere else. For example, in New Orleans he knew only drug dealers, whose lifespan is pretty short, in general. In East Texas, his neighbors were all quite old even at the time. But in South Texas, Burroughs met everyone because of Kells's social contacts. Otherwise, who would remember Billy? Grauerholz has also told me that what distinguishes these people's accounts of Burroughs is that they saw him before he was known as a writer, and they thus provide a picture of him that is very accurate in some respects — and often quite unflattering. Burroughs encouraged Ted Morgan to find people who would say critical things about him, but not much of that made it into *Literary Outlaw*. The South Texans and Mexicans I have interviewed give us that glimpse of Burroughs before anyone had any reason to guess they were in the presence of someone who would become an icon of the twentieth century. The book thus captures Burroughs at his unguarded best and worst.

His view of the Valley reflects both of these aspects. When I first read Burroughs's account of the Valley in *Junky* and then read his letters, I was floored by how much my own feelings, as an outsider to the Valley, matched Burroughs's strong impressions. There was some level of energy I couldn't tune in to, much as if I lacked a radio receiver to pick up the music. Of course, if you don't speak Spanish, that makes sense, but it was more than a language barrier. It was a feeling that I was in a foreign country rather than in the States. I no longer feel that way, but I did at one point, as did Burroughs. He also characterized the type of outsiders who come here as people drawn to self-destruction and maintained that they don't learn their lesson about the Valley: They try to leave but keep coming back, until finally the place gets them. That was a story I heard over and over when I first came down here. Burroughs depicted those impressions in his factualist style of the time, and no other record by any writer of that period captures the place and the outsider's relationship to it so well. I often recommend those passages in *Junky* to Valley newcomers.[2]

Yes, Burroughs was accurate and even prophetic about the Valley in some respects, but, crucially, he also did not understand the place. He says that people come to the Valley to die — "the dying cell gravitates to the Valley" — but that's true from only one point of view. As Juan Ochoa has explained to me, from the point of view of the Mexicans who come across the border to find a better life, the opposite is true: The Valley is a place you come to *live*, not to die. Burroughs argued that Mexicans came here because they could make more money working in the States than in Mexico, but beyond that he has little to say about the field hands or the social reality lived by Mexican Americans in the Valley in the 1940s. He thus fails to discuss the clear racial segregation that was going on in the area. In Edinburg at that time, some restaurants had signs reading "No Dogs or Mexicans."[3] A cartoon from the 1940s shows the great Mexican comic, Cantinflas, getting kicked out of a restaurant in the States and then going back to Mexico and imagining a sign over a restaurant there proclaiming "No Texans." Such discrimination was a fact of life in the Valley, and Burroughs never recorded it. The Beats in general failed to write about the same issue with regard to African Americans; instead, as did Kerouac, they romanticized them as outsiders and longed for their same outcast status — as if they were the best form of bohemian.

In the States, it was thus all too easy for men like Kells and Burroughs to act the part of landed gentry, complete with dark-skinned workers doing all of the real labor at slave wages. They ran the country club, grew their own marijuana, and even made some quick money. Moreover, just across the border in Mexico was almost anything you could desire, and during the 1940s Reynosa was in its heyday. It was the perfect place for such black sheep of wealthy families. However, built in was the price of their freedom. During the years that Billy was here, we know Kells began to change into the Jekyll-and-Hyde alcoholic playboy of the Western world (to quote Ted Morgan and Peter Elvins). Burroughs, too, was significantly changed by his experiences in the Valley, both positively and negatively. Perhaps that's why the Valley recurs, like a dream, in almost every book he wrote. In a positive sense, the Valley served the same purpose for him that his hometown of St. Louis had for pioneers headed west in the nineteenth century: It was a staging ground for crossing into the frontier. Had Burroughs never come to the Valley and lived among its people, picking up some Spanish and a knowledge of Mexican culture, it is unlikely he would have been so well prepared for living in Mexico City. It is also improbable that he would have studied the Mayan culture, which became a central part of the mythology he creates in his novels. Moreover, I doubt he would have undertaken the dangerous and difficult trips he made into Central and South America in the early 1950s. Burroughs was, at heart, an explorer, and his life in the Valley turned out to be a test run for — and a pathway to — his future explorations.

There is, however, a much more crucial way that Burroughs changed and developed during his time on the border and in Mexico. In the later stages of writing this book, I came to see how different the William S. Burroughs who came to South Texas in 1946 was from the man who left Texas in 1949 and Mexico just a few years later. In 1946 he was not yet a writer, nor did he have any ambition to be one. He was a man with a wife and (later) two children, and he needed to support them. He took this responsibility seriously, as you can see in his letters to Allen Ginsberg about Neal Cassady, whom Burroughs attacked for financing his "on the road" trip with money that "could have been a down payment on a house to take care of his family" and for leaving his "wife and child without $ one."[4] Burroughs, by contrast, chose to settle down and farm as his way of supporting his family, and he made a more (South Texas) or less (East Texas) serious effort at it. In his letters to Ginsberg and Kerouac from 1946 to 1950, you can hear the drive to make money and the endless scheming about how to do it.

However, by September of 1951 (the month of Joan's death), his schemes for making money were now being expressed only in the most desperate terms: Maybe he could open a bar on the border or go into ranching in South America. In "International Zone," written in 1954, he provides this self-portrait of his string of failures: "He could have been a successful business executive, anthropologist, explorer, criminal, but the conjunction of circumstances was never there. He is always too late or too early."[5] To this list of failures he could have added "farmer in Texas." Therefore, Burroughs's increasingly self-destructive and dangerous behavior after leaving Texas was undoubtedly related to his inability to solve his family's financial problems.

Burroughs must also have realized that his life with Joan was at a dead end. Joan even reflected this physically. When Hal Chase met her on the streets of Mexico City just weeks before her death, he was shocked: The formerly beautiful young woman he had known at Columbia in 1945 now had thinning hair and open sores on her arms and walked with a limp. "I'm not going to make it," she told Chase. After the accident, more than one of Joan's friends who had seen her near the end of her life would say that Joan had already accepted her doom and that in some strange way she might even have willed the bullet to miss the glass that night.[6]

If she were somehow trying to provoke Burroughs, she knew exactly the right way to do it — by playing on his insecurities about their future and his ability to support his family. Immediately preceding the William Tell act that killed Joan, Burroughs had once again been talking about buying some land for ranching or farming, this time in Panama or perhaps Ecuador. There was some discussion about what they would do if they became stranded in the jungle. Joan, drunk and rightly skeptical, scoffed at the idea that Burroughs, after years of addiction, could still shoot straight enough to provide food for her and her children by hunting wild game. Provoked by her challenge, Burroughs attempted the William Tell trick. The result was that he no longer had to worry about supporting his wife or his children, who subsequently went to live with their respective grandparents. Instead, Burroughs became a writer, perhaps less by choice than by fate.

The Valley was a major setting for this drama of life and death and emerging genius at great cost. Almost as much as this is a book about William S. Burroughs, the Valley, the border, and its people are also lead characters. South Texas is a place of endless, fascinating stories, many of them waiting to be told. It seems fitting that, among everything else that was happening here in the Valley at midcentury, Billy would go unnoticed. Repeatedly, I was told, yes, he was an interesting person in some ways, but there were a lot of intriguing people. They just didn't happen to go on to write books that English professors like to read and teach. My research on Burroughs has allowed the people of the Valley to tell their stories, too, and, whenever possible, I have let them do so unedited and in their own words.

ACKNOWLEDGMENTS

I would like to thank all of the people I interviewed for this book, most of whom are named, but some of whom preferred to remain anonymous. Their cooperation was essential; I consider them my coauthors. Several of these informants have passed away since I interviewed them: Anna Mae Kelly, John Snider, and Rodolfo Villarreal. I hope this book serves as a type of memorial to them. Many people assisted me in my research over the years, and I would like to thank the following in particular: Ellen Volk, for listening to this story unfold, for finding Kells Elvins's grave in McAllen (by impersonating his "niece"), and for exhaustively researching Walter Benson and Politte Elvins; Lisa Travis, my research assistant at the University of Texas–Pan American (UTPA), for locating Burroughs's Edinburg land and for accomplishing numerous other research chores; George Gause, for his magic Rolodex, which led me to many of my sources throughout the Valley, and for his unfailing interest in and support of my research; Virginia Gause, for inviting me to discuss my work at the Hidalgo County Historical Society annual meetings; George Avellano, for funding my research assistants at UTPA; and Rodolfo Arevalo, UTPA provost, for providing the release time from teaching that I needed to write and complete this book. Others who provided support and encouragement include William T. Pilkington, Ivo Slavnic, David Rice, René Saldaña Jr., Eric Miles Williamson, Liza Porras and the staff at the UTPA Department of English, Gavin Schultz, Mike Reed, the Folsom and Heath families, Bob and Sondra Johnson, the Moore family, Ed Simmens, Kurt Hemmer, Tim Bradford, Gordon Ball, Dave Moore, Carolyn Cassady, Don Graham, Chris Carmona, Keith Fitzgerald, Kev Ring at *Beat Scene,* the Trannies in McAllen, the staff at Barnes and Noble (McAllen), Sheriff Robert Horn (Beeville), Helen Snider, Matt McClung, Paul Steckler, Tila and Amy Ochoa, and Kathleen Alcalá. I would especially like to thank Donna Johnson for telling me that my own story was a key part of the book; Erika Garza, for helping me complete the book and this part of my life; and Dashiell Johnson, my son, for trying to understand his father's book and for his delightful and patient company on all of our research trips. Finally, I would like to thank James Grauerholz and Juan Ochoa. I could not have written this book had James not been the true generous Beat soul he is, always helping to "let a thousand flowers bloom." Nor could I have written this work without Juan Ochoa, who has been my guide to the border, my good friend, and, most important, my Mexican lawyer. Billy, Kells, Tiger Terry, Joan, and Walter — I hope I got it right.

NOTES

"The Beatest State in the Union": William S. Burroughs in Texas

1. Two full-length biographies summarize the facts of Burroughs's life: Ted Morgan, *Literary Outlaw: The Life and Times of William S. Burroughs,* and Barry Miles, *William Burroughs: El Hombre Invisible.* See also the introductory essays in James Grauerholz and Ira Silverberg, eds., *Word Virus: The William S. Burroughs Reader.*

2. See Michael Schumacher, *Dharma Lion: A Biography of Allen Ginsberg,* for an account of Ginsberg's stay in New Waverly (83–85). There is no biography of Cassady, but his life story is covered in biographies of Kerouac. See, for example, Gerald Nicosia, *Memory Babe: A Critical Biography of Jack Kerouac.* See also Carolyn Cassady, *Off the Road.* For Huncke's version of these events, see Herbert Huncke, "Bill Burroughs" (parts 1 and 2), *The Herbert Huncke Reader,* 146–61.

3. Ann Charters, ed., *The Selected Letters of Jack Kerouac,* vol. 1, 196.

4. Barry Miles, *Ginsberg: A Biography,* 80.

5. Morgan, *Literary Outlaw,* 129.

6. Still, it wasn't as if I were the only person down here interested in Burroughs. For many years rumors of his past presence had excited the local Beat enthusiasts and scattered Valley bohemians. In fact, I was in something of a race with an ambitious undergraduate who was independently trying to find Burroughs's land. (He got there first but wouldn't tell me where it was.) I have also heard of a friend of a friend who grew up here and knows the location of the house in Pharr where Burroughs, his wife, Joan, and their two children lived for about six months in 1949. This friend of a friend, however, has never materialized, and I am pretty sure the house no longer exists. Even more apocryphal is a story about South Texas hippies who stole the remains of Burroughs's famous "orgone accumulator" (more on that later) in the early seventies. Letter quoted from Oliver Harris, ed., *The Letters of William S. Burroughs, 1945–1959,* 40.

7. "Introduction" by Allen Ginsberg in William S. Burroughs, *Junky,* edited by Oliver Harris, 157.

8. Burroughs, *Junky,* 91.

9. Peter Elvins, letter to author, Mar. 15, 2000.

10. Morgan, *Literary Outlaw,* 111–28. Huncke, *The Herbert Huncke Reader,* 256.

11. My source for Burroughs's purchase of 50 acres of land in 1946 is Morgan, *Literary Outlaw* (129). However, there is no record in Hidalgo County of

this purchase. Burroughs did buy 40 acres of land in Edinburg from Roy Hines on May 6, 1948. In 1945, Kells Elvins had bought 80 acres from Hines, and he probably referred Burroughs to him. In May 1949, Burroughs sold his 40 acres plus 10 more he had acquired from Elvins. When he left the Valley for Mexico in the fall of 1949, he tried to sell some additional land, possibly the land Morgan says he bought in 1946. In late 1950 he found a buyer but was still trying to collect the money on the sale in May 1951. No record exists of either the purchase of this land or the sale. In Burroughs, *Letters,* see Burroughs to Jack Kerouac, Mar. 10, 1950; Burroughs to Allen Ginsberg, Jan. 1, 1951; and Burroughs to Jack Kerouac, May 1951.

12. Burroughs's decision to leave South Texas and move to New Waverly is somewhat mysterious. James Grauerholz suggested to me that it was because growing pot in the wide-open landscape of the Valley would have been unwise.

13. Morgan, *Literary Outlaw,* 128–51.

14. Burroughs to Jack Kerouac and Allen Ginsberg, *Letters,* 21.

15. William S. Burroughs, *Naked Lunch,* 20.

16. Burroughs, *Junky,* 66–79.

17. Ibid., 89.

18. Ibid., 88.

19. William S. Burroughs, *The Western Lands,* 105.

20. "Bentsen, Lloyd Millard, Sr.," *The Handbook of Texas Online.*

21. Population figures for Starr, Hidalgo, and Cameron counties in 1945 and 1946 come from "Population History of Texas Counties from 1850 to 2000" in *Texas Almanac 2004–2005* (Dallas: *Dallas Morning News*, 2005).

22. Burroughs, *Junky,* 88.

23. J. Gilberto Quezado, *Border Boss: Manuel B. Bravo and Zapata County,* 108.

24. Jack Kerouac, *On the Road,* 275–91.

25. This general information on Valley life and farming in the 1940s comes primarily from interviews with John Snider and from an interview with Betty Jo Noser, John Noser's daughter. The price-cost squeeze on midcentury U.S. farmers is discussed in *Subsidies for Farmers,* edited by Robert E. Summers, 38–39.

26. John Houghton Allen, *Southwest,* 13. For biographical information on Allen, see "An Anglo Vaquero of the Brush Country: John Houghton Allen," in Bert Almon, *This Stubborn Self: Texas Autobiographies,* 194–211.

27. Burroughs, *Junky,* 88–89. Valley-born writer and filmmaker David Rice has produced a short film titled "Odyssey One: Chicanos in Space," which once again tells this story of the Valley's strange pull on its people. In the film, two

Chicanos from the Valley are sent into space as part of a top-secret government program of the 1950s. They are lost in a black hole and disappear for forty years. When their spacecraft crash-lands, it does so, of course, back in the Valley (at Delta Lake, near Edcouch). As Burroughs says, the place reels you in, no matter where you go — even into a black hole.

28. Benson's house, where Burroughs stayed, was probably located in Pharr at 329 W. Kelley, the address listed for Walter Benson in a March 1948 phone book. Burroughs interview with James Grauerholz, June 4–16, 1974.

29. Rob Johnson and Juan Ochoa, "The South Texas Beats."

30. Burroughs, *Junky,* 90.

31. Deed, Hidalgo County Courthouse. Marianne Woolfe (Kells Elvins's second wife) described the effects of this freeze to me in a letter dated June 14, 2002.

32. Burroughs, *Letters,* 65.

33. My conclusions concerning what Burroughs learned about the United States by being a South Texas cotton farmer are similar to Ted Morgan's: "Burroughs's experience as a farmer in the Rio Grande Valley reinforced his conviction that conventional morality was a hoax, and that the line between the criminal and the law-abiding citizen was blurred" (*Literary Outlaw,* 149).

34. "Heir's Pistol Kills His Wife; He Denies Playing Wm. Tell," *New York Daily News,* Sept. 8, 1951, 3. See James Grauerholz, "The Death of Joan Vollmer: What Really Happened?" (available at www.lawrence.com/Burroughs/deathofjoan-full.pdf) for the facts surrounding Joan Burroughs's death.

The South Texas Beats

1. See, for example, Jack Kerouac, *The Vanity of Duluoz;* John Clellon Holmes, *Go: A Novel;* Carolyn Cassady, *Off the Road;* Joyce Johnson, *Minor Characters* and *Doors Wide Open;* and Joan Haverty, *Nobody's Wife: The Smart Aleck and the King of the Beats.* Films about the Beats include *Beat* and *The Last Time I Committed Suicide.*

2. Letter from Peter Elvins to author, Mar. 15, 2000.

3. Ted Morgan, *Literary Outlaw,* 69. Dan Lohr met Kells on the golf course in Edinburg in 1936 and is the source for Kells's sojourn in the Valley in the midthirties.

4. This information comes from several sources: Peter Elvins's letters to the author, Politte Elvins's obituaries ("Death Claims Politte Elvins," "Former Congressman Dies"), and Estate of Politte Elvins, Probated Will, #2405.

5. McAllen City Directory, 1938.

6. William S. Burroughs, *Last Words,* 198: "Said about me by Politte Elvins, Kells's father, who later went nuts with paresis." Various characters, alter egos of Politte, say this about Burroughs's young protagonists in his books.

7. The current owner of Politte's house claims an old gringo haunts the place — Politte? — and was interested in knowing about Kerouac's description of the crazy house because it has almost no right angles. See Jack Kerouac, *On the Road,* 150–51.

8. "Death Claims Politte Elvins."

9. Estate of Politte Elvins, Probated Will, #2405.

10. Because of his research, Ted Marak is my source for Elvins's dismissal from Huntsville.

11. Letter from Peter Elvins to author, Jan. 11, 2001.

12. Interview with Pat Lohr Paris.

13. The information on Obie Dobbs comes primarily from my interviews with Pat Paris, Ted Marak, Anna Mae Kelly, and an informant (interviewed in the summer of 2003 in Mission, Texas) who wishes to remain anonymous. This informant knew Dobbs in Mission from junior high school on and contributed the information about Dobbs's family and the story of the phone conversation at the Circle Inn.

14. William S. Burroughs, *Interzone,* 33.

15. Ibid., 93.

16. The photo is one of several accompanying Paul O'Neil's article on the Beats ("The Only Rebellion Around").

17. Ted Marak, telephone interview by author, 2002.

18. Kerouac, *On the Road,* 149.

19. To this day, Reich is a controversial figure and the subject of several biographies. His most famous book, in the context of the Beats, is *The Function of the Orgasm,* which Mardou Fox and Leo Percepied (Kerouac) are reading in *The Subterraneans,* by Jack Kerouac. Burroughs read Reich's *Cancer Biopathy* (1948) while he was living in the Valley. Burroughs's essay in *The Adding Machine,* "My Experiences with Wilhelm Reich's Orgone Accumulator," is a concise introduction to Reich and his theories. Burroughs says Reich "considered that cancer occurs where the electrical charge @ the surface of the cells falls to a suffocation point. To offset this condition and tone up the cells he developed orgone therapy." Ted Marak's comment about the accumulator was made in the 2002 interview.

20. Burroughs, "My Experiences with Wilhelm Reich's Orgone Accumulator," 164–66.

21. Burroughs, "International Zone," in *The Adding Machine,* 50. See also *Interzone:* "hardest fabric known, beat ramie hands down and cocks up" (137).

22. John Snider believes that Ted Marak and his friends were actually at a McAllen nightspot called the Wagon Wheel, where J. Connally Kelly (Anna Mae Kelly's deceased husband) was famous for feeding his dogs steaks. Pat Paris also objected to Marak's story. As a charter member of the McAllen Country Club, she would have heard of such antics taking place on a Saturday night.

23. Pat Paris, 2002. Interview by author at Paris's home in McAllen, Texas.

Tiger in the Valley

1. William S. Burroughs, *Junky,* 89.

2. Ibid., 88–89. On Burroughs's fascination with the Sargasso Sea eels, see, for example, a letter from Burroughs to Allen Ginsberg and Jack Kerouac (Oct. 23, 1955) in Oliver Harris, ed., *The Letters of William S. Burroughs, 1945–1959,* 294.

3. Interview with Nancy Roberts; letter from Nancy Roberts to author.

4. John Taylor provided the biographical information on Eugene Terry in an interview in the summer of 2001.

5. Rob Johnson, "William S. Burroughs: South Texas Farmer, Junky, and Queer."

6. Victor Bockris, *With William Burroughs: A Report from the Bunker,* 165.

7. William S. Burroughs, "Word," in *Interzone,* 152.

8. Fran Alger, telephone interview by author, Spring, 2001.

9. Interview with Jim McKone (Summer 2002); Bryce Armstrong, "Lion Kills San Juan Man at Night Club in Reynosa," 1–2.

10. Armstrong, "Lion Kills San Juan Man," 2.

11. Burroughs to Allen Ginsberg, Oct. 10, 1955, *Letters,* 285.

12. Elvins moved to Mexico City two months after Terry was killed and probably told the story to Burroughs. James Grauerholz sees Burroughs's use of this story as an example of how Elvins functioned in Burroughs's life the same way Neal Cassady did in Jack Kerouac's: He introduced him to people and situations that then became the basis of his writings.

13. Burroughs to Allen Ginsberg and Jack Kerouac, Oct. 23, 1955, in *Letters,* 294–95.

14. Burroughs, "Word," in *Interzone,* 152.

15. William S. Burroughs, *Naked Lunch,* 116.

16. William S. Burroughs, *Last Words,* 250.

17. William S. Burroughs, *The Place of Dead Roads,* 200–201. For the Beat

character of the punch-drunk fighter, compare Burroughs's description in *Dead Roads* to Jack Kerouac's description of Neal Cassady's mentor, Tom Watson, in *Visions of Cody*: "[T]his Tom Watson so tragically interesting, so diseased and beautiful, potent because he could beat anybody yet be so obscurely defeated" (58). John Clellon Holmes and others also describe the Beat character in this "doomed but not defeated" way.

18. Burroughs to Allen Ginsberg, Feb. 7, 1955, *Letters,* 263.

19. William S. Burroughs, *Queer,* xviii–xxiii.

20. The first mention of the story is in an Oct. 10, 1955, letter to Ginsberg (*Letters,* 285). Kerouac sent the story to his agent, Sterling Lord, in November of 1955 (Ann Charters, ed., *The Portable Beat Reader,* 530).

21. Jack Kerouac to Sterling Lord, Nov. 10, 1955, *Selected Letters,* vol. 1, 530.

22. William Burroughs, "The Finger," in *Interzone,* 14.

23. Actually, the young lioness that killed Terry was not destroyed. Instead, Joe — ever the shrewd businessman — told authorities Terry had been killed by an old, ailing lion, and it was this less valuable lion that was destroyed. Soon thereafter, though, Joe began thinning his stock of wild animals. The scotch-drinking bear, Joe's favorite, was the last to go. Joe donated the bear to the Brownsville Zoo, and years later, Luis Alejos spotted him in a cage. He called to it by name, and the bear came straight to him, raising its paws up in its old drinking posture, begging for liquor.

24. As Burroughs wrote to Jack Kerouac on Nov. 2, 1949, "Also considering the project of opening an American Bar on the border (Mexican side, of course. I *no sabe* U.S. side of The Border.)" (Nov. 2, 1949, *Letters,* 56). The insights about mordidas come from Juan Ochoa's unpublished essay, "Desportando Leones," as does the interview with El Soplado.

25. Translated by Juan Ochoa.

26. Letter from Marianne Woolfe to author.

The Wetback Deal

1. William Burroughs, *Junky,* 73–74. The City College quotation comes from James Grauerholz, "The Death of Joan Vollmer: What Really Happened?" Ed Simmens of the Universidad de los Americas (formerly Mexico City College) provided Grauerholz with this information. The second quote is from the *New York Daily News,* Sept. 8, 1951, 3.

2. Interview with Burroughs by David Moberg, New York, 1975. Sylvère Lotringer, ed., *Burroughs Live: The Collected Interviews of William S. Burroughs,* 317.

3. Herbert Huncke, *The Herbert Huncke Reader,* 262.

4. Burroughs to Ginsberg, Jan. 11, 1951. Oliver Harris, ed., *The Letters of William S. Burroughs, 1945–1959,* 78.

5. Burroughs to Ginsberg, Oct. 10, 1946. Ibid., 8.

6. Although it's accurate to say Burroughs's patrician background comes through in these letters from the 1940s, it is also fair to point out that, in later years, Burroughs was an outspoken critic of colonialism. For example, in *The Job,* a book-length interview with Burroughs conducted by Daniel Odier, Burroughs was asked what he thought the major contribution of the Beat generation was, and he replied, "[T]he literary importance is perhaps not as obvious as its sociological importance. . . . [I]t really has transformed the world and populated the world with Beatniks. It has broken down all sorts of social barriers. . . . The old settlers are stuck back in the 19th century. 'These people are charming really but of course we'll never understand them not really.' The Beatniks do not have this folkloric viewpoint. They assume that the Arab way of thinking is not basically different from their own and make direct contact" (53).

7. Ted Morgan, *Literary Outlaw,* 36–55.

8. Burroughs to Ginsberg, Jan. 11, 1951. *Letters,* 78–79.

9. Letter from Peter Elvins to author, Mar. 18, 2001.

10. This quotation combines statements Burroughs made in an interview with Ted Morgan on Nov. 2, 1983 (tape 10), and Dec. 13, 1984 (tape 20).

11. Burroughs to Ginsberg, Feb. 7, 1949. *Letters,* 40.

12. Burroughs to Ginsberg, Nov. 9, 1948, and Jan. 10, 1949. Ibid., 23, 33.

13. Burroughs, *Junky,* 91.

14. Danny Lohr, interview by author, 2002.

15. Carrol Norquest, *Rio Grande Wetbacks: Mexican Migrant Workers,* 21–23.

16. Henry Nash Smith, *Virgin Land: The American West as Symbol and Myth,* 253. Frederick Jackson Turner first proposed his frontier thesis in a talk titled "The Significance of the Frontier in American History," July 12, 1893. My analysis of Burroughs's ideas about farming as they relate to Jackson and Smith is influenced by Leticia M. Garza-Falcón's discussion of Walter Prescott Webb as historian of the American West. See *Gente Decente: A Borderlands Response to the Rhetoric of Dominance,* 30–32.

17. Burroughs to Jack Kerouac, Nov. 30, 1948. *Letters,* 40.

18. Burroughs to Allen Ginsberg, Feb. 7, 1949. *Letters,* 40.

19. Ibid., Nov. 30, 1948. *Letters,* 25. A popular story from this period makes the same point: A farmer was called in for jury duty and found himself in line behind two other farmers trying to get out of serving. Both told the judge they were unable to serve that day because they needed to get a crew of wetbacks

across the river and out in the fields to pick their onion crop. The judge excused them. The third farmer then told the judge he had family business he needed to attend to. The judge ordered him to serve anyway. "Now wait a minute, Judge," the farmer objected. "We're living in a free democracy, and we're all here in a court of law, and you just excused two people from jury duty so they could take care of hiring some wetback laborers." The judge almost fined the farmer for contempt of court but ended up dismissing him just to get him out of his courtroom. This is the story of the "honest South Texas juror."

20. Norquest, *Rio Grande Wetbacks,* 4.

21. Much of the following information on the braceros and the use of illegal labor in Texas is drawn from Rodolfo Acuña, *Occupied America: A History of Chicanos,* 144–48. See also George O. Coalson, *The Development of the Migratory Farm Labor System in Texas: 1900–1954.*

22. "Braceros Ill Treated, Consul Reports."

23. See "Mexican Workers Stage Mass River Crossing at El Paso"; "North of the Border"; "Farming: The Mexican Wetbacks."

24. "Mexican Workers Stage Mass River Crossing at El Paso," 2.

25. For national coverage of this event, see "North of the Border" or "Farming: The Mexican Wetbacks." Burroughs read *Time,* we know, and he may have sent the *Time* magazine story to Ginsberg. The San Antonio and Brownsville papers also ran stories, featuring a local angle. Local Immigration and Naturalization Service (INS) officials claimed, rather defensively, that what was going on in Laredo was not happening in the Valley. Burroughs's letter of Dec. 22, 1948, to Ginsberg shows that this was not true (*Letters,* 28).

26. Burroughs, interview by John Tytell, 1974. Reprinted in *Burroughs Live,* 250. I have been unable to confirm Burroughs's stories of Valley guards armed with machine guns.

27. "Report on Abusing Wetbacks Called 'Lie' by Washman."

28. "Facts, Not Propaganda."

29. "Report on Abusing Wetbacks."

30. Burroughs to Jack Kerouac, Mar. 15, 1949. *Letters,* 43.

31. "Braceros Jam Border Area."

32. "Farmers Not Enthused over Legal Braceros."

33. Burroughs to Allen Ginsberg, May 1, 1950. *Letters,* 65–68; John Tytell, "Interrogations," in Sylvère Lotringer, *Burroughs Live,* 249.

34. Burroughs, *Junky,* 109. See also Burroughs to Jack Kerouac, May 27, 1949 (*Letters,* 49): "This Valley is full of bankrupt farmers."

35. Burroughs to Ginsberg, May 1, 1950. *Letters,* 66–67.

36. Quoted in Coalson, *The Development of the Migratory Farm Labor System,* 81. Norquest's *Rio Grande Wetbacks* is a singularly balanced and valuable account of these times. Norquest farmed a few miles from Kells and Billy. He notes instances of employers having their field hands busted by the Border Patrol just before payday and other examples of exploitation of the workers (102–103). However, he says, the worst offenders were "Americanized Mexicans" who treated their "cousins" from across the border worse than the Anglos did.

37. Burroughs, *Junky,* 90.

38. One man I talked with believed that Burroughs might have been referring not to the Bentsens but to the Benson family of San Benito and Sinton, Texas. J. W. Benson owned the San Pat Vegetable Company, which ran a produce shed in Pharr. Burroughs's friend Walter Benson was a member of this family and worked at the San Pat Vegetable Shed. However, this Benson family was not nearly so powerful as the family Burroughs described: They were hardly "swallowing up the Valley," as Burroughs says, and they were not "the bank." Moreover, I simply did not hear any stories about this family's business interests in the Valley, whereas stories about the interests of the very powerful Bentsen family were ubiquitous. I am thus assuming that Burroughs was confusing the homonymic Bentsen/Benson names. Kells Elvins knew the Bentsens well enough to be invited to a party at Lloyd Jr.'s house (according to Ted Marak), and Burroughs bought his land in Edinburg from Roy Hines, one of the Bentsens' land agents. For these reasons, I identify the "Big Holders" as the Bentsens, rather than Walter Benson's family. For information on J. W. Benson and his sons, I consulted the Texas Citrus and Vegetable Growers and Shippers 1953 *Yearbook* (41). I would like to express my thanks to Helen and John Snider for providing me with a copy of this book.

39. For the history of the Bentsen family up to the 1940s, see Joan R. Sloan Johnson, *The Bentsen Family: From Denmark to Texas.*

40. "Bentsen, Lloyd Millard, Sr." *The Handbook of Texas Online.*

41. Ibid.

42. George Norris Green, *The Establishment in Texas Politics: The Primitive Years, 1938–1957,* 59.

43. The current unemployment rate in Hidalgo County is 13.5 percent, more than double the national average (5.5 percent). See the *Texas Almanac 2004–2005,* 207.

44. Burroughs to Jack Kerouac, May 27, 1949. *Letters,* 49.

45. See, for example, Ezra Taft Benson, *Farmers at the Crossroads (as Told to Carlisle Bergeron),* 22–23; Burroughs to Jack Kerouac, May 27, 1949. *Selected Letters,* 49.

46. Robert E. Summers, ed., *Subsidies for Farmers,* 18.

47. William S. Burroughs, *Queer,* 58–59.

48. William S. Burroughs, *The Last Words of Dutch Schulz,* 84.

49. See Summers, ed., *Subsidies for Farmers,* 66–69.

50. Burroughs to Jack Kerouac, June 24, 1949. *Letters,* 50.

51. Benson, *Farmers at the Crossroads,* 22–23.

52. Summers, ed., *Subsidies for Farmers,* 115.

53. Ibid., 29.

54. Ibid., 158; Burroughs, *Junky,* 104–105.

55. Lotringer, *Burroughs Live,* 329.

56. Ibid.

57. John Snider, telephone interview, 2001.

58. Doug Grant's quotation is posted at www.geocities.com. For negative reactions to the Nike ad, see, for example, Doug Nufer, "Muckrakers," or David L. Ulin, "The Disappearing Bohemian."

Willy El Puto

1. Letter to author from Peter Elvins, Jan. 22, 2003.

2. Ibid.

3. William S. Burroughs, *Junky,* 111.

4. William S. Burroughs, "Word," in *Interzone,* 156–57.

5. Letter from James Grauerholz to author, May 2004.

6. Rob Johnson and Juan Ochoa, "The South Texas Beats."

7. Pamela Colloff, "Looking for Bill." In the summer of 2001 Juan Ochoa, James Grauerholz, and I gave Colloff the "Beat" tour of the Valley and Reynosa.

8. "Border Beats" is a short documentary on Burroughs in the Valley that Juan Ochoa and I cowrote; filmmaker Matt McClung of Austin, Texas, directed and produced it. In 2002 and 2003 McClung filmed interviews with Ted Marak, Pat Paris, Fran Alger, "Blondie," and others.

9. William S. Burroughs, *Queer,* 52–53.

10. Ibid., 33–34.

11. Burroughs, *Junky,* 108–10.

12. Ibid., 163 (Oliver Harris's "Notes").

13. Ibid.

14. Burroughs, "Introduction" to *Queer,* 52–53.

15. Letter from James Grauerholz to author (Summer 2002).

16. Burroughs's common-law marriage was considered legal in Mexico,

thus the necessity for a divorce. See Ted Morgan, *Literary Outlaw: The Life and Times of William S. Burroughs,* 176, 202.

17. Ibid., 173.

The Texas Oilman Routine

1. William S. Burroughs, interviews by Ted Morgan, tape 20, Dec. 13, 1984.

2. Ibid.

3. William Burroughs to Allen Ginsberg, Oct. 14, 1948. *Letters,* 23.

4. Ted Marak, subsequent interviews by Matt McClung, July 2002 and September 27, 2002.

5. William S. Burroughs, *Queer,* 29–30.

6. "Most of the Oilman routine was secondhand. Most of it was from Kells." Burroughs-Morgan interviews, tape 20, Dec. 13, 1984; Burroughs, *Queer,* 29–33.

7. James Grauerholz in a letter to the author (summer 2002).

8. Burroughs, *Queer,* 30–33.

9. Burroughs, *Queer,* 29–33.

10. Burroughs-Morgan interviews, tape 20, Dec. 13, 1984.

11. John William Rogers, *The Lusty Texans of Dallas,* 288.

12. Ibid.

13. Jerrell Dean Palmer, "David Harold 'Dry Hole' Byrd."

14. Burroughs-Morgan interviews, tape 10, Nov. 2, 1983.

15. "Murchison, Clinton Williams, Sr.," *Handbook of Texas Online;* Ernestine Orrick Van Buren, *Clint: A Biography,* 214; John Snider (on the "garrulous" nature of Murchison in McAllen), interview.

16. *Centennial History of Corpus Christi,* 124–27.

17. Burroughs-Morgan interviews, tape 20, Dec. 13, 1984.

18. Charles J. V. Murphy, "Texas Business and McCarthy."

19. William S. Burroughs, *Roosevelt after Inauguration and Other Atrocities.*

20. Dick Russell, *The Man Who Knew Too Much,* 521–23.

21. Burroughs to Jack Kerouac, Mar. 15, 1949. *Letters,* 43.

22. William S. Burroughs, *Nova Express,* 150. Late in his life, Burroughs often discussed environmental issues quite passionately: "I'm doing paintings on the seven deadly sins, and also writing on each one, showing the ravages of, well, avarice, for example. That's at the back of all this destruction of the environment. Companies — they don't care what happens to the rain-forests or anything, so long as they can make a good show in front of their stock-holders." From "A Bleak Picture," 1996, in Sylvère Lotringer, ed., *Burroughs Live,* 775.

23. William S. Burroughs, *Interzone,* 91.

The Wrath of God and the Liberal Imagination

1. Lionel Trilling, *The Middle of the Journey*. For the political orientation of intellectuals during these years, see Trilling's "Introduction," xxi.

2. William Burroughs to Allen Ginsberg, Nov. 9, 1948. *Letters*, 23.

3. Allen Ginsberg, "Introduction" to *Junky*, 157.

4. Burroughs to Ginsberg, Nov. 9, 1948. *Letters*, 24.

5. Ginsberg, "Introduction" to *Junky*, 157.

6. In *Spontaneous Mind: Selected Interviews, 1958–1996*, Allen Ginsberg coins this political label in the following exchange about the drug problem in the United States:

> AG: "So there would be ways of ameliorating the problem that the neoconservative 'Big Brother off our back people' would agree would be better. . . ."
>
> Steve Silberman: "A lot of the conservatives, actually."
>
> AG: "Yeah, the *libertarian* conservatives. That's the libertarian understanding. Then there's the right wing Stalinoid conservatives who really want to impose a police state, basically" (562–63).

7. My information about Ginsberg's parents and his formative years comes from Barry Miles, *Ginsberg: A Biography*, 10–35.

8. Ibid., 43.

9. Ibid., 127.

10. Conrad Knickerbocker interview with Burroughs, in Sylvère Lotringer, ed., *Burroughs Live: The Collected Interviews of William S. Burroughs*, 75.

11. This information on Burroughs's family and his formative years comes from Ted Morgan, *Literary Outlaw*, 14–41. The quotation on Marxism is from Morgan, 57. See also William S. Burroughs, *Queer*, 40–41.

12. Burroughs to Ginsberg, Dec. 24, 1949. *Letters*, 57. Pegler's anti-union and anti-Roosevelt columns are collected in two works by Westbrook Pegler, *'T Ain't Right* and *George Spelvin, American and Fireside Chats.*

13. Jack Kerouac, *On the Road*, 145.

14. Ibid.

15. Jack Kerouac to John Clellon Holmes, June 24, 1949. *Selected Letters*, vol. 1, 200.

16. My psychoanalysis of Ginsberg here is indebted to Miles's analysis in *Ginsberg*, 74–75.

17. William S. Burroughs, *Naked Lunch*, 112–13.

18. Burroughs to Ginsberg, Sept. 1, 1946. *Letters*, 7.

19. Burroughs to Ginsberg, Feb. 19, 1947. Ibid., 11.

20. Burroughs to Ginsberg, Nov. 9, 1948. Ibid., 24.

21. Burroughs to Kerouac, June 24, 1949. Ibid., 51.

22. Burroughs to Ginsberg, Nov. 9, 1948. Ibid., 25.

23. Burroughs to Ginsberg, Feb. 19, 1947. Ibid., 11.

24. Louis Menand, review of *Before the Storm: Barry Goldwater and the Unmaking of the American Consensus.*

25. Burroughs's famous routine "Roosevelt after Inauguration," for example, closely resembles in content and style Pegler's "Pop Bottle Barrage," both of which are absurd routines about Roosevelt's stacking of the Supreme Court in order to fast-track his New Deal legislation. See Pegler, "Pop Bottle Barrage," in *'T Ain't Right.* "Roosevelt after Inauguration" is the title piece in *Roosevelt after Inauguration and Other Atrocities.*

26. Burroughs might have been borrowing this line when he wrote to Jack Kerouac that a "Jean de Brasse here [Mexico] ranks with a street-car conductor." Burroughs to Jack Kerouac, Jan. 1, 1950. *Letters,* 61.

27. Westbrook Pegler, "The Evolution of the Liberal," in *George Spelvin, American and Fireside Chats,* 21–24.

28. Burroughs to Allen Ginsberg, Nov. 9, 1948. *Letters,* 24.

29. In his biography of Ginsberg, Miles says Ginsberg was too preoccupied with a mystical experience he had in his Harlem apartment in the spring of 1948 — in which he heard William Blake recite "The Sick Rose" and other poems — to be much concerned with headlines about communist witch hunts or other political events. However, Burroughs was clearly engaging him in political discussion. It is also likely, though, that Burroughs was making an effort to yank Ginsberg out of the world of mysticism with his letters about the price of carrots.

30. Burroughs to Allen Ginsberg, Dec. 2, 1948. *Letters,* 28.

31. David McCullough, *Truman,* 565–66, 586.

32. There may well have been violence against striking workers in the Valley in the late 1930s and 1940s, but it has not been well documented and remains a subject for further investigation. Hart Stilwell's fact-based novel about the lower Valley in the late 1930s and early 1940s, *Border City* (1945), includes a scene in which union organizers in the Valley (from San Antonio) are beaten by the police. The Communist Party in Texas at this time was headed by the legendary Emma Tenayuca, who led a strike by pecan shellers in Central Texas in 1938 that made national news.

33. Burroughs to Allen Ginsberg, Dec. 2, 1948. *Letters,* 28–29.

34. Allen Ginsberg, *Deliberate Prose: Selected Essays, 1952–1995*, 386–90.

35. Burroughs to Allen Ginsberg, Mar. 18, 1949. *Letters*, 44.

36. Burroughs to Allen Ginsberg, Apr. 16, 1949. Ibid., 47.

37. Miles, *Ginsberg*, 113–16.

38. John Clellon Holmes, *Go: A Novel*, 291.

39. Miles, *Ginsberg*, 119.

40. Burroughs to Jack Kerouac, June 24, 1949. *Letters*, 51.

41. Quoted in Miles, *Ginsberg*, 58–59.

42. Burroughs's comments on Trilling are quoted in Michael Schumacher, *Dharma Lion: A Biography of Allen Ginsberg*, 357. Trilling's views on what makes up a liberal society are of interest here. After all, he was about to become famous as the author of *The Liberal Imagination: Essays on Literature and Society* (1950).

Those who have not read the book (and few under the age of forty have) probably mistake the book as an endorsement of "liberal" thinking because of its title. In fact — and evidently unknown to Burroughs — Trilling's views are remarkably similar to Burroughs's individualistic, factualist views in the late 1940s, if less forcefully expressed. Trilling's generation of the 1930s had embraced communism only to see it turn into the brutality of Stalinism. By the 1940s, however, when he was writing the essays collected in *The Liberal Imagination*, Trilling and his former liberal associates were deeply suspicious of the motives of powerful governments. So it may be surprising for contemporary readers to find Lionel Trilling criticizing the expanding powers of government in a book titled *The Liberal Imagination*.

43. See, for example, Jon Lance Bacon, *Flannery O'Connor and Cold War Culture*, for a discussion of how writers in the 1950s were pressured to express pro-U.S. sentiments in their writings. Citing the 1952 issue of *Partisan Review*, Bacon says, "'Our Country and Our Culture' announced that intellectuals had shifted from a viewpoint antagonistic to American society, in the decades before the World War II, to a position affirming the American way of life during the Cold War" (42). Newton Arvin, in the same issue, argues more pointedly that the "disaffected" intellectuals in U.S. society must, as a duty to country, identify with — rather than repudiate — dominant U.S. "culture" (quoted in Bacon, 43).

44. Lionel Trilling, "The Kinsey Sex Survey," in *The Liberal Imagination*.

45. Interview with Barry Farrell, Feb. 11, 1966, in Ginsberg, *Spontaneous Mind*, 65.

46. Miles, *Ginsberg*, 122.

47. Ibid., 123.

48. Burroughs to Allen Ginsberg, Dec. 24, 1949. *Letters,* 57.

49. Quoted in ibid. (footnote by Oliver Harris, ed.).

50. Burroughs to Jack Kerouac, Jan. 1, 1950. *Letters,* 61.

51. Schumacher, *Dharma Lion,* 127.

52. For a discussion of the significance of May 1 in Mexico, see José Antonio Burciaga, *Spilling the Beans: Lotería Chicana,* 135–45.

53. Burroughs to Allen Ginsberg, May 1, 1950. *Letters,* 66–67.

54. Ibid., 68.

55. Ibid., 69.

56. Burroughs to Allen Ginsberg, May 5, 1951. Ibid., 85.

57. Ginsberg, *Deliberate Prose,* 253.

58. For Ginsberg's disillusionment with communism (or any form of organized government), see his interview with the *Paris Review* (Spring 1966), reprinted in Ginsberg, *Spontaneous Mind,* 52. "Prose Contribution to Cuban Revolution" is Ginsberg's best essay on his youthful ideal of being a leader of the masses developing over time into a distrust of all forms of government: "I have no notion of future state or government possible for man" (*Deliberate Prose,* 135–45).

59. *Spontaneous Mind,* 33.

60. Sylvère Lotringer, ed., *Burroughs Live,* 810.

The Wild West

1. Hal Chase quotation in James Grauerholz, "The Death of Joan Vollmer: What Really Happened?" 25.

2. Jack Black, *You Can't Win,* 180.

3. Partially quoted and summarized in Ted Morgan, *Literary Outlaw,* 148. The full text here is from the original Morgan tapes, composed of more than one hundred hours of interviews Morgan conducted with Burroughs in the early 1980s. James Grauerholz graciously provided me with a transcript of the South Texas material contained in these interviews.

4. Margaret Lyne Moser, *The Biography of a Particular Place: Bee County from the Days of the Spanish Missions through September 11, 2001,* vol. 2, 465–67.

5. William S. Burroughs, *Last Words,* 149.

6. "Texas Hellbent Sheriff." Reprinted in Moser, *The Biography of a Particular Place,* vol. 2, 479–80.

7. Barry Miles, *Ginsberg: A Biography,* 71.

8. The facts related to Ennis's service as sheriff of Beeville are recorded in

"Vail Ennis: An Anachronistic Phenomenon," by Richard Rudeloff, in Moser, *The Biography of a Particular Place,* vol. 2, 457–78.

9. As for Burroughs's "sympathy" with Ennis, this can be overstated. Burroughs hated Southern lawmen and attaches the epithet "nigger-killing" to almost every Southern sheriff he writes about.

10. "Vail Ennis," in Moser, *The Biography of a Particular Place,* vol. 2, 458.

11. The *Time* magazine article on Ennis, which Burroughs apparently read, briefly discusses the incident. Burroughs could also have heard about it from Kells or read about it in the McAllen paper.

12. Interview with Carlos Guerrero; "Beeville Sheriff Shoots Three Men." See also Moser, *The Biography of a Particular Place,* vol. 2, 463–65.

13. William S. Burroughs, Interviews by Ted Morgan, South Texas interview.

14. Evan Anders, *Boss Rule in South Texas,* 143.

15. General information on Mayfield's career comes from Sue Stevens, *Tom Mayfield.* Stevens has based her book on the research of Tom Webb and Robert Norton, who proposed establishing a Texas highway marker dedicated to Mayfield back in the 1980s. The marker now stands before the San Juan Hotel in San Juan, Texas (down the road from Pharr). The research of Norton and Webb is housed in the University of Texas–Pan American, Lower Rio Grande Valley Collection.

16. For information on the career of A. Y. Baker, I consulted Mary Margaret McAllen Amberson, James A. McAllen, and Margaret H. McAllen, *I Would Rather Sleep in Texas: A History of the Lower Rio Grande Valley and the People of the Santa Anita Land Grant,* 442–44. Américo Paredes also tells the story of Ramon de la Cerda and A. Y. Baker in *With His Pistol in His Hand* (29–30). In *Kings of Texas,* Don Graham presents both the Anglo and Texas Mexican side of the story (199–200).

17. Anders, *Boss Rule in South Texas,* 232–33.

18. For a summary discussion of the violence along the border during this period, see Benjamin Heber Johnson, *Revolution in Texas,* 119–20. See also James A. Sandos, *Rebellion in the Borderlands,* chap. six.

19. Walter Prescott Webb, *The Texas Rangers,* 478.

20. The "killing Mexicans on sight" quotation comes from Johnson, *Revolution in Texas* (21); for Tom Mayfield's role in the breaking up of the Plan de San Diego, see Amberson, McAllen, and McAllen, *I Would Rather Sleep in Texas,* 472. See also Stevens, *Tom Mayfield.* According to Johnson and Anders, however, Mayfield's role in the arrest of the revolutionary was minimal.

21. Stevens, *Tom Mayfield,* 14.

22. David Montejano, *Anglos and Mexicans,* 122.

23. See Johnson, *Revolution in Texas,* 120.

24. Interview with John Snider.

25. Virginia Armstrong, "Witness Says Ramsour Told Plans to Kill Benson."

26. "Police Officers Describe Scene of Slaying in Trial of Ramsour."

27. Virginia Armstrong, "Accused Slayer Hits Character of Gun Victim."

28. "Ramsour in Jail as Attorneys Study Whether to Appeal 10-Year Sentence."

29. Interview with John Snider regarding Governor Daniel's motivation for pardoning Ramsour. I have no independent confirmation of this story. See also "J. Loy Ramsour Starts Ten-Year Pen Sentence" and "Ramsour Given Full Pardon."

30. For a history of the border ballad, see *With His Pistol in His Hand* by Brownsville native Paredes.

31. See ibid. for the story of Gregorio Cortez; for information on Treviño, see Américo Paredes, *A Texas-Mexican Cancionero: Folksongs of the Lower Border.*

32. William S. Burroughs, *The Place of Dead Roads,* 45–74. *Cities of the Red Night* by Burroughs tells essentially the same story (255–65).

33. Burroughs, *The Place of Dead Roads,* 98–99.

34. William S. Burroughs, *Port of Saints,* 29.

35. Burroughs, *The Place of Dead Roads,* 156.

36. Burroughs, *Cities of the Red Night,* 302–303.

37. Ibid., 75.

38. Burroughs, *Interzone,* 186.

39. Burroughs, *Port of Saints,* 127.

40. William S. Burroughs, *The Western Lands,* 30.

On the Road in South Texas

1. Information on Kerouac's Brownsville trip comes from "Wild Night in Brownsville," Kerouac's journal entry for July 1952, in *Windblown World: The Journals of Jack Kerouac 1947–1954,* 352. More than half a century later, the Hotrod Johnny Bowen that Kerouac writes about still lives in Brownsville. He does not specifically remember picking up Kerouac but told me he quite often gave a lift to hitchhikers at the border during those years, when he was about twenty-two years old. After I read Kerouac's journal entry from *Windblown World* to him, Bowen confirmed he was in fact the Hotrod Johnny Bowen Kerouac refers to: Bowen's wife was pregnant in the summer of 1952 (as is the wife of Johnny Bowen in *Windblown World*), and his sister worked at a drive-in restaurant (as does the sister of Johnny Bowen in the journal entry). In my telephone interview with

Bowen, he identified the drive-in as Davico's, formerly located at East Fourteenth and Boca Chica Boulevard in Brownsville.

2. Ann Charters notes several instances in which Cassady's letters to Kerouac show up in Kerouac's novels. See, for example, *The Portable Beat Reader* (193). In a recent interview my students conducted with Carolyn Cassady, she also noted Neal's "authorship" of parts of *On the Road.*

3. Burroughs to Kerouac, Jan. 1, 1950. *Letters,* 61.

4. Jack Kerouac to Sebastian Sampas, Mar. 25, 1943. *The Selected Letters of Jack Kerouac,* vol. 1, 61.

5. The manuscript of this book, cowritten by Burroughs and Kerouac, is currently unpublished. I would like to express my thanks to James Grauerholz for alerting me to this reference to farming in *Hippos.*

6. Jack Kerouac to Hal Chase, Apr. 19, 1947. *Selected Letters,* vol. 1, 108.

7. Kerouac to Burroughs, July 14, 1947. Ibid., 109.

8. Ibid., Sept. 13, 1947, 129.

9. Kerouac to Neal Cassady, May 10, 1948. Ibid., 149.

10. Ibid., June 27, 1948, 155.

11. Ibid., July 10, 1948, 159.

12. William S. Burroughs, *The Place of Dead Roads,* 114–15.

13. Burroughs to Jack Kerouac, May 27, 1949. *Letters,* 49.

14. Carolyn Cassady, interview by author (Fall 2001).

15. Quoted in Carolyn Cassady, *Off the Road,* 71.

16. Burroughs to Allen Ginsberg, Jan. 30, 1949. *Letters,* 37.

17. Kerouac, *On the Road,* 144–45.

18. Jack Kerouac to Neal Cassady, Aug.26, 1947. *Selected Letters,* vol. 1, 113.

19. Kerouac, *On the Road,* 68–73.

20. On May 20, 1948, Kerouac recorded his excitement over the news that Jesse James was still alive: "The news that Jesse James is still alive is very thrilling news to me. . . . The amazing feeling of the American nineteenth century carrying over into the 1940s — with its evocations of Mark Twain, Bill Hickock, old Abilene, Bill Cody, the James Boys, the Overland, the Pony Express, Melville, Walt Whitman . . . and Sitting Bull." Kerouac, *Windblown World,* 83.

21. Burroughs to Jack Kerouac, Jan. 22, 1950. *Letters,* 63.

22. Kerouac, *On the Road,* 273.

23. William S. Burroughs, *Junky,* 90.

24. Kerouac, *On the Road,* 274, 294.

25. Burroughs to Allen Ginsberg, Dec. 24, 1949. *Letters,* 57.

26. Burroughs to Jack Kerouac, Jan. 1, 1950. Ibid., 62.

27. Kerouac, *On the Road,* 285.

28. Burroughs to Jack Kerouac, Sept. 26, 1949. *Letters,* 53.

29. Kerouac, *On the Road,* 279, 274.

30. Burroughs to Jack Kerouac, Jan. 22, 1950. *Letters,* 63.

31. Burroughs to Allen Ginsberg, May 1, 1950. Ibid., 69.

32. Burroughs to Kerouac, [May 1951]. Ibid., 91.

33. Burroughs to Allen Ginsberg, May 5, 1951. Ibid., 84.

34. See Oliver Harris's discussion of the composition of the "Junk" manuscript: "Introduction," *Junky,* xxvi–xxx, and "Notes" (ibid.), 159–66.

35. Burroughs to Kerouac, [May 1951]. *Letters,* 91.

36. For a discussion of Beat views of Mexico and Mexican views of the Beats, see Howard Campbell, "Beat Mexico: Bohemia, Anthropology, and 'the Other,'" in *Critique of Anthropology* 23(2): 210–30. Today Kerouac and Burroughs would both be accused of "orientalism" in their view of Mexico, a term drawn from Edward Said's seminal postcolonial study, *Orientalism.* In Said, the term refers to the way in which outsiders view indigenous people as "other," projecting onto them either highly romantic qualities (as in Kerouac's *On the Road*) or highly negative qualities, from an "Ugly American" perspective (as in Burroughs's view of Mexico as "gloomy and sinister and chaotic"). However, unlike the typical Ugly American, Burroughs actually liked the special chaos of Mexico. Anthropologist Howard Campbell argues that Burroughs's picture of Mexico is often "pure Orientalism," but, contrastingly, he also has "a sharp eye for the contradictory currents of freedom and corruption, spontaneity and decadence, and beauty and ugliness that permeated life in Mexico in the 1950s" (220).

37. Kerouac, *On the Road,* 97–98.

38. John Houghton Allen, *Southwest,* 57.

39. "Well, he wouldn't mind being re-born a Mexican," Kim (one of Burroughs's alter egos) thinks in *The Place of Dead Roads* (14).

40. Herbert Huncke, *The Herbert Huncke Reader* (256), an excerpt from *Guilty of Everything.*

41. Kerouac, *On the Road,* 152.

42. William S. Burroughs, "My Experiences with Wilhelm Reich's Orgone Box," in *The Adding Machine,* 164.

43. Burroughs to Jack Kerouac, June 24, 1949. *Letters,* 51.

44. Burroughs, interview by James Grauerholz, 1974.

45. Burroughs, *The Adding Machine,* 164.

46. E-mail correspondence with author (summer 2002).

47. One other possibility exists: Cassady saw Kells's and Tiger Terry's or-

gone accumulator, which, as far as I can tell, existed back in 1946 or early 1947. If that's the case, though, it's hard to tell why Burroughs seems never to have seen one until 1949.

48. Burroughs, *Junky,* appendix 1, 136.

Asustado: The Death of Joan Burroughs

1. These and other facts about Joan Burroughs's death are cited from the definitive essay on the subject: James Grauerholz, "The Death of Joan Vollmer: What Really Happened?" The essay will be part of Grauerholz's full-length biography of Burroughs.

2. William S. Burroughs, "Introduction," in *Queer,* xxii.

3. Pat Paris, interview by author, 2002.

4. Jim McKone, interview by author, 2002.

5. Both stories are from the Sept. 8, 1951, issue of the *Valley Morning Star,* published in Harlingen, Texas.

6. "Pistol Slip Killed Wife, Pharr Man Says"; "Ask Freedom for Burroughs."

7. Letter to author, June 25, 2002.

8. Quoted in Grauerholz, "The Death of Joan Vollmer," 33–34.

9. This quotation is a compilation of two statements Marak made for Matt McClung's *Border Beats* film.

10. Conrad Knickerbocker, "White Junk." Interview with Burroughs, 1965, reprinted in Sylvère Lotringer, ed., *Burroughs Live,* 76.

11. Quoted in Grauerholz, "The Death of Joan Vollmer," 59.

12. Ibid., 35–36.

Atrophied Afterword

1. The epigraph comes from Burroughs's 1990 interview with Kristine McKenna (Sylvère Lotringer, ed., *Burroughs Live,* 727). The Peter Elvins quotation is from a letter to the author dated Mar. 18, 2001.

2. John Houghton Allen's *Southwest* (1952) also dramatizes this outsider status of the Anglo in South Texas. Allen's book is set near Laredo, Texas.

3. Ruben Navarrette Jr., "Ruben Navarrette Jr., Tony, and Me," *Texas Monthly,* Oct. 2002, 23.

4. Oliver Harris, ed., *The Letters of William S. Burroughs, 1945–1959,* Jan. 30, 1949, 37.

5. William S. Burroughs, *Interzone,* 50.

6. Ted Morgan, *Literary Outlaw: The Life and Times of William S. Burroughs,* 193.

SOURCES

LETTERS

Elvins, Peter, to author. January 11, 2001; January 18, 2001; January 19, 2001; March 18, 2001; February 14, 2003; February 18, 2003.

Moore, Dave. January–February 2002.

Roberts, Nancy. Librarian, Corsicana High School, Corsicana, Texas. February 27, 2001.

Taylor, John. Summer 2001 and Summer 2002.

Woolfe, Marianne Elvins. June 14, 2002.

INTERVIEWS

Alger, Fran. Telephone interview by author, Spring 2001.

Anonymous. 2002. Interview by author concerning Obie Dobbs's family and past. August 12. Mission, Texas.

Burroughs, William S. Interviews by James Grauerholz, June 4–16, 1974, New York City. Transcript provided by James Grauerholz.

Evins, Jim. 2001. Telephone interview by author. Summer.

Garcia Garza, Ernesto ("El Blondie"). 2001. Interview by Juan Ochoa. Summer.

Guajardo, Berto ("El Soplado"). 2002. Interview by author. Summer.

Guerrero, Carlos. 2004. Telephone interview by author. Summer.

Kelly, Anna Mae. 2001. Telephone interview by author. Spring.

Lohr, Danny. 2002. Interview by author. September 10. McAllen, Texas.

Marak, Ted. 2002. Telephone interviews by author, 2003, 2003. June. Subsequent interviews by Matt McClung, July 2002 and September 27, 2002.

McKone, Jim. 2002. Interview by author. Hidalgo County Museum (now the Museum of South Texas History). Summer. Filmed by Matt McClung for *Border Beats,* Summer 2002.

Norton, Robert. 2004. Telephone interview by author. Summer.

Noser, Betty Jo. 2001. Interview by author at the Renaissance Hotel, McAllen, Texas. Spring.

Paris, Pat. 2002. Interview by author at Paris's home. June. McAllen, Texas.

Roberts, Nancy. 2001. Telephone interview by author. February. Corsicana High School Library, Corsicana, Texas.

Snider, John. 2001. Telephone interview by author. December.

Taylor, John. 2001. Telephone interview by author. February 27.

Villegas, Antonio, Jr. 2004. Telephone interview by author. Summer.

Woolfe, Marianne Elvins. 2001. Telephone interview by author. February.

WORKS CITED

Acuña, Rodolfo. *Occupied America: A History of Chicanos.* 1981. Reprint, New York: Pearson Longman, 2004.

Allen, John Houghton. *Southwest.* Philadelphia: Lippincott, 1952.

Almon, Bert. *This Stubborn Self: Texas Autobiographies.* Fort Worth: Texas Christian University Press, 2002.

Amberson, Mary Margaret McAllen, James A. McAllen, and Margaret H. McAllen. *I Would Rather Sleep in Texas: A History of the Lower Rio Grande Valley and the People of the Santa Anita Land Grant.* Austin: Texas State Historical Association, 2003.

Anders, Evan. *Boss Rule in South Texas.* Austin: University of Texas Press, 1982.

Armstrong, Bryce. "Lion Kills San Juan Man at Night Club in Reynosa." *Valley Evening Monitor,* November 9, 1950, 1–2.

Armstrong, Virginia. "Accused Slayer Hits Character of Gun Victim." *Valley Evening Monitor,* March 3, 1957, 1–2.

———. "Witness Says Ramsour Told Plans to Kill Benson." *Valley Evening Monitor,* March 4, 1957, 1–2.

"Ask Freedom for Burroughs." *Valley Evening Monitor,* September 9, 1951, 5.

Bacon, Jon Lance. *Flannery O'Connor and Cold War Culture.* New York: Cambridge University Press, 1993.

"Beeville Sheriff Shoots Three Men." *Valley Evening Monitor,* July 8, 1945, 2, Sunday morning edition.

Benson, Ezra Taft. *Farmers at the Crossroads (as Told to Carlisle Bergeron).* New York: Devin-Adair, 1956.

"Bentsen, Lloyd Millard, Sr." *The Handbook of Texas Online.* http://www.tsha.utexas.edu/handbook/online/articles/BB/fbebb.html (accessed June 20, 2005).

Black, Jack. *You Can't Win.* New York: Macmillan, 1927.

Bockris, Victor. *With William Burroughs: A Report from the Bunker.* New York: Seaver, 1981.

"Braceros Ill Treated, Consul Reports." *Valley Evening Monitor,* October 3, 1948, 1.

"Braceros Jam Border Area." *Valley Evening Monitor,* July 15, 1949, 1.

Burciaga, José Antonio. *Spilling the Beans: Lotería Chicana.* Santa Barbara: Joshua Odell Editions, 1995.

Burroughs, William S. *The Adding Machine.* New York: Arcade, 1993.
———. *Cities of the Red Night.* New York: Henry Holt, 1981.
———. *Interzone,* edited by James Grauerholz. New York: Penguin, 1990.
———. *Junky,* edited by Oliver Harris. Fiftieth anniversary edition. New York: Penguin, 2003.
———. *Last Words.* New York: Grove, 2000.
———. *The Last Words of Dutch Schulz.* New York: Arcade, 1993.
———. *Naked Lunch.* New York: Grove, 1991.
———. *Nova Express.* New York: Grove, 1992.
———. *The Place of Dead Roads.* New York: Henry Holt, 1981.
———. *Port of Saints.* Berkeley: Blue Wind Press, 1980.
———. *Queer.* New York: Viking, 1985.
———. *Roosevelt after Inauguration and Other Atrocities.* San Francisco: City Lights Books, 1979.
———. *The Western Lands.* New York: Penguin, 1987.
———. Interviews by Ted Morgan. Ted Morgan Papers. Special Collections. Department of Archives and Manuscripts. University Libraries, Arizona State University, Tempe.
Cassady, Carolyn. *Off the Road.* New York: Penguin, 1990.
Centennial History of Corpus Christi. Corpus Christi: *Corpus Christi Caller Times,* 1952.
Charters, Ann, ed. *The Portable Beat Reader.* New York: Penguin, 1992.
———. *The Selected Letters of Jack Kerouac,* vol. 1. New York: Penguin, 1995.
Coalson, George O. *The Development of the Migratory Farm Labor System in Texas: 1900–1954.* San Francisco: R and E Research Associates, 1977.
Colloff, Pamela. "Looking for Bill." *Texas Monthly* (October 2001): 38, 40, 44, 46, 48.
"Death Claims Politte Elvins." *McAllen Evening Monitor,* January 15, 1943.
Estate of Politte Elvins. Probated Will, #2405, Hidalgo County Courthouse, Edinburg, Texas.
"Facts, Not Propaganda." *Valley Evening Monitor,* June 15, 1949, 5.
"Farmers Not Enthused over Legal Braceros." *Valley Evening Monitor,* July 28, 1949.
"Farming: The Mexican Wetbacks." *Newsweek* (October 25, 1948), 80–81.
"Former Congressman Dies." *Valley Morning Star,* January 15, 1943.
"Friend Sure Case Accident." *Valley Morning Star,* September 8, 1951.
Garza-Falcón, Leticia M. *Gente Decente: A Borderlands' Response to the Rhetoric of Dominance.* Austin: University of Texas Press, 2001.

Ginsberg, Allen. *The Collected Poems.* New York: Random House, 1981.

———. *Deliberate Prose: Selected Essays, 1952–1995,* edited by Bill Morgan. New York: HarperCollins, 2000.

———. *Spontaneous Mind: Selected Interviews, 1958–1996,* edited by David Carter. New York: HarperCollins, 2001.

Graham, Don. *Kings of Texas.* Hoboken, N.J.: John Wiley and Sons, 2003.

Grauerholz, James. "The Death of Joan Vollmer: What Really Happened?" Unpublished essay.

———, and Ira Silverberg, eds. *Word Virus: The William S. Burroughs Reader.* New York: Grove, 1998.

Green, George Norris. *The Establishment in Texas Politics: The Primitive Years, 1938–1957.* Westport, Conn.: Greenwood, 1979.

Harris, Oliver, ed. *The Letters of William S. Burroughs, 1945–1959.* New York: Viking, 1993.

Holmes, John Clellon. *Go: A Novel.* New York: Thunder's Mouth Press, 1997.

Huncke, Herbert. *The Herbert Huncke Reader.* New York: William Morrow, 1997.

"J. Loy Ramsour Starts Ten-Year Pen Sentence." *Valley Evening Monitor,* January 22, 1958, 1.

Johnson, Benjamin Heber. *Revolution in Texas.* London: Yale University Press, 2003.

Johnson, Joan R. Sloan. *The Bentsen Family: From Denmark to Texas.* Austin: Hart Graphics, 1985.

Johnson, Joyce. *Minor Characters: A Beat Memoir.* New York: Penguin, 1999.

Johnson, Rob. "William S. Burroughs: South Texas Farmer, Junky, and Queer." *Southwestern American Literature* (Spring 2001): 7–36.

———, and Juan Ochoa. "The South Texas Beats." *Beat Scene* 42 (Early Spring 2003), 38–45.

Kerouac, Jack. *On the Road.* New York: Penguin, 1976.

———. *The Subterraneans.* New York: Grove, 1958.

———. *The Vanity of Duluoz.* New York: Penguin, 1994.

———. *Visions of Cody.* New York: Penguin, 1972.

———. *Windblown World: The Journals of Jack Kerouac 1947–1954,* edited by Douglas Brinkley. New York: Viking, 2004.

———, and Joyce Johnson. *Door Wide Open: A Beat Love Affair in Letters, 1957–1958.* New York: Penguin, 2001.

Kerouac, Joan Haverty. *Nobody's Wife: The Smart Aleck and the King of the Beats.* Berkeley: Creative Arts Book, 2000.

Lotringer, Sylvère, ed. *Burroughs Live: The Collected Interviews of William S. Burroughs.* Los Angeles: Semiotext(e), 2001.

McAllen City Directory, 1938. McAllen Public Library, McAllen, Texas.

McClung, Matt. *Border Beats.* Unreleased documentary film, 2002–2003. With Rob Johnson and Juan Ochoa. Includes interviews with Luís Alejos, "Blondie," Fran Alger, Jim McKone, Pat Paris, Ted Marak, and others. Transcripts in author's possession.

McCullough, David G. *Truman.* New York: Simon and Schuster, 1992.

Menand, Lewis. Review of *Before the Storm: Barry Goldwater and the Unmaking of the American Consensus. New Yorker* (March 26, 2001), 92–96.

"Mexican Workers Stage Mass River Crossing at El Paso." *Valley Evening Monitor,* October 15, 1948.

Miles, Barry. *Ginsberg: A Biography.* New York: Simon and Schuster, 1989.

———. *William Burroughs: El Hombre Invisible.* 1992. Reprint, London: Virgin, 2002.

Morgan, Ted. *Literary Outlaw: The Life and Times of William S. Burroughs.* New York: Henry Holt, 1988.

Moser, Margaret Lyne. *The Biography of a Particular Place: Bee County from the Days of the Spanish Missions through September 11, 2001,* vol. 2. Beeville, Tex.: Beeville Publishing, 2002.

"Murchison, Clinton Williams, Sr." *Handbook of Texas Online.* http://www.tsha.utexas.edu/handbook/online/articles/MM/fmu10.html.

Murphy, Charles J. V. "Texas Business and McCarthy." *Fortune* (May 1954), 101.

Nicosia, Gerald. *Memory Babe: A Critical Biography of Jack Kerouac.* New York: Grove, 1983.

Norquest, Carrol. *Rio Grande Wetbacks: Mexican Migrant Workers.* Albuquerque: University of New Mexico Press, 1972.

"North of the Border." *Time* (November 1, 1948), 38.

Nufer, Doug. "Muckrakers." *Washington Free Press* 22 (July/August 1996). http://www.washingtonfreepress.org/22/Muckrakers.html (accessed August 8, 2005).

Ochoa, Juan. "Desportando Leones" (unpublished essay).

Odier, Daniel, ed. *The Job.* New York: Penguin, 1989.

O'Neil, Paul. "The Only Rebellion Around." *Life* (November 30, 1959), 114–16, 119–20, 123–24, 126, 129–30.

Palmer, Jerrell Dean. "David Harold 'Dry Hole' Byrd." *Handbook of Texas Online.* http://www.tsha.utexas.edu/handbook/online/articles/BB/fby13.html (accessed August 8, 2005).

Paredes, Américo. *George Washington Gómez: A Mexicotexan Novel.* Houston: Arte Publico, 1990.

———. *A Texas-Mexican Cancionero: Folksongs of the Lower Border,* 2d ed. Austin: University of Texas Press, 1995.

———. *With His Pistol in His Hand.* Austin: University of Texas Press, 1958.

Pegler, Westbrook. *'T Ain't Right.* Garden City, N.Y.: Doubleday, Doran, 1936.

———. *George Spelvin, American and Fireside Chats.* New York: Scribner, 1942.

"Pistol Slip Killed Wife, Pharr Man Says." *Valley Evening Monitor,* September 9, 1951, 1.

"Police Officers Describe Scene of Slaying in Trial of Ramsour." *Valley Evening Monitor,* March 1, 1957, 1–2.

President's Commission on Migratory Labor. "Report on Migratory Labor in American Agriculture." Washington, D.C.: Government Printing Office, 1951.

Quezado, J. Gilberto. *Border Boss: Manuel B. Bravo and Zapata County.* College Station: Texas A&M University Press, 2001.

"Ramsour Given Full Pardon." *Valley Evening Monitor,* February 2, 1962.

"Ramsour in Jail as Attorneys Study Whether to Appeal 10-Year Sentence." *Valley Evening Monitor,* March 6, 1957, 1–2.

Reich, Wilhelm. *The Discovery of the Orgone,* 2d ed. Vol. 2: *The Cancer Biopathy.* New York: Orgone Institute Press, 1948.

"Report on Abusing Wetbacks Called 'Lie' by Washman." *Valley Evening Monitor,* June 14, 1949, 2.

Rivera, Tomás. *Y no se lo tragó la tierra* [And the Earth Did Not Devour Him] (1971). In *Tomás Rivera: The Complete Works,* 2d ed. Edited by Julian Olivares. Houston: Arte Publico Press, 1998.

Rogers, John William. *The Lusty Texans of Dallas.* New York: Dutton, 1951.

Russell, Dick. *The Man Who Knew Too Much: Hired to Kill Oswald and Prevent the Assassination of JFK.* New York: Carroll and Graf, 1992.

Said, Edward. *Orientalism.* New York: Vintage, 1979.

Sandos, James A. *Rebellion in the Borderlands.* Norman: University of Oklahoma Press, 1992.

Schumacher, Michael. *Dharma Lion: A Biography of Allen Ginsberg.* New York: St. Martin's Press, 1992.

Smith, Henry Nash. *Virgin Land: The American West as Symbol and Myth.* Cambridge: Harvard University Press, 1978.

Spence, Ruth Griffin. "The Nickel Plate Highway to Hell: A Political History of Hidalgo County 1852–1934." Copy available at McAllen Public Library, Main Branch.

Stevens, Sue. *Tom Mayfield.* Privately printed; available at the University of Texas–Pan American, Lower Rio Grande Valley Collection, Edinburg, Texas, 1999.

Stilwell, Hart. *Border City.* Garden City, N.Y.: Doubleday, Doran, 1945.

Summers, Robert E., ed. *Subsidies for Farmers.* New York: H. W. Wilson, 1951.

Texas Almanac 2004–2005. Dallas: *Dallas Morning News,* 2005.

Texas Citrus and Vegetable Growers and Shippers Association. *Yearbook.* Mission, Texas, 1953.

"Texas Hellbent Sheriff." *Time* (November 24, 1947), 30.

Trilling, Lionel. "The Kinsey Report," in *The Liberal Imagination: Essays on Literature and Society.* Garden City, N.Y.: Doubleday, 1953, 216–35.

———. *The Middle of the Journey.* New York: Harcourt, Brace, Jovanovich, 1975.

Ulin, David L. "The Disappearing Bohemian," in *Beat Down to Your Soul,* edited by Ann Charters. New York: Penguin, 2001, 577–83.

Van Buren, Ernestine Orrick. *Clint: A Biography.* Austin: Eakin, 1986.

"Wealthy Pharr Man Held in Death of Wife." *Valley Morning Star,* September 8, 1951.

Webb, Walter Prescott. *The Great Plains.* New York: Ginn, 1931.

———. *The Texas Rangers,* 2d ed. Austin: University of Texas Press, 2003.

INDEX